TITLE SHOT

INTO THE SHARK TANK
OF MIXED MARTIAL ARTS

Kelly Crigger

**VICTORY
BELT**

First Published in 2008 by Victory Belt Publishing.

Copyright © 2008 Kelly Crigger

ISBN 10: 0-9815044-0-X

ISBN 13: 978-0-9815044-0-7

Victory Belt ® is a registered trademark of Victory Belt Publishing.

Printed in the United States

Cover Design by BRIAN RULE

PROLOGUE

ONE: TEAM QUEST

TWO: GRACIE JIU JITSU

THREE: SPORTFIGHT XIX & IVAN SALAVERRY

FOUR: JACKSON'S MMA

FIVE: SITYODTONG

SIX: THE IFL FINALS

SEVEN: AMERICAN TOP TEAM

EIGHT: THE MODERN ARMY COMBATIVES TOURNAMENT

NINE: VEGAS BABY

ACKNOWLEDGEMENTS

I had no idea how many people it takes to write a book. Credits are generally ignored by the readers, but without the cooperation of the following people this would still be a dream.

My wife–How can I adequately thank my loving wife for all she's done to support my disgusting habit of writing stories about strange, sweaty men with violent tendencies? My wife is a trooper. I've left her on several occasions for official duties in foreign countries and she never complained. So when I said I was taking on this project, I expected a bit of well-deserved ball busting that never happened. She's always believed in me and will always be my faithful "Ranger Buddy."

Mike Carlson–Without a doubt a huge amount of credit goes to my friend and mentor Mike Carlson at *Real Fighter* magazine. Though I'm several years older and infinitely wiser, Mike guided me through the publishing and MMA worlds. Mike gave me my first break as a writer for which I will be forever indebted. If I live to write a hundred books or write for a hundred magazines, I will always owe a debt of gratitude to Mike and *Real Fighter*. That sounds overly compassionate, but he's the most creative guy I've ever known and has a penchant for putting thoughts into words that few can match.

Erich Krauss for publishing this book and guiding me through the whole process. Aside from being my publisher, he's been a friend and confidant.

Raffi Nahabedian for hooking me up with Erich Krauss

My two dads for instilling me with self-confidence and ripping it from me at the same time. They always knew when to pat me on the back and when to kick me in the ass. Too bad I was too immature to see it. They made me who I am, plain and simple.

My Mom for always correcting my verbage. I will always know the difference between a verb and an adverb because she never let me forget it. If I write well it's because she never relented on forcing me to use correct English. It was always annoying, but was worth it in the long run.

Schoolhouse Rock for teaching me about English when Mom wasn't around and for having the coolest songs about diction in the world. How can you beat Conjunction Junction, We the People, and I'm Just a Bill?

Greg Sierra for bringing my sarcastic side out. Until we met I was stiff and mildly funny, but Greg took my smart-assery to a whole new level. He's been a true friend and always reminds me not take things too seriously.

Tommy Macias for introducing me to some of the best sports writing in the world, including the effervescent sportswriter Rick Reilly. My writing is greatly improved because of them.

Sean Kirschner for being a soundboard for my writing, a fellow website supporter, UFC sidekick, and the guy who always calls when there's MMA on TV.

S.E. Hinton and Francis Ford Coppola for writing making the most influential movie of my life, "The Outsiders." Diane Lane for being so hot as Cherry Valance.

Bob Kaplan, Homer Hickam, and Chris Ayre for writing great books that inspired me.

Major Dennis Heaney and Doctor Chuck Bass for giving me the time off to write this book. Captain Phil Brown and Colonel Ben Hagar for approving it.

Bill Curry for his extremely helpful class on photography 101. I met Bill at American Top Team where we had spirited debates about politics and government conspiracies. Someday I want to take his Libertarian ass to the Republican National Convention just to see if he would explode like the drummer from Spinal Tap. My photography improved 100% as a result of his tutelage.

Carlos Sanchez for his fantastic insight into the IFL expansion.

All the people who threw open their doors and showed me such great hospitality along the way of this journey, especially Matt "The Law" Lindland, without whom the book would have never gotten out of the starting gates. Ivan "The Terrible" Salaverry, Cesar "The Timekeeper" Gracie, Greg "The Two Hundred Pound Brain" Jackson, Ricky "Pretty Boy" Kottenstette, Kurt "The Commissioner" Otto, Mark "The Sanitizer" Dellagrotte, "The Godfather of Army Combatives" Matt Larsen, Ricardo "The nicest guy in MMA" Liborio, Richie "Puma" Guerrerio, Donovan "The Dinner Host" Craig, Jen "The PR Machine" Wenk, and even Dana White, who gave me all the time I wanted despite others trying to pull him away.

The Screaming Eagles Combatives Team – LTC Kevin Petit, 1SG Mike Lamkins, Ze Mario Esfina, and John "The Saint" Renken who let me tail them during the All-Army Combatives Tournament.

Last, but certainly not least, my UFC fight club. Every month we would gather to imbibe spirits, tell tale tales, and watch our favorite sport while the wives hung out in the kitchen gossiping and the kids went upstairs to destroy things. There were many members, all of whom were deeply opinionated on their favorite fighters, how the UFC killed Pride, and which beer goes best with haggis. Thanks to Otto Liller, Haydn Hungerford, Jamie Burns, Sean Kirschner, Blaine Hedges, Jim Bonner, Matt "The Smadge" Barnes, Todd "Quaz" Emoto, Mike Kenny, Steve Stowell, Dan Hill, Phil Brown, and "The Blonde Sheik of Zormat" Matthommad Gomlakian.

PROLOGUE

"It is not the critic who counts; not the man who points out how the strong man stumbles, or where the doer of deeds could have done them better. The credit belongs to the man who is actually in the arena, whose face is marred by dust and sweat and blood, who strives valiantly; who errs and comes up short again and again; because there is not effort without error and shortcomings; but who does actually strive to do the deed; who knows the great enthusiasm, the great devotion, who spends himself in a worthy cause, who at the best knows in the end the triumph of high achievement and who at the worst, if he fails, at least he fails while daring greatly. So that his place shall never be with those cold and timid souls who know neither victory nor defeat."

—Theodore Roosevelt

"BJ Penn really wants to do something for the troops," the e-mail started.

I was only days away from returning home after a short tour of duty in Afghanistan when I got this message from BJ's lawyer and pseudo-manager, Raffi Nahabedian. "Could you arrange a visit with the troops at Fort Lewis when you get back?"

Sure I could. It was easy, but did I want to take three days out of my life to play chaperone to a rich, twenty-eight-year-old kid and his little brother instead of spending that time with my family? Hell, no.

But I was a fan of MMA. I knew that having BJ Penn visit my unit to train them for free was a golden opportunity that only a fool would pass up. I'd written a couple of freelance articles for *Real Fighter* magazine and knew the value of such a visit, especially since BJ offered to do the whole thing out of his own pocket. So I gathered up all the professionalism that Army officers are known for, put together a three-day itinerary, made sure his logistics were taken care of, and stepped up to the plate.

BJ Penn fires an M4 Carbine at Fort Lewis, Washington. Dec, 2006.

I couldn't have been happier that I did.

BJ was nothing like I thought he'd be. He was gracious, humble, and genuinely happy to spend time with the soldiers of Fort Lewis, Washington. He gladly trained fifty troops for two hours and then socialized with them for a couple more, grappling with a line of about ten troops who wanted to test themselves against "The Prodigy." With each person who tapped out, he would make a point of teaching him exactly what he did wrong, including me.

BJ Penn left Fort Lewis with a lot of new fans in his wake, and I was certainly one of them. His professionalism and patriotism made me wonder why the general public had such a negative view of mixed martial arts fighters. People who didn't follow MMA viewed these men as little more than former convicts and thugs engaging in barroom brawls behind the masquerade of a sport. Admittedly, many people had only been exposed to the early "no-holds-barred" UFC events, where the slogan was "there are no rules," and it wasn't uncommon to see a fighter get his groin pummeled or his hair pulled.

Because of those early days, despite all the rule changes and the athleticism the combatants now possessed, the general public still had very little insight into the human side of the fighters, which wasn't helped by the unwillingness of mainstream media outlets like ESPN and Fox Sports

Network to grant the sport exposure. As a fan of MMA and occasional writer on it, I knew a little about the human stories behind the four-ounce gloves and sponsor-covered shorts, but my time with BJ left me wanting to know more. That desire grew inside me every time I heard someone give MMA a bum rap based upon the early years. I became certain that there was a wealth of untapped followers who only needed a glimpse inside modern MMA to become full-fledged fans.

Living in close proximity to Team Quest, one of the premier MMA training facilities, I decided to skip down there to learn more about the fighters and their sport. My crusade was twofold.

First, I wanted to answer the basic question, "Why fight?" I'm no pacifist, but I had a hard time understanding why men engage in such risky activity when there is so little to be gained from it. Mixed martial arts pays very little compared to other sports, and yet the MMA fighter trains longer and harder than almost any other athlete. After all, it's a fight, and it's potentially life altering if you're on the wrong end of a high kick to the head. I could understand why cops, firemen, and especially the military choose to take this path despite the ever-present specter of death that looms over their professions. They do it for the greater good of the community and country. But what drives fighters to expose themselves to such danger when the basic human instinct is to avoid conflict?

The second thing I wanted to find out was why the media failed to portray fighters accurately. Most fighters are finely tuned athletes who grew up under the strict values and traditions of the martial arts. Why was BJ Penn, one of the most genuine people I'd ever met, mostly seen as a cocky, arrogant, self-centered kid? Was this bad-boy image the fault of promoters because the clean-cut, kid-next-door image was too boring? They certainly stood to profit more if they advertised a match as bad blood and got the athletes to make rude public statements against each other. Unfortunately, this kind of thing costs the man in the ring fans who might otherwise support him and gives fighters a public image 180 degrees off from their true persona.

I learned a lot about MMA during the time I spent at Team Quest, like how some fighters find a peaceful coexistence with God and how crippling a kick to the liver is. However, the answers I had come searching for still eluded me. I still didn't understand why these driven young men beat their bodies raw in training for the chance to climb into the ring, and I still didn't understand why all their hard work and charisma was portrayed in such a negative light by the media. I repeatedly saw examples of the media latching on to their faults instead of their virtues in order to sell tickets, which I felt was unfair to the person wearing the gloves.

I decided to turn my few days' adventure into a yearlong journey. Certain that answers were out there waiting to be found, I would visit some of the top MMA gyms in the country and spend time with the fighters. I would crawl inside their minds and learn what made them and their sport tick.

On a personal level, my journey was also a search for personal courage. Some people seem to harbor a burning need to confront danger by any means possible. I'm not one of them, but I've always been curious to know who they are and what drives them.

As a young boy I was on the losing end of several fights I never started, yet I turned to the military as a career. I did it because it was a family tradition. There I found the courage and self-confidence I needed in life and even sought out combat when the war on terrorism began.

But I knew there was a fundamental difference between military warriors and MMA fighters. For one thing, our conflict occurred at a distance of anywhere from fifty to a thousand meters, depending on the weapon system in your hands. For fighters, distance was measured in inches, and even a one-inch reach advantage could mean disaster. It seemed to me that it took more personal courage to engage your enemy at such a close distance.

Along the way, this project expanded into so much more. I discovered the convoluted business side of MMA and the twilight zone where martial arts meets capitalism and decisions are made for money instead of the good of the sport. I discovered the athletes' integrity and their intolerance for charlatan martial arts instructors who cheapen their profession.

And sushi—I found lots of sushi.

Mixed martial arts lies squarely at the intersection of beauty and pain. It's a rough place to live, but it was my privilege to sojourn there and train among these men. I hope you enjoy it as much as I did.

TEAM QUEST

Now this is the Law of the Jungle—as old and as true as the sky;

And the Wolf that shall keep it may prosper, but the Wolf that shall break it must die.

As the creeper that girdles the tree-trunk, the Law runneth forward and back—

For the strength of the Pack is the Wolf, and the strength of the Wolf is the Pack.

—Rudyard Kipling, *"The Law of the Jungle"*

"Ⓘf you have questions, ask me. Don't fucking stand around talking!" Matt Lindland said in a low raspy voice that wasn't intimidating by itself, yet carried the weight of Stonehenge in its tone. It was my first day in a mixed martial arts gym and already there was conflict.

February in Portland is miserable. It is an Eskimo's version of a vacation paradise, yet here I was in the rain and cold using up my hard earned leave from the Army so I could hang out with MMA fighters. I stood in the middle of Team Quest on the brink of a ten-day mission to get into the heads of these combatants, but secretly wondered if I was out of my own.

Lindland's berating was mercifully focused on two of his fighters instead of me. They were slacking off during practice so "The Law," as he was nicknamed, decided it was time for corrective action. It was no different than me getting into a soldier's ass for avoiding work while his fellow soldiers toiled away maintaining their equipment. Whether it was a Fort Lewis motor pool or one of the best MMA training camps in the world, the unwillingness of those in charge to tolerate laziness was the same. Some things transcend boundaries.

Lindland's warning was smartly heeded. His guys immediately went back to sparring without protest, the sure sign that he was the top dog in the building. He ought to be since he built it along with his training partners, Robert Follis and Randy Couture, in 1997. With other friends and relatives, the three transformed the former car lot and garage by hand. Now it was one of the most respected MMA training academies in the world.

The space was huge and I watched intently as Lindland and Follis put their guys through several five-minute rounds of boxing followed by their signature style, ground and pound. During this time, my lungs embraced a unique mixture of steam, Clorox, and sweat. The aroma thrived like a living organism in the climate of an overworked heater compensating for the Oregon February cold. In all the gyms I would travel to over the next year, none would deliver a first-impression punch to the chest the way this one did. The pungent odor was far from enticing, but eventually I learned to appreciate it, because not all gyms took the time and effort to maintain standards of cleanliness like Team Quest. Fighters are tough, but a staph infection can be brutal.

I watched them train for nearly an hour, my emotions swaying wildly between fierce adulation and abject sympathy. After the sparring session was over, I gazed around the gym and spotted four recognizable fighters packing equipment into worn-out lockers and throwing sweats on over their T-shirts. Chris Leben, Nate Quarry, Ed Herman, and Josh Haynes were minor celebrities in Gresham after being plucked from their spartan Oregon training facility and dropped into a luxurious Las Vegas home for the Spike TV reality show *The Ultimate Fighter*. A strange mix of *Big Brother* and *Survivor*, TUF gave sixteen fighters a chance to compete for a multifight deal with the UFC. Cut off from the world, every moment was taped and broadcast around the country for the entertainment of MMA fans. It turned out to be the best thing they ever did. The finale of *The Ultimate Fighter*'s first season on April 9, 2005, brought about a rapid and massive expansion of MMA that was unlike any other single event in professional sports.

By season three, the TUF experiment was tested and true, but no less exciting for Herman and Haynes when they entered the house to be sequestered with fourteen other fighters. They were coached by Tito Ortiz and Ken Shamrock, bitter rivals if there ever were any, and thrust into the blazing spotlight of invasive television. The two rode the blast wave of the media frenzy all the way to the bank. The show got them so much exposure they could walk down the street with Matt Lindland, a renowned fighter of considerable seniority to both men, and they would get recognized first.

"We were used by the UFC," Haynes said, reclining on a bench press machine after the workout. "But it was fine. The massive exposure they gave us was something we couldn't have gotten anywhere else. What was strange to me, and still is, is the number of people out there who live, breathe, and eat this show up. I was amazed how many people recognized me after it."

But it was stressful as well, and the life of a minor celebrity took its toll on Haynes, who once weighed over three hundred pounds. "We were in the middle of the hype machine. I mean there were cameras everywhere in the house for one thing, but then the publicity that led up to the finale was huge also. There were media events, videos of my home life, trailers and commercials to film, photo shoots, the works. There was even wagering on the finale in the sports book rooms. I was so glad when that thing was done, just because I could relax and get back to my life. Don't get me wrong. I'd do it again in a heartbeat, but it was a stressful time, too."

Haynes, adorned in all his tattoos had just finished a rigorous training session and was tired—a perfect time to assault him with questions and get inside his head.

"I fight to pay the bills, plain and simple," he blurted out. "I mean, if I could play chess and make this kind of money, I'd do it. But for me, this is what I'm good at." It was a politically correct statement, but it was crap. Only a few moments later, he negated it by admitting, "There's a feeling you get when you're in the cage, and there's only one way out—through the other guy. It's like a fix. I imagine some people get it from other things . . . skydiving, bull riding, whatever. But for me, it's fighting. If I don't get that feeling every couple of months, I don't like it."

At the time, Josh was in danger of losing that rush, at least on the big stage. He was winless in the Octagon, which is not something UFC's boss Dana White tolerated for long. He was set to face another TUF alumnus in Luke Cummo the following month, and the writing was on the wall—this was his last chance.

Josh fought for tangible reasons, a paycheck, but it also provided a feeling that was almost like an addiction. He liked the rush of getting into the cage and hearing the door slam behind him, the look in his opponent's eyes, the swell of adrenaline. It was a high nothing else could replace.

But this rush also came at a price, one that economists would call an opportunity cost. Instead of building a career with his computer science degree from Southern Oregon University, Haynes managed a strip club at night, which afforded him the daylight hours to train. The prize purses are not extravagant in MMA and certainly not enough to live off of unless you are a championship belt holder. Some fighters have corporate sponsors, but that revenue is usually minimal at best. Thus, many sacrifice a better life to train for combat in the Octagon. Maintaining a day job is the reality for most fighters, and for a father of three like Josh, it's a necessity.

Josh's son, Thor, was born with a brain cancer called medulla blastoma, a condition he underwent numerous surgeries and chemotherapy sessions to treat. Thor was mostly out of the woods, but his care left the Haynes family with a multitude of medical bills. Most reasonable men would take this as a situation calling for working several jobs to earn money for the family, but not Haynes.

"I get decent cash from fighting," he said.

"But you could get more if you entered the job market full-time, right?"

"Yeah, but that would be a boring life," he responded chuckling. "I mean it would be hollow without doing the thing I love. Don't get me wrong; my family means everything to me, so if they were ever in jeopardy of losing the house or going hungry, I'd quit this in a second. But we're getting by now, so I'll keep training."

"So the thrill of fighting overrides the desire to have a bigger house or a stockpile of cash in the bank?"

"Yeah, I guess so. But here's the thing. Even if I got the huge contract to fight like the bigger guys get, I'd still work. It's in my blood, you know. So it's a strange parallel. On the one hand I could stop training and make more money with another job, but then again, if I had plenty of money and didn't have to work, I probably would anyway. I don't know what I'd do with myself if I didn't have to work."

Josh went on to describe his time as a soldier. He'd enlisted for four years in the infantry and achieved the rank of sergeant at Fort Benning, Georgia, but not before a lot of miserable days as a lowly private.

In the Army, privates don't know much and are entrusted with only enough rope to hang themselves with. They are generally delegated menial tasks, are seldom happy, and are rarely instilled with any sort of responsibility. But most of all, privates are not in control of their own destiny. Their entire day, from start to finish, is planned for them, and even their weekends are closely monitored.

In the MMA world, fighters fresh off the street are the privates. Even a fighter who has been around the amateur circuit or has three professional fights to his credit is a private because he still has so far to go before reaching his potential. These fighters toil daily for little or no gain and always have a job outside the gym or teaching inside it. Their sponsors are either nonexistent or somebody like Joe's Vacuum Repair down the street that pays him fifty bucks to wear the company name on his shorts. But they can take solace in the fact that every fighter has to endure this rite of passage, starting at the bottom and working his way up laboriously.

At Team Quest, Greg Thompson, Jon Krohn, Mike Dolce, and Ian Loveland were "privates." Though accomplished in their own respects, none had a real say in their own destiny. They were not in a position to turn down a fight, lest they risk an early departure from the sport. They stepped up to the plate when their manager told them to and always stayed ready so they wouldn't miss an opportunity.

During my stay at Team Quest, three of the starting fighters for Matt Lindland's Portland Wolfpack were suddenly pulled out of an upcoming match in Atlanta against the Toronto Dragons. Aaron Stark had a rib injury, Ryan Schultz was still under suspension "for his own safety" after a vicious knockout, and Chris Wilson decided it was time to take control of his career and move on to greener pastures. So Jon Krohn took the light heavyweight spot on the team for Aaron Stark. Mike Dolce stepped into the 170-pound welterweight position, and Ian Loveland, a well-known figure in a smaller circuit called Sportfight, filled the lightweight slot for Schultz.

All three had earned their shot at the big time and were excited about the opportunity. None really had the ability to say no when Matt asked, especially since the prize money and exposure were so much greater than anything they'd had before. Such was the life of the private; take what you can get and make the most out of it.

"You know, I could have turned it down, but when is an opportunity like that gonna come along again?" Jon Krohn said. "Unless it's the UFC or Pride, there's nothing better than the IFL." Though he didn't say it, I suspected loyalty to Team Quest and Matt Lindland played just as much a factor in his decision.

* * * * *

Matt Lindland could never be accused of being a "pretty boy." You'll never see him flashing ripped abs in a Calvin Klein ad or parading around in the newest line of clothing with hot chicks hanging off him. Even if he had a perfect head of thick hair, he wouldn't be caught dead flipping it over his shoulder to plug the latest gel or shampoo like Johnny Damon or Mike Piazza. Matt is also a rather boring guy. He isn't flashy, cocky, or a man of many words. He rarely trash-talks an opponent and is the last guy to brag about his accomplishments. He's a meat-and-potato eater who prefers an untucked button-down shirt and a pair of boots to a custom leather jacket and slacks.

But Matt makes up for all that in brass cajones, a razor-sharp focus on his goals, and a steadfast plan for achieving them. He recognizes that a passion for the sport of MMA isn't enough to be successful. A good business sense and financial acumen are just as critical, not only for fighters, but for managers as well.

We met in his office, which doubled as a storage room for sweatshirts and other fight gear. The walls were void of any memorabilia to look at despite a lifetime of wrestling and MMA achievements. Only one poster-sized pencil drawing was worthy of a look, barely visible in the bad lighting of the closet-sized office where million-dollar deals were made.

"What's this?" I asked.

He didn't even look at what transfixed me. "That's me at the ninety-eight World Wrestling Championships," he said.

"Did you win?"

"I got fourth actually."

"Disappointing?"

"Yeah. To me you have to expect to win. That's what we teach everyone here. You just have to go out there and fully know in your heart and soul that you're going to be victorious." He sat in a rickety metal chair while I sat on the floor, leaning up against a file cabinet. "If you enter a fight, a soccer game, or a game of cards without expecting to win, you're bound to lose."

Matt Lindland's standard is to win, period. He expects it. But the desire to win in itself only goes so far when it comes to getting paid. The underlying motivation for Lindland striding into a ring and entering in unarmed combat with another man is money. But not to build wealth, gain fame, or buy toys. Like I said, he's as plain as vanilla yogurt. He isn't like Chuck Liddell, with a mansion, a Ferrari, and a Hummer. Lindland would rather spend his money on his ranch to keep his family safe and solvent for years to come.

"My motivations have never changed," he said. "I want to make sure my family is taken care of, my kids can go to college, my wife has a place to live comfortably. Those are the reasons I'm in this business."

But how would history treat the great Matt Lindland? Despite over twenty MMA victories over high-profile opponents and being ranked as the world's number one middleweight, Matt never won a championship belt.

"Why should I?" he asked, shrugging his shoulders. "What's so special about winning a belt?"

"Well," I replied, "as much as you may not like it, the world won't remember you as fondly without one. We're a materialistic society, after all."

"If it got me a bigger paycheck, then yeah, I would pursue it." He rubbed his bald head. "But a belt doesn't put food on the table. It doesn't keep my family sheltered against the Oregon weather. It doesn't get you to heaven, and it isn't a value. So why should I focus my life on winning one?"

"It signifies the top dog of the heap," I said. "Your friend Dan Henderson, for example, has two belts and is all over the covers of magazines right now."

"Fighting the best guys is more important to me. I pursued Rich Franklin for years when he was the UFC middleweight champion. I've made it clear that I want a shot at Anderson Silva (the current middleweight champion). I took the fight with Fedor [Emelianenko] despite being two weight classes lighter because he's the best in the world. I'd rather be the guy who puts himself in the line of fire against the best fighters in the world than the guy who wins a belt and sits on it year after year."

This point was indisputable. As much as Matt shuns championship belts as shallow and materialistic, he could not be accused of avoiding anyone. In fact, he'd gone out of his way to fight bigger and better fighters. In 2006 he fought a heavier and more dangerous Quinton "Rampage" Jackson in the upstart promotion, the World Fighting Alliance. In a very close match, he took Jackson the distance and lost a decision that could have gone either way, but he gained a ton of respect in the process. And in a sport where toughness is common, respect is the only true way to separate the great from the mediocre.

During my stay at Team Quest, Lindland was three weeks away from his biggest challenge ever. He was set to fly to Russia, at a thirty-pound weight disadvantage, to fight the man most experts considered the best fighter on the planet, Fedor Emelianenko. It was a fight he didn't have to take, but he sought it out because of the type of person he was—a perfectionist.

He was also convinced that he was the best fighter in the world at any weight class, but his modest attitude kept him from proclaiming it, unlike many who feel the need to channel Muhammad Ali.

But there was one thing that had to be a sore subject. "How did you feel when Nate Quarry, one of your own fighters, was offered a title shot at Rich Franklin in 2006 and you weren't?" I asked.

"That was after the UFC got rid of me, but it still pissed me off because of the way it was handled. It was bad business."

"Bad business?"

"Yeah." He narrowed his eyes, his face changing as if I'd touched a nerve. "They [the UFC] went straight to Nate instead of coming through me, as his manager. They thought they could make him an offer and promise a bunch of money on the back end, like I wouldn't find out. It's bad business. This sport isn't big enough to get away with something like that. I mean, we all talk to each other, especially in the same camp, so what did the UFC think? That I wouldn't find out?"

"Did you want the shot instead of Nate?" I asked.

"Yeah, of course. But I wasn't in good with them at the time, so I just tried to be happy for Nate and support him. We felt he was ready at the time."

Unfortunately, Nate wasn't as ready as Matt thought. Midway through the first round, he was knocked out cold by a wicked overhand right that landed cleanly on his nose. With a weird, frozen expression of astonishment, his body stiffened as he fell to the mat like an ironing board. The punch made highlight reels forever. Casual fans and those unfamiliar with the sport will only remember Nate Quarry for being the guy who got knocked out by Rich Franklin.

The media is something Lindland understands and, more important, knows how to use to his advantage. The constant hospitality he showed me and other journalists I saw him with underscored a mutual understanding that each party benefited from the engagement as long as the rules are adhered to.

"But here's the thing I get antsy about," he told me. "People will base their perceptions off a video snippet or an interview and either be a fan of a fighter or hate him because of it. People will see an interview with Ed Herman, let's say, and if he comes across well, they'll think, 'I like this guy. He's a really good guy,' based off that interview. But we all have character flaws, you know? We're all human. If they knew us on a more personal level, they might not like us. Then again, they might like us more."

This point was along the lines of what I was out to prove, though we saw the problem from different angles. As far as his own image was concerned, I had never seen or read an interview with Matt that discussed his family values. It just wasn't something the hype machine focused on because it didn't sell magazines or DVDs. But after spending time with him and learning about his commitments to his wife and kids, I respected him more for it.

But this is the life of a professional athlete. It's the life these guys strive to achieve, and it has to be expected. Fighters like Matt and his stable are at the forefront of the MMA explosion. They interact with fans on a daily basis, either in person or through their websites. They do radio shows, sign autographs, and have followers who hang on their every word. And this behavior will only increase as MMA becomes more mainstream.

My time with Matt ended for the day when he did something that continued to underscore the kind of guy he was. A young fighter was in town practicing with Team Quest. His name was Zach, and since he was only seventeen, his father—like a responsible father should—accompanied him from Oklahoma to survey and approve the training program his son aspired to be part of.

Zach's dad was impressed with Team Quest and thanked Matt for the time he'd spent developing his son over the past week. The conversation soon turned to each man's favorite hobby, fishing. After a couple of quick "one that got away" tales, Matt invited Zach and his father to go fishing for Pacific salmon with him and his own son the next day. It was a moment that said so much about who he is because those private moments are few and far between and not meant to be interrupted by strangers.

Zach's dad caught a steelhead.

* * * * *

The next day I drove to the gym down Stark Street. The road was littered with strip clubs, pawnshops, tattoo parlors, bilingual restaurants, graffiti, and low-income housing—a familiar sight for anyone who's been to an Army post.

I caught up with Chris Wilson at his kickboxing class. Though not a household name among UFC fans, Chris "The Professor" Wilson was well known in the sport of MMA, especially among International Fight League fans. During the 2006 season, Wilson defeated league standouts Rory Markham and Jay Hieron the old fashioned way—by beating the hell out of them. Wilson is a world-class striker with an array of punches and kicks that leave opponents devastated and unable to continue. His ground game is good, but it is his legs that are truly impressive. They're like nine irons with feet. He could probably kick a golf ball from 150 yards out and stick it 6 inches from the hole with backspin if he was challenged to do so.

But being a striker means he's always on the losing end of a corporate decision. Under the unified rules of MMA, striking an opponent with a downward elbow is illegal. Kicking and kneeing an opponent to the head when he's down is also outlawed to ensure the safety of the fighters.

"Rule changes always hurt the strikers," Chris complained as he prepared for class. "They always take out the strikes. You never see any rule changes that affect the grapplers. It's biased."

"You don't think it's in the best interest of the athletes?"

"It is, but it's also done to increase viewership. If the average fan saw someone take a soccer kick to the head like they do in Brazilian Vale Tudo, they'd say it's too brutal to watch. Here's where it can get you into trouble though—it gives fighters a false sense of security because they can't get kicked. They think they don't have to worry about it so they don't train for it. And then suddenly they find themselves in Pride, where it's legal—or worse, out in the streets—and they take one to the head. Wham! I knee and elbow the shit out of people because that's my style."

Chris's fighting style is indeed "smash-mouth." His speed and agility are formidable and his reputation as an in-your-face striker is well earned. But he is also a jovial, candid, twenty-something who was more than likely a class clown at some point in his academic career. As his students gathered and donned their equipment, one asked him how he should move his hips when he threw a kick. Instead of demonstrating the proper technique, Chris threw his arms in the air like a Spanish Flamenco dancer and said, "If you can do this, you can kickbox." He broke into a gyrating salsa dance.

What was really funny, though, was that he was dead serious. He made light of the question, but there was a practical message to the joke. "Salsa is the same as kickboxing. The hip movement is exactly the same. Trust me," he told the class. (I later took his advice and discovered an important lesson—I can't salsa).

Chris gave me a basic kickboxing lesson, going through the numbered strikes one through ten, followed by a thirty-minute heavy bag session. Kickboxing strikes are easy as long as you remember that your lead hand (in my case the left because I'm right handed) is an odd number and the nonlead hand (my right) is the even number. For example, one is a left jab. Two is a right jab. Three is a left hook. Four is a right hook. The strikes continue with uppercuts, straight kicks to the sternum, and finish with high kicks to the head. Sounds easy, right? I thought so too.

The students paired up, and one held pads while the other went through the strikes as Chris called them out. At first it was easy. "One!" Chris commanded, and we all threw a left jab. "Two!" he shouted, and we all threw a right jab.

"No sweat," I thought. But then it got harder.

"One, four, ten!"

I froze, trying to think what that combination would be. It was a left jab, right hook, and right kick. But my brain forgot to tell my arms and legs that.

"Left, right, kick," my partner whispered.

"Yeah. Of course," I threw the combination.

"One, one, four, eight!" I remembered the one-one-four, but failed at the eight. My patronizing partner smiled. "Nice try."

"One, two, one, switch, nine!"

Now I was really confused. I waited for Chris to demonstrate. He threw a left jab, right cross, left jab, and followed it up by switching his feet and throwing a left kick. The difficulty with this combination is that the second jab leaves the striker's legs in the wrong position to throw an effective left kick. So the feet have to be quickly switched in order to deliver the kick with force. Not that it mattered in my case, since I could hardly muster enough velocity in my legs to scare a ballerina.

The punishment continued, and I eventually discovered that the secret to kickboxing is learning by rote—doing something so many times that your body reacts without thinking. Some call it muscle memory. I call it slow-motion pain.

Every time Chris called out a combination, I would have to watch how the other students did it in order to get it right. Later I would feel firsthand the difference between a novice striker who took an occasional class and a professional, world-class kickboxer. For all his lanky build, Chris Wilson had developed a style over many years that was incredibly efficient at delivering a solid kick. Even through thick training pads and leaning into it, his kicks nearly knocked me off my feet. Everyone knows how the body adapts to its surroundings—bodybuilders build muscle, runners shed it, swimmers develop long, lean frames that cut through the water. It has been proven in air tunnel tests that professional cyclists become more aerodynamic over time. On the receiving end of a Chris Wilson kick, my liver felt firsthand how technique and repetitive training changed the limbs of a striker into rigid, formidable weapons.

His metamorphosis into a human weapon started when his missionary parents brought him to live in São Paulo, Brazil as a child. Chris went native and immersed himself in the culture, learning Portuguese and Brazilian jiu jitsu.

"I started out like most kids wanting to take a martial art. I did tae kwon do, a little kung fu, and wrestling, but found out it wasn't for me. It wasn't practical enough."

"It wasn't practical enough?" I asked after the class.

"Yeah. For me it had to be usable in a real situation. Every art, if you do it long enough, allows you to spar and that stuff, but usually only after a lot of practice at the noncontact forms and positions. I wasn't interested in that. It was boring. I liked getting in there and mixing it up."

"In a ring?"

"Yeah, or wherever. You'd be surprised how similar the arts are when they're for real. They start to look the same when it goes to full contact. Karate, kung fu, tae kwon do—the moves look similar when it's a real fight. Speed, agility, timing, range—all that makes the difference. It doesn't matter what your favorite punch is or what kick you prefer. It just matters that you land it."

It was nice to hear that schoolyard fights were no different in the Southern Hemisphere.

After graduating high school, Chris earned a scholarship to Syracuse University because of his high SAT scores and a paper he'd written on his life experiences outside the States. But instead of becoming an Orangeman, Chris became an Oregonian.

"Fighting is simply a contest of skill." He leaned back against the wall mats like they were a La-Z-Boy. "I want to prove I can strike you before you can stop it. I want to show that I have better control, technique, and conditioning than my opponent, that I can control my breathing, my adrenaline, and focus at outwitting him. No one skill will do; you have to be well-rounded in everything, and that's what I love about this sport."

"But isn't that egotistical? If you walk out of the ring proving you're better than someone, what does that mean?"

"Well, there's a sense of achievement involved, sure. But I don't do it because I have a superiority complex. I do it to show that I have the level of skill necessary to go anywhere the fight goes and win it. If it stays on the feet, I'm good. If it goes to ground, I can win there, too. I do it to show that I can take advantage of a good situation and get out of a bad one. I train hard, I cut weight, I do drills, I do cardio, I work out two or three times a day, I learn new skills, I get beat up learning new skills, I see my family less than I want to. Winning is the reward and culmination of all that."

"Do you walk into the ring hating your opponent, or telling yourself you should hate him?"

"I don't hate anyone," he said without hesitation. "I'll admit that I want to embarrass someone by winning convincingly, but I don't want to hurt him in an injury sense. It's a professional matter. I want him to leave the ring saying, 'Wow, I wasn't ready for that guy,' then shake his hand and go drink beer with him and his family. I don't take anger into the ring like some other guys do. I'm too cerebral for that," he laughed.

At the time, Chris was in between promotions, which was the MMA equivalent of being unemployed. He'd left the International Fight League at the height of his career for bigger and better paydays when they denied him a one-year contract. He'd defeated two of the best the IFL had to offer and felt it was time to capitalize on his success. Chris would probably fight for free if MMA were still in the early stages of the mid-nineties. But these were the days of full arenas and come-and-go MMA promotions with the start-up capital to attract names like him. I had the distinct impression Chris would find one to work for.

* * * * *

Near the end of my time in Oregon, I had the good fortune of watching the team completely out of its element. A local TV camera crew arrived to take short interviews and training video of the Wolfpack that would air the following month when the IFL debuted on local television. Being a gentleman as always, Matt was more than happy to accommodate the crew, and though it interfered with training, the party was on.

The reporter was everything you'd expect in a newswoman covering an MMA team—she was cute, wore tons of makeup, over accentuated her lines, and didn't know a thing about MMA. After carefully placing Matt in a spot where the team would be practicing in the background, she started the interview, but immediately encountered problems.

To begin with, the fighters had just finished several five-minute rounds of sparring and were in no mood to look good for a camera. Hugh Heffner and ten Playboy bunnies could have walked in and gotten no warmer of a welcome. But when the boss says cooperate, the minions fall in line. So, with a hand gesture from Matt Lindland, the boys put on their best smiles and did what was asked of them.

"I'm [insert hot reporter chick name here]. I'm here with the Portland Timberwolves and we're about to watch them work out."

"Cut," the soundman said.

"How was that?" the reporter asked.

"Well . . . ," Matt started, trying hard to be nice. "We're actually the Wolfpack, not the Timberwolves. It's right here on our shirts." He pointed to the word WOLFPACK emblazoned across his blue and gray T-shirt.

"Oh. Okay," she said. "Let's do it again."

The crew reset the shot as the fighters snickered.

"Hi. I'm [re-insert hot reporter chick name here]. I'm here with the Portland Timberwolves and. . ."

I wondered how she could have messed it up again. Lindland, for all his manners, ventured a smile as he spoke into the camera without missing a beat. "Well, the Wolfpack is Portland's local IFL Team, and we train in MMA, which is Mixed Martial Arts."

"Stop," the cameraman said, knowing the footage was no good.

"I did it again?" the reporter asked.

"Yeah," Matt said, following it up with a quick ego stroke. "But I think there used to be a baseball team called the Portland Timbers. You're probably confusing us with them."

"You're probably right," the reporter said, taking the out he gave her.

Later, each member of the team got his own individual interview. For all their physical prowess, most of the fighters were completely stiff when the cameras rolled and they were forced to say something. For "Judo" Jon

Krohn, it was just plain alien. His nervous gaze darted around the gym like he was a cocaine smuggler. Jon is an easy-going guy but a life in front of the camera is probably not in the stars for the light heavyweight. Nevertheless, Jon at least managed to give politically correct answers. When asked why he fought, Jon stated, "I want to test myself against other fighters. It's a contest of skill, and I want to prove I'm the best." Well put.

Mike Dolce did the same. "I want to prove I'm better than the other guy in the ring."

Ian Loveland, on the other hand, needed some public relations coaching. "I like to punch people in the face," he said without hesitating. "It's fun."

The reporter learned a hard lesson in interviewing fighters immediately after a workout session. It was like talking to a drunk. They'd just pushed their minds and bodies to their limits and were going through the recovery period when energy and rational thought were at very low levels. It was a time when the brain didn't function at a hundred percent and tolerance for people who didn't understand them was fleeting. It was also the best time to get the truth out of them.

Lindland was completely considerate of the invasive crew and obliged them at every opportunity, no matter how inconvenient it was to him and his fighters. He knew thousands of people would see this broadcast and form opinions about him and his guys from it. This was the edge of the expanding MMA explosion, the interface between fighter and fan, the point where the sport's future was determined by how well the athletes interacted on a personal level with the viewers and made a connection through the media. Overall, Team Quest knew it and profited from it.

Matt Horwich used his camera time to quote scripture and compare his fighting career to that of ancient holy warriors. "The Bible says the faith of a mustard seed can move mountains," he said into the camera. "So with the Lord by my side, I can do the same."

They called him "Suave" because of the way he talked, which was slow and deliberate. He took the time to pronounce every syllable and to think before responding to a question. With his wide eyes and a wrinkled forehead, his delivery was a bit odd and, if you didn't know him, you would wonder if he'd been hit in the head a few too many times.

Like Chris Wilson, Horwich used religion as proof that fighting was a virtuous way of life. He'd made a name for himself by entering the ring carrying a Bible and praying for the men he'd knocked out as physicians tried to revive them.

"Religion and MMA are not separate," he said. "They're mutually supporting. Exodus says, 'God is a warrior, mighty in battle.' Proverbs says, 'From many wise advisements and wise counsels battles are won.' God wired it into our hearts to be warriors. We grow up playing Risk and war, cowboys and Indians, you know. Just because it's violent doesn't mean it goes against good faith and Christian values."

As a teenager with no direction, Matt Horwich had done what many do—drank beer, hung out with friends and tried to decide what he wanted to be when he grew up, not realizing that he was already halfway there. He was taken in by a Christian family and suddenly decided he wanted what they had—good faith and family. Since then, he'd dedicated his life to others, living clean, and spreading the good word.

"I like hanging out with fans and talking about spirituality," he said. "I started giving out autographed Bibles instead of scratch paper with my signature on it. I figured I'd give them something to help them make their dreams come true."

Balancing religion and violence is a remarkable thing in an age where we're made to feel guilty about everything from eating a Big Mac to choosing plastic bags instead of paper at the checkout counter. So it was remarkable not only to hear him espouse a clean lifestyle and dedication to his job, but also to see him live it.

Most fighters train hard or they wouldn't be in this sport, but Matt Horwich is an anomaly of dedication and drive. When the team took a break, he kept going. When he got tapped out, he'd say, "Let's do that one again." When no one wanted to grapple with him, he grabbed Tyson "The Janitor" Jeffries and worked on submissions until he couldn't anymore. He punched, sprawled, and shot in for a takedown like a kid on a never-ending Kool-Aid sugar buzz and forced his teammates to defend themselves or get slammed.

Horwich eats a steak every night for protein, doesn't own a car, and has no driver's license. By his own admission, his life consists wholly of God, fighting, heavy metal, and maintaining his MySpace account, where he has 1,640 cyber-friends. His goals in life are to win the IFL middleweight championship and to buy a piece of property where he and his friends can grow organic food, play music, and hang out. On my last day at Team Quest, Horwich was still going strong after practice and followed Greg Thompson around the gym, prodding him relentlessly with jabs and light armlocks as Greg tried to get work done.

"Cut it out, Suave! Practice is over. Go hit a bag."

But Horwich wasn't having it. He threw punches at Thompson's arms and eventually picked him up, but decided to let him down easy on the carpeted floor. "See what I have to deal with?" Thompson implored, his arms outstretched.

After one last spider roll at the unnamed sushi bar on 181st Avenue, I left Team Quest on a rare clear winter day with Mount Hood dominating the horizon to the east. Weeks later, Matt Lindland lost his fight against Fedor Emelianenko in the first round. Just moments into the fight, Matt clinched Fedor in a Greco-Roman wrestling hold and attempted to take him to the ground. Fedor grabbed the ropes and used the leverage to get himself into a dominant top position. It was a move Matt would never recover from. But he had proved himself a fighter once again. When he got back to Oregon, he would still have his ranch and his family and his team of young fighters and the work that he loved.

Of course, it would still be raining too.

CESAR GRACIE JIU JITSU

Oh the shark has pretty teeth dear
And he shows them pearly white.

—Bertolt Brecht, *"Mack the Knife"*

If you were Asian American in the 1970s, people assumed you knew the deepest secrets of kung fu, and they would cross to the opposite side of the street to avoid the throwing stars secretly hidden in your sleeves. Kung fu was all the craze, made popular by Bruce Lee's freakishly fast hands and casual swagger, as well as Carl Douglas's timelessly cool groove, "Kung Fu Fighting." After Lee's death, Bruceploitation went into full swing, as impersonators like Bruce Li and Bruce Le sprung up to capitalize on the fallen screen legend and founder of Jeet Kune Do—one of the first true mixed martial arts. Bruceploitation and the kung fu craze also fueled sham artists who made a killing by setting up dojos and promising to pass along those secrets to the gaijin for a hefty fee.

Fast-forward to the early twenty-first century, where the new martial arts craze is Brazilian jiu jitsu, due mostly to the exploits of the Gracie family. A quick perusal of the back-page advertisements in Black Belt magazine will yield no less than thirty self-proclaimed masters of Brazilian jiu jitsu offering instructional videos and books. As long as these masters don't have a prior engagement to battle a mutant ninja, you can usually convince them to make a personal appearance at a price. After all, learning how to fight evil isn't cheap. A discerning eye is a must when ferreting out these bogus pedigrees and shady associations, most of which carry no more weight than Napoleon Dynamite's "Rex Kwon Do."

But anything named Gracie is usually a safe bet. America's free-market economy makes it possible for entrepreneurs to develop, market, and sell a product or service that people want to buy. They can set the price as high as they think it's worth, and Gracie Jiu Jitsu is worth a lot. If you're unfamiliar with the storied history behind the family modifying traditional jiu jitsu and inventing the Brazilian fighting style, then allow me to briefly summarize in the same style that Jon Stewart summarized the history of America.

Mitsuyo Maeda was a highly skilled judokan trained by the founder of the art, Jigoro Kano. In the early twentieth century, he decided to take his show on the road. Wandering with his nomadic friends throughout North America and Europe, he challenged anyone and everyone to judo-style matches. His skill earned him the moniker "Count Combat," which would become the first MMA nickname. The world tour headed south in 1908, presumably because they couldn't get a bitchin' tan in London. For six years they wandered through Cuba and Central America kicking ass and eating chili con carne.

In 1914 Maeda and his troupe heard of the famous Carnivale celebration in Rio and decided to check it out. Unfortunately, they were unable to convert time zones and missed the party by three days. But something about Brazil tickled Maeda's fancy, and he stayed, marrying a local woman and forsaking the vagabond lifestyle. Throughout his life, Maeda reportedly won over 2,000 times and lost only twice.

In 1915 he ended up in Belem, Brazil, where he met a student named Carlos Gracie, a third-generation descendant of a Scots immigrant with a family the size of a Mormon cult. As the oldest of five brothers, Carlos learned jiu jitsu from Maeda and his assistant instructors, eventually developing his own techniques.

In 1925 Carlos opened his own jiu jitsu academy in Belem, but spent the majority of his time establishing the family name by challenging other schools to fights, as Maeda had done during his travels. His younger brothers, Osvaldo, Gastao, Jorge, and Helio did the majority of the actual fighting while Carlos managed and trained them. The youngest brother, Helio, was sickly and frail, but ended up as the badass of the family. It is reported that in all his extended life, Helio Gracie only lost two fights, one to Masahiko Kimura and the other to Valdemar Santana, a match that lasted three hours and forty-five minutes.

And you thought the Eco-Challenge was the first endurance sport.

Helio modified his jiu jitsu style to accommodate his smaller stature. He refined his techniques so that they were less reliant on strength, allowing him to defeat larger, stronger opponents with skill. Today, Gracie Jiu Jitsu gives hope to small, picked-on nerds everywhere, due to the exploits of his sons, Royce (pronounced Hoyce) and Rickson (pronounced Hickson).

The siblings advanced the family's trademark combative style through challenges of other martial arts disciplines for years. It was through these challenges that the UFC was born. Rorion (pronounced Horion—notice a pattern?) Gracie commercialized these challenges by establishing the pay-per-view show in 1993.

Keeping track of the Gracie family lineage is difficult at best, morbidly fascinating at worst. Every member of the clan is tied to jiu jitsu in some way or another, and Cesar Gracie is no different. The son of Carlos's daughter, Sonja, he moved to Los Angeles at the age of seven, where he fell into the family business and learned the art from his uncle Rilion (pronounced Helion—this is the last time, I swear). He was eventually awarded the prestigious BJJ black belt from the Federation of Brazilian Jiu Jitsu, which was run by his uncle, Robson (pronounced Hobson—I can't help it!) Gracie.

In Northern California, just east of the Bay and south of Napa, is Pleasant Hill. As its name implies, it's pleasant and has a hill. Thankfully not all towns get their names in this way or lots of us would live in "Thisplacesuckstown." Pleasant Hill is blessed with moderate temperatures, roads lined with manicured flora and fauna, and those soothing fountains that adorn upscale apartment complexes. Although it's no Tahiti, it's still a far cry from Gresham, Oregon. In 1993, Cesar set up Gracie Jiu Jitsu here and in 2006 expanded to Antioch, California, where he established a second gym among the farmlands of the San Joaquin Valley.

Traveling down Contra Costa Boulevard toward Gracie's studio was a stark contrast to Stark Street, which is the avenue leading up to Team Quest. Stark Street is littered with strip clubs and pawnshops. Contra Costa Boulevard is loaded with organic burger joints, bagel cafes, and in-ground sprinklers. Not a bail bondsman in sight.

Cesar's academy was nestled in the corner of a tiny strip mall between TugBoat's Fish 'n Chips and Honda's Sushi. The building had hanging vines that provided a natural shade. Confused, I checked my directions to be sure I was in the right spot. I was, and since the "OPEN" light wasn't on yet, I decided to try Honda's Sushi next door. The Lion King roll tasted as good as its picture.

When Cesar's staff arrived and opened the gym, I found little more than a bare-bones, come-as-you-are operation. There was a ring, eight heavy bags, a rack of pads, a couple of weight machines that were in need of maintenance, a huge grappling pad, a couch for visitors, and, of course, a portrait of Cesar's grandfather, Carlos Gracie. For all the favorable atmosphere Cesar's Academy had the aura of a plain old, no-frills gym where both ordinary and extraordinary men gravitated to sweat, bleed, and struggle to achieve their Octagon dreams. Among those men were four extraordinary pupils who were quickly making names for themselves in MMA.

Jake Shields and Gilbert Melendez are very talented fighters, but when the UFC abolished its lightweight division in 2003, it closed the doors to not only them but all athletes of smaller stature. Some chose to move up to welterweight, but these two chose to stay light and hock their wares in Japan, quickly rising through the ranks of Shooto and Pride's Bushido tournaments to become champions. When the MMA craze exploded in the United States, they were largely left out because the UFC didn't bring back the lightweight division until 2006. Consequently, Shields and Melendez were not household names, despite their huge success overseas.

Both trained at Cesar Gracie's Jiu Jitsu alongside his other two rising stars, Nick and Nathan Diaz. But Jake and Gil hadn't gone completely unnoticed, and on my first day at Cesar's, I learned that the world was about to become more interested in Pleasant Hill.

* * * * *

Jake had recently signed a three-fight deal with MMA start-up EliteXC, which had a broadcasting deal with Showtime. He would be fighting on their next show in just six weeks, which meant the hype machine was in full swing to promote him. Showtime sent a film crew to Pleasant Hill to make a documentary on Jake, and chose this day to get lots of footage.

The shoot was scheduled to start at noon, so when 12:30 rolled around, the young Californian grew noticeably concerned at the absence of his stablemates and kept looking at his watch like an Kenyan waiting for the start of a marathon. Fighters are never on time and the simple fact that Jake was punctual was a triumph of timekeeping. Cesar finally arrived fifteen minutes later. And the last two men everyone was really waiting for, Nick and Nathan Diaz, came in at 12:50. They shook hands with Jake, apologized for being late, and took their gear to the back room to change while Jake warmed up.

When the brothers were ready, Showtime finally got what it wanted—grade A pugilism. But it seemed to me that the producer had ulterior motives for putting Nick Diaz in the ring to spar with Jake first. On the surface, this was to profile Jake alongside a fighter with more name recognition, but Nick Diaz had a bad-boy reputation and was known for being angry at the world. Every good show needs a hero, a villain, and conflict to draw viewers in and invest them emotionally. The hero here was Jake Shields, the young, clean-cut, All-American wrestler with the boyish charm of the kid you babysat in grade school, everybody's friend next door, brought up by responsible parents. The villain was Nick Diaz, a gruff-looking, darker-skinned man who could have the appearance of a Middle-Eastern terrorist with the right camera angles and strategic lighting.

It was classic good versus bad, only lacking the damsel in distress. The producers were making sensationalized TV that reflected the sentiments of a paranoid society, and it had a simple goal—bring in more viewers. Two men who trained together were squeezed into cartoon shapes of good and evil by media magnates.

In front of the camera, Jake was as classy as a young Clark Gable in a pair of board shorts. He made the cameraman's job easy by making his face available wherever he went, especially in the clinch. He even rested against the ropes with a sports drink in hand like Michael Jordan.

And the hype machine smiled.

Jake's rise to popularity was partly due to good timing. After winning for years in Japan, he was noticed by Calvin Ayre and his fledgling MMA promotion, BodogFight. They put him on the reality show Costa Rica Combat. The show gained the attention of Japanese fight promoters K-1

HEROs and their partners EliteXC and Showtime, who put him squarely in front of the camera to hype their upcoming event in Los Angeles. Jake was definitely a rising star, and if he continued to win and avoid the pitfalls of poor contract decision making, he was destined to be a household name.

Though he wasn't living on Easy Street yet, he'd managed to earn his way into the promised land of MMA that so many fighters strive for—no more day job. Jake had earned enough prize and sponsorship money that he had the luxury of being able to train full-time and avoid punching a clock for eight hours a day, a situation that an estimated 60 percent of fighters in the sport couldn't claim. He taught jiu jitsu part-time at the Fairtex gym in San Francisco, but mostly for his own self-fulfillment.

Just as Jake was a natural in front of the camera, Nick Diaz was equally as savvy behind it. After sparring one round with Jake, he insisted one of the younger fighters, whose name was Jimmy, climb into the ring to get some film time. "Just get a round in and get yourself seen," he told him. Nick knew how much the young guns struggled to get exposure in a sport that was becoming harder and harder to break into. It was a quick lesson in the economics of MMA that Jimmy was grateful for. But Nick wasn't finished telling his pupil how things worked.

"When they interview me, I'll get camera time, but I'll be wearing Jake's T-shirt. If he gets interviewed about me in the future, then he'll wear mine. Everyone wins. You gotta take advantage of this kinda thing." Sure enough, Nick donned a "Jake Shields American Jiu Jitsu" T-shirt just before his own interview to show support for his training partner.

With this phase of filming complete, Jake and the camera crew packed up and headed to the Fairtex gym in San Francisco, leaving the Diaz brothers, Val Ignatov, and me at Cesar's. I waited patiently for Nick as he continued to train. There was no doubt he loved his job. He studied every move in detail and then practiced it repeatedly to make sure he had it right. He grappled with Val like he was a rodeo cowboy in his seventh second on Beelzebub the Killer Bull until everyone but him got tired, including his younger brother Nathan.

Taking a moment to lean back against a padded wall, Nathan opened up about growing up in the shadow of a rising-star.

"I don't mind it," he said. "Nick's been a great big brother. We live together, train together, hang out together. It's all good."

"Did you get your start in MMA from him?"

"Yep. But it was different back then."

Nate is only nineteen years old, so I had to chuckle when he said, "back then."

"The money sucked," he said. "I got like two hundred and fifty bucks for my first show. Now it's a lot more. It's taken off so fast that everyone wants to get behind it and the prize money is getting bigger, but it's still not enough. I see it this way. We train three times as hard as boxers so we should get three times the money they do. I mean we work Muay Thai, jiu jitsu, kickboxing, boxing, wrestling, but boxers only have to train one thing: boxing. We should be paid more for all the time we train and all the effort we put into it, but we're not. Boxers get millions for a fight, but no one in MMA is getting that much except Chuck [Liddell] maybe."

"Did you get paid while you were in the house?" I asked referring to his time on season five of *The Ultimate Fighter*, which he eventually won.

"Nope. That place sucked. We couldn't do anything. We couldn't leave, couldn't watch TV, couldn't do shit. I almost went crazy the night my brother fought Gomi. I wanted to jump over the fence and run down to buy a ticket."

When Nick fought Takanori Gomi on Pride Fighting Championship's adventurous foray into U.S. territory, it was one of the best fights of the year. Nick handed the planet's top lightweight a resounding defeat while Nathan was locked up just a few miles away making sure the hype machine saw his mug.

"It's cool. I mean people recognize me now and I get some perks from it, so I can't bitch about being there too much."

Nathan's experience was right in line with the men from Team Quest. While the process of being sequestered to film a show was a temporary burden, it paid huge dividends in the long run in exposure. Name recognition also put young Nathan Diaz at the front lines of the MMA explosion. Months later when he won *The Ultimate Fighter* finale against Manyel Gamburian, he would be instantly vaulted into "rising star" status and learn what it's like to be a minor celebrity, something his brother knew all too well.

Ironically the hype machine had led me to believe Nathan was a total punk, which wasn't the case. That was surprising because he fit the profile of a kid who could easily become one. He and Nick were raised by a single mother and virtually no father in Stockton, California. They'd had a ton of hurdles to overcome as youths, not the least of which was anger management, so the word on the street was that they were difficult and self-centered.

But just as Matt Lindland said about fans making judgments based on an interview or two, I had misjudged Nathan based on what I'd seen in a few episodes of *The Ultimate Fighter*. On the show, he nearly started a fight with Robert Emerson over a trivial matter and then another one with Karo Parisyan over a misunderstanding. Fortunately, cooler heads prevailed, but the damage was done. Nathan Diaz was portrayed as a self-destructive hothead who could easily be goaded into a fight.

However, I saw a side of him that the cameras never seemed to capture— that of a thinking man who knows more about his surroundings than the casual observer would suspect. He was affable, bright, and willing to help others in need. This view was underscored when he and Nick offered their house to the young fighter named Jimmy while he trained in Stockton.

Nick Diaz continued to grapple long past the time I was told to be in San Francisco for the continuation of Jake Shields's documentary. Although I desperately wanted to spend time with the man *Real Fighter* magazine had profiled in a story called "Angry Young Man," I had to go. I was sure there would be time to catch up with him later. But, as I later learned on several more occasions during the week, Nick Diaz has his own agenda.

* * * * *

The founder and chairman of the Fairtex Corporation of Thailand is a man known as Phillip Wong, mostly because his given Thai name (Bujong Busarakamwongs) is too difficult to pronounce. The Fairtex Company got its start in 1958 by producing textiles at a fair price, which is where its name comes from. Mister Wong had a passion for the national sport of Muay Thai, and in 1975 he opened a gym for poor children and troubled young men to give them a second chance in life through the sport he loved. In

1994, he began producing high-quality training equipment and provided it to martial arts instructors and students in North America.

In the last two decades, Fairtex opened Muay Thai gyms in Europe and Japan, as well as two in the United States—one in Mountain View, California, and the other in downtown San Francisco. Fairtex has sponsored thirty Muay Thai champions and recently expanded to sponsoring mixed martial arts fighters, but not in the usual way. Instead of giving athletes cash payments for living expenses, Fairtex provides them with gear, such as gloves, pads, shorts, hand wraps, and anything else they need in order to train effectively. It's not much, but it gets them started in the right direction until they earn money for themselves.

I know all this because Mike Bruno, a Fairtex public relations representative with a lazy afro, told me the entire company history as we watched Jake being filmed at the Fairtex gym in San Francisco. In between history lessons on the company, Mike sprinted to a back room to get Fairtex T-shirts to put on any fighter in the background of the shoot. I asked for a freebie, but got denied like O.J. Simpson gets denied bail.

The Fairtex facility was impressive. Besides being on prime real estate downtown, it was large by MMA gym standards, clean, well lit, and outfitted with a multitude of weights and cardio equipment. There were more heavy bags than I'd seen anywhere and enough mat space for an entire collegiate

Jake Shields prepares to spar for the cameras.

wresting team. The walls were adorned with the history of Fairtex fighters and the normal stench of sweat was masked by a faint aroma of what I believe was incense mixed with Tiger Balm.

In the middle of the gym, surrounded by several large, flat-screen televisions, was a boxing ring placed well enough away from the walls that bleachers could be brought in for a public event. The gym was high tech to say the least.

Jake had slightly more composure than the guys at Team Quest, but was still as stiff as the IRS on April 15 in front of the camera. The short, nerdy Showtime producer instructed him to "lift your chin more, bring your chest up," as he tried to achieve a look that eluded him.

Thirty onlookers, mostly other fighters, acted like they were sparring, but really watched from outside the camera's view as Jake tried hard to emulate a GQ model. The producer shouted over the noise of the gym, "Give me something more intense," which sounded idiotic. I didn't think the producer wanted to see the kind of "intensity" Jake was accustomed to summoning. Saying those words was like dangling a T-bone stake in front of a starving bear. Although sitting in front of a camera doing little should be easy work, Jake's demeanor made it clear that it was grating on his nerves. But patience and tolerance are necessary when your image is at stake.

I caught his eye in between shots and gave him a sarcastic smile as if to say, "Look at the big bad fighter posing like a pretty boy" just to poke fun at him. In return, I received a glare that made me feel like a piggy bank looking at a ten-year-old with his dad's hammer.

Sometimes being a smart ass isn't a great idea.

It was a ballet of media exposure. Mike played musical shirts while the camera crew manipulated themselves into contortionist positions to get a shot and I went around asking questions. But very little in the way of actual training was taking place. The Showtime producer was demanding and cared nothing about how disruptive his presence was, going so far as to stage a sparring match between Jake and Gilbert with a ladder in the middle of the ring. As the cameraman perched high above the fighters, I watched in curious delight, waiting for one of them to plow into the ladder.

Josh McDonald, who was up next to spar with Jake, was stopped and repositioned by the crew to get a better shot. Out of breath and clearly frustrated, Josh confessed they were a distraction. "Yeah, this isn't much fun," he admitted. "But in the end it's a good thing. It'll benefit us all"

Moments later, Gilbert Melendez broke ranks. "Mike, can I take this off now?" he pleaded, referring to his Fairtex shirt that was two sizes too small and constricting his arms. "My shots are done and it's bothering me." Mike reluctantly agreed, stripping Gil's shirt off him and putting it on someone else, sweat and all.

Oh, the price of fame.

It was the intersection of art and business, where hard work and intense training crash headlong into the rigors of success and celebrity. Here was where a young fighter's dreams came true, that all-important big break when someone with power took notice and decided he was worth a sizable investment. Here was the next level of media exposure, the first real payoff. Here's where the law of diminishing returns meant nothing and the future looked as bright as could be, where big dreams got even bigger and new dreams were born.

I wanted to hear more about the business side of the sport. It was time to corner the man who managed these fighters and who came from a family that built its own fortunes on fight promotions.

* * * * *

Cesar Gracie has his own time zone. As I said before, fighters are never on time; it's like a culture of lateness with them. But Cesar's even worse. If he says he's going to be somewhere at a certain time, be sure to add at least thirty minutes to it. I arrived at his Antioch gym two minutes late for our 10:30 appointment. Cesar arrived at 11:00 sharp, perfect if you live in Cesar Standard Time.

Cesar is an odd mix of laid-back skateboard slacker and Andrew Dice Clay without the Mother Goose stories. Settling into his office chair and never removing his sunglasses, he provided glowing insight on the sport of MMA as his phone consistently vibrated. To his credit, he never answered it until Gary Shaw, the owner of EliteXC, called.

"The UFC is a monopoly, which I thought was illegal in this country," he said. "Don't get me wrong. I don't hate the UFC, but I don't think monopolies are fair, and they're certainly a monopoly. If anyone were to get their shit together and sue the UFC for illegal business practices, they'd win. But no one has the resources to do that, except maybe the IFL, so it'll never happen."

Zuffa, the parent company of the UFC, had just purchased its only major competition, the Japan-based Pride Fighting Championships. The UFC's status as the giant of the sport was undisputable and threatened everyone who didn't fight in the octagon, but other promotions were enjoying moderate success. Strikeforce, BodogFight, King of the Cage, the IFL, and K-1, whom Jake Shields fought for, were pulling in profits, though they certainly struggled to do so against the UFC and its marketing abilities. But comparing them to true monopolies in American history, such as nineteenth-century Pennsylvania railroads, U.S. Steel in 1920, or AT&T in the 1980s isn't really fair. Those conglomerations regularly practiced anticompetitive business strategies and secured legislation from corrupt politicians who received benefits in return.

"So we'll just play their game until the world looks the way they want it to," Cesar continued.

"And what's that?" I asked.

"The Nevada State Athletic Commission [NSAC] standards. Now that Zuffa owns Pride, they're already looking at unified weight classes and unified rules to make everything the same. Instead of a fighter being able to move from the UFC to Pride like Nick [Diaz] did to find a better venue for his style, he'll only find the same thing he left and may have to compete in a different weight class where he's at a disadvantage."

The lightweight division in the UFC is 146–155 pounds, but it's 161 and under in Pride. It's not a huge amount, but when someone like Jens Pulver, who walks around normally at 155 pounds, has to put on weight to make himself equal to his opponent, it can slow him down and put him behind the power curve. Pride also uses a boxing-style ring with four ropes instead of an enclosed cage. This changes a fighter's game plan when he doesn't have solid cage walls to use for leverage.

But the rule set was where the two organizations existed in parallel worlds. In the UFC, kneeing or kicking an opponent when he's on his knees is illegal, but it's allowed in Pride, as are foot stomps. This changes a fighter's strategy altogether, especially for Brazilians like Mauricio "Shogun" Rua, who loves to heel-stomp a downed opponent.

All this changed just a few weeks prior to my stay at Cesar's when Zuffa, the parent company of the UFC, bought Pride Fighting Championships, altering the MMA landscape forever. The melding of Pride and the UFC meant fighters whose style fit the Pride ring better than the UFC Octagon would no longer have the refuge of moving from one promotion to the other where they fit in best. Fighters would have to accommodate the UFC and their unified MMA rule set or seek out a different (and smaller) promotion.

"Nick's treatment after the Gomi fight was a travesty," he continued. "First, it was the first time a fighter was given a no-contest ruling for testing positive for marijuana. Secondly, since when does the NSAC overturn an international competition? I mean this event took place in Nevada, but it's a Pride decision. It's not the NSAC's jurisdiction."

Diaz's treatment was certainly unique, but so were the conditions that led to the fight in the first place. Nick Diaz was not an international sport figure like "The Fireball Kid" Takanori Gomi. After losing three high-profile fights in a row, all by decision, Nick's future in the UFC was in question. He then racked up two victories, but they were minor wins and weren't televised, so he left the organization with a so-so reputation. Nick opted to fight for Pride and was immediately put up against Gomi, who was considered one of the best fighters in the world. Nick wasn't even considered in Gomi's league, a perception that was reinforced early in the fight when Gomi nearly knocked him out. But the scrappy kid from Stockton had the heart of a champion and came back to win, only to see his victory overturned by the NSAC for testing positive for marijuana. Despite the ruling, he redefined the term "spoiler" in the MMA world.

"Pride is an international sports organization that tarnished Nick's record with a bullshit "no contest" decision. And why?"

I shook my head.

"Because the UFC owns the NSAC," Cesar said. "The Nevada State Athletic Commission will do whatever the UFC asks it to do. They just hired that guy Ratner from the NSAC, so now all of them are looking for a sweet deal from the UFC and want to keep them happy to get it."

In 2006 Marc Ratner, who had been with the NSAC for twenty-two years, thirteen of which were as the commission's executive director, was hired by the UFC. In Cesar's opinion, the NSAC was bowing to the whims of the UFC in order to set themselves up for bigger paychecks after their time in the commission was done. It wasn't unlike the "kissing up" that some military officers engage in to cultivate cozy relationships with companies like Boeing, General Dynamics, and Raytheon. By getting in good with these companies, they secure themselves a job when the Army, Navy, or Air Force is done with them. It's not illegal, but it does venture into the realm of ethically questionable, especially if tangible items, such as cash and/or benefits are proven to have changed hands. Then again, Marc Ratner may have been the most qualified candidate for a legitimate job opportunity in the UFC that was made public and above the table. Not everything is an "Area 51" or "Grassy Knoll" conspiracy.

Diaz had been given no chance to win in his bout against Gomi, but he did—in spectacular fashion on a huge stage. He was supposed to be just another highlight reel in Gomi's career, a stepping-stone on Gomi's way to superstardom on a night Pride picked to go all-out in the American market with a massive show.

"Nick was picked for that fight to be the villain to Gomi's hero. He was supposed to go in there, flip off the cameras, make everyone hate him and lose so Gomi would be the triumphant victor and get more famous. But it didn't happen that way," Cesar said.

"Well, he flipped off the cameras."

Cesar flashed a smile. "That was his way of saying he wasn't going to let the spectacle of the moment get to him. It was his way of saying he wasn't nervous."

Nerves or not, showing your middle finger to the world is rarely taken well. "So why does Nick have such an image problem?" I asked.

"Does Nick have an image problem?" Cesar retorted.

"Well, you said yourself everyone perceives him as a villain," I said, remembering the earlier sparring session between Nick and Jake. "He comes across on camera as having a chip on his shoulder."

"So how is that a problem?" Cesar again asked.

I paused, not sure why he didn't grasp my point. "Well, it's not going to win him many fans."

"But it gets lots of people talking about him—like yourself," he said, almost disappearing behind his pearly white smile.

Then it all became clear. William Randolph Hearst once said, "You can say anything you like about me. Just be sure to spell my name right." His point? There's no such thing as bad press. It's present everywhere in our society. When a celebrity does something wrong, like Paris Hilton going to jail, Mel Gibson spouting an anti-Semitic tirade, or O.J. Simpson committing a double homicide, it's instantly all the rage. Every media outlet in the world scrambles to cover it, and average citizens are bombarded ad nauseam with the minutiae of the subject. When celebrities do as they should and conduct themselves as model citizens, they fade from the public vision. But once they step out of line, you can be sure the paparazzi will be there to splash it across the front pages, TV, and Internet.

Nick Diaz was the MMA version of a bad boy making headlines. Still, it seemed to me that behind his unassuming smile and smoky sunglasses, Cesar Gracie was the man pulling the strings and using his own hype machine to tout Diaz. Gracie's way, probably because he lacked the resources of the UFC, was completely negative. Nick Diaz, though certainly no cherub, was somewhat a victim of his manager's aspirations.

Despite his public image there was no denying Nick's fighting prowess. He sported a winning record, as did all of Cesar's roster, no doubt in part because of the Gracie Jiu Jitsu system.

"I think we're so successful because we take an open-minded approach," Cesar said. "A lot of jiu jitsu schools are close-minded. You can't do this and you can't do that. No footlocks and all these other restrictions. It's too closed off. I encourage my guys to do whatever works, which is what my grandfather started the art to be like in the first place. But as it became a business, people did things they knew and shied away from venturing out. I was more like, 'If you learn something show it to me.'"

Cesar's form of jiu jitsu was known for incorporating Sambo, leglocks, and spending a considerable amount of time without a gi, the standard dress for martial arts. "We train a lot with both gi and no gi. It is a fight, after all, and there aren't any in the streets, you know? But it's the open-minded attitude that probably sets us apart. We try whatever works best and promote a healthy atmosphere with no rivalries in the gym, no egos, that kind of stuff. Otherwise the talent pool gets depleted."

"If you want to see a gym with no egos, check out Team Quest," I joked.

"I like the guys at Team Quest. Some of the hardest working people are in Oregon. But their technique sucks."

I gave him the sideways confused puppy dog look.

"Here's what I think. As you go from south to north, technique goes down while dedication goes up. You see the people in L.A. are pussies. They don't want to work. They want the rewards without putting in the time to earn them. They're not dedicated and hard working people. They're all flash. But as you go north, that changes and people get harder. Their work ethic gets better until you get to Oregon. Technique is another story. Technique in L.A. is good. They know how to use the principles of jiu jitsu. It actually gets better as you come north to here and then gets worse as you go farther north to Oregon. Up there they're all wrestlers, which is fine if that's the style you're comfortable with. But wrestling is not jiu jitsu."

"So the best technique is here in Northern California?"

"Of course," he smiled.

It was an interesting theory, but there was a major variable that he wasn't considering—the takedown. Submission wrestling, as practiced by Team Quest, was not the same as Gracie's style of Brazilian Jiu Jitsu. Wrestlers are trained from an early age to achieve the goal of pinning their opponent's shoulders to the mat. As they emerged in MMA, wrestlers had to relearn their art and incorporate new moves to achieve a different outcome—a submission instead of a pin. Jiu jitsu, on the other hand, did not have to alter its goal; it was conceived around the principles of using leverage and chokes to achieve submissions, and it borrowed selected moves from other martial arts. But another difference between the two, which favored wrestling, was their starting positions. Most jiu jitsu classes started from the knees instead of standing. The opponents faced each other while already in a downed position instead of on the feet. Jiu jitsu fighters never had to learn the art of the takedown like wrestlers did. Therefore, jiu jitsu practitioners were not as proficient at taking their opponents down.

Cesar felt jiu jitsu practitioners had better technique, which might be true, but only after the fight went to the ground. Wrestlers actually had better technique when it came to taking their opponent off of his feet.

The whole philosophy of jiu jitsu is about efficiency—that a man of smaller stature with good technique will not have to work hard to defeat a man of larger and stronger size. The same, according to Cesar, was not true of wrestlers.

* * * * *

Back in the gym I found a fire hydrant that ate a surfer. Josh McDonald was a short, Hawaiian-looking bruda with a scar like a map of the Panama Canal running from his knee to his ankle. I figured he had suffered the injury on the playing field of his choice. Sports injuries in America are almost a rite of passage, as common among the nation's youth as working in a fast food restaurant. It is rare, however, to hear a wrestler or grappler tell a tale of how he had a fourteen-inch rod placed into his leg after having it broken during practice.

"I was rolling with another guy and got cranked backward before I could get my legs underneath me and it just snapped." His surgical scars were truly admirable. Almost like colorful tattoos, they stuck out and drew a cringe at the thought of a leg breaking like a dry branch under the weight of another man.

But Josh's scars were probably the least interesting facet about him. At twenty-seven years old and a relative newcomer to MMA, Josh was the baby-faced, clean-cut, voted most-likely-to-succeed boy next door, much like Jake Shields. The son of good parenting who aspired to be a good parent himself, Josh was what many people strove to be like as human beings, if not necessarily as fighters.

After high school, he wrestled for San Francisco State University alongside (coincidentally) Jake Shields and Gilbert Melendez. But after his life in academia ended, Josh suffered from the same condition that afflicts most wrestlers—the dreaded what-to-do-with-these-skills-now disease. Many wrestlers face an uncertain future after years of training in a sport that has no professional counterpart. Football, basketball, and baseball players can try to transition to the professional ranks once their collegiate careers end. But for wrestlers, unless they're talented enough to coach, the choices of how to use their finely honed skills are limited.

Until now.

MMA has opened up a whole new marketplace for the former wrestler, and thanks to pioneering fighters like Matt Hughes and Dan Henderson, all respectable MMA training camps have a resident wrestling coach to develop ground skills. Josh fit this scenario to a tee. When his fellow alums started achieving success in MMA, he naturally followed suit and got into the fight game.

On the other hand, like Jake, Josh could have done anything in life. He was a high school stud who helped look out for his siblings while his dad worked two jobs and studied to be a pilot. He never got into trouble as a kid, had the benefit of a diverse upbringing that exposed him to different cultures, and was imbued with good moral standards by parents who took the time to mentor him. After a couple of community colleges and various wrestling programs, he earned his degree from San Francisco State, but was undecided on a career field after school.

He started working with kids at a daycare/gym where he taught basic gymnastics and received training on childcare, which became his focus, but he needed more. He enjoyed watching kids learn and grow, but after a while he realized he had some maturing of his own to do. With the help of his SF State wrestling buddies, he turned to MMA.

"I had to learn more about myself. I had to force myself out of the comfort zone and try to exceed my own expectations."

"Can't you do that sailing the open seas or climbing a midsize mountain?" I asked. "Mount Shasta isn't too far away."

"Not risky enough," he chuckled.

"I'm sure someone who's climbed it would disagree with you."

"I needed more. It was important to me to know what kind of person I was under duress. I needed something risky. I can't imagine a life without it. I think people are too afraid to see where their talents will take them. I tried to get on *The Ultimate Fighter* and made it to the final fifty, but didn't get picked."

"How do you think the kids you work with would be affected if they saw you on TV beating someone up?"

"They probably wouldn't understand it, so I'd have to explain it to them. I'd have to show them that it's a sport and there's a winner and a loser and that no one really gets hurt, at least not permanently—especially me," he laughed, gesturing toward his scar. "Kids are remarkably adaptable. I love watching them learn and grow. I wish adults were the same."

* * * * *

After watching fighters for several days, I was feeling the itch to compete. I'd grappled with soldiers as part of the Army's combatives program, but that was part-time at best and had a completely different objective from sport fighting. Now I was in the company of professional fighters, which made me ask the logical question, "How would I fare against them?"

Jake Shields was teaching a jiu jitsu class that night at the Fairtex gym in downtown San Francisco and invited me to join in. The opportunity to take a grappling session from a decorated Gracie student and professional fighter who'd never been submitted was an opportunity only a fool would pass up, and my momma didn't raise any of those.

Unfortunately, I'd misjudged the driving time from Cesar's gym in Pleasant Hill and arrived at five o'clock, which meant I had two hours to kill, plenty of time to find sushi. Unable to find any, I ended up opting for clam chowder in a sourdough bread bowl on Pier 39. This was great for my palate, but it turned out to be a bad mistake for the rest of my body. By the time I got back to Fairtex gym and began the physical exertion of submission wrestling, I was a wee bit queasy.

Grappling is demanding. It requires every muscle in the body to get involved to its maximum potential. As a novice grappler I knew this, but I was confident that my physical conditioning in the Army could handle a stomach full of clam chowder and grappling at the same time. This might have been true if I were working with Frodo and some hobbits. But these were talented jiu jitsu practitioners who'd been taught by one of the best, and I was in for ass pain from the beginning.

I first grappled with Travis, a large man who bordered on obese and didn't look very intimidating, but he slapped an armbar on my right elbow like it was child's play. An armbar is accomplished when one grappler secures an opponent's arm, hooks his legs over the upper torso, and arches backward to concentrate all his body weight onto the elbow joint, bending it at an angle it was not designed for. It is very painful, and unless the person caught in the submission taps out quickly, it can snap like a twig.

Novice grapplers are always in danger of getting caught in an armbar when they're in someone's guard, meaning in between their legs. And it is infinitely more painful than it appears. Travis trapped my arm by grabbing the wrist and threw his legs over my head, bending my arm back before I could say, "Oh, shit." I tapped his leg, signaling I'd had enough and to please release me from this ride before my arm broke. A tap out is the MMA version of an S&M safe word, which I had no problem using at this point.

After five minutes of utter domination, I was embarrassed and breathing hard, and my clam chowder dinner was bubbling up. It's important to note that everybody in Jake's class grapples on a common mat, just inches away from each other. Normally this doesn't pose a problem unless some new guy loses focus of where he is and rolls too close to another pair of grapplers.

About the time I realized that Travis and I were dangerously close to Jake and Brett "The Angry Hick" Bergmark, I was introduced to one of Jake's heels (I believe it was the left one) that crashed into my eye as he spun around to reverse Brett.

As the timer went off, signaling the end of the round, I joked with Travis. "Lucky for you I'm jet lagged."

"I'm just taking whatever I can get," he replied modestly. I later learned Travis was a BJJ black belt, which made my lack of performance against him less humiliating, if not less painful.

Next I grappled with a smaller, skinnier man whose name I think was Brett, though definitely not Brett "The Angry Hick" Bergmark, who was on the other side of the mat. He introduced himself and slapped my hand, and once again I found myself in a quick and painful armbar on the same arm that Travis had graciously decided not to break off and use as a yard mallet. Since grappling rounds in Jake's class lasted five minutes and I'd been submitted in less than one, I had a ways to go still, and Brett wasn't going to let me off easy.

We went at it again. Brett immediately pulled me into his guard, which felt like skinny vise grips around my waist. It might be threatening to a straight man's ego to find himself between the legs of another man. But I was more focused on not getting caught in another painful submission than my self-esteem. My competitive spirit was driving me on to find a way to win, no matter how much the local clam chowder disagreed with me.

Brett immediately went for a leg triangle choke, wrapping his legs around my head and one arm. It's a move that squeezes the jugular veins and stops the flow of blood to the head, causing the recipient to pass out. He almost secured the choke on me, but relying on brute strength and ignorance, I postured up and muscled my way out of it. However, this left me vulnerable to yet another armbar, which he took advantage of. I tried to hold out this time, but the pain was too much. You would think tapping out gets easier after the third time, but trust me, it doesn't.

Now I found myself with three long minutes left in the round and an aching right elbow. This was agonizing. Seeing that I was susceptible to an armbar, Brett attempted it a few more times, which I managed to slip out of with a great amount of effort and a lucky layer of sweat. Here I learned a lesson known to most fighters. Sweat makes submissions difficult to secure, especially near the end of a fight when the two combatants, not wearing shirts, are covered in it. It's a less tasteful part of the strategy of the sport.

Although I had managed to avoid Brett's final submission attempts, I had been constantly on the defensive, despite a forty-pound weight advantage and apparent strength superiority. The man's technique was incredible, and it frustrated me. He defeated my size and strength by knowing exactly which joint to attack and when. I was always blocking his moves, never able to go on the offense. Each time I tried to pass his guard, he blocked me and went for a finishing move of his own. It was the practical application of the most basic technique of jiu jitsu—using technique and leverage to compensate for a smaller stature. Brett was nothing to admire in the strength and size department, but he was at home when the fight went to the ground. When the timer sounded to end the round, relief engulfed me.

Sweaty and tired, I cornered Jake and Gilbert Melendez as they cooled down from the workout. Jake heard my full-time job was in the Army and despite me being there to ask him questions and delve into his personal life, he threw one back at me that caught me off guard.

"Can we win in Iraq?" he asked bluntly. "I mean the Sunnis and Shiites have hated each other for centuries. What makes us think we can go in there and create a situation where they'll stop their tribal fighting and live peacefully?"

Before this moment, I was certain no one under the age of thirty cared about anything other than which video game console they were going to buy next. So having Jake Shields, a man who specializes in inflicting pain and competes in a sport where the athletes are generally regarded as idiots, ask this question blindsided me.

"What makes us think we can install a democracy overnight when ours took, what, two hundred plus years to perfect?" Jake asked.

Jake's understanding of and interest in world affairs was inspiring. I proceeded to explain my side of the issue from the perspective of a career Army officer who'd never been to Iraq. Having witnessed definite progress in Afghanistan, I could convey the sense of promise there, but could only tow the party line or pass on the things my friends had told me about Iraq. It wasn't my forte, but I tried to provide as much insight as I could.

It was Thursday night and the "dynamic duo" was headed to a private viewing party of *The Ultimate Fighter* for Nathan Diaz. Gilbert and Jake were roommates, and from what I'd heard, had legendary sparring matches in the middle of their apartment after a night on the town. Allegedly the pair had cleared out the coffee table and gone at it more than a few times, but in a purely competitive manner rather than a full fight.

"It's overhyped," Jake said. "We have this big living room and a couple of times it's turned into a wrestling mat." He shrugged his shoulders and smiled. "We both think we're better than each other. What can you do?"

Jake threw a shirt on (not a Fairtex one) and tossed his gear into a gym bag. "You going to Nate's party?" he asked me.

"No. I'm going out to Cesar's in Pleasant Hill to get some time with Nick," I said as we parted ways. Cesar had carved out some one-on-one time for me and Nick, but it never happened. The meeting was supposed to take place at 7:00 p.m. at Cesar's gym, so when 9:00 rolled around and I was still waiting, I was baffled. Eventually one of his friends told me he'd already gone to San Francisco to meet with Nate. It was frustrating, but I still had a couple of days to corner him.

Sometime during my match with Brett I must have also caught a forearm or hand to the face because I had a shiner over my left eye the next day. I wore it like a badge of honor from Jake Shield's jiu jitsu class.

* * * * *

The next day I traveled to Santa Rosa, California, to see one of Cesar's disciples at work. Santa Rosa is the largest city in Sonoma County, with an easy climate that makes it ideal for wine production. David Terrell grew up here, and it's where he returned to when it was time to open his own gym. He's what you would expect from a suburbanite Californian: athletic, perfect teeth, and good-looking to the point that you don't notice his array of tattoos. He first started training with Cesar when he was eighteen, making the hour-and-a-half drive from Santa Rosa to Pleasant Hill three times a week because Cesar offered the best training around and at the best possible price.

"He let me train for free until I could afford to pay him," he said. "I guess he saw something in me and that's why, I don't know."

Terrell had a healthy 4-1 MMA record in Pancrase and smaller shows when he burst onto the UFC scene in 2004. At UFC 49 David brutally knocked out Matt Lindland in twenty-four seconds, announcing his coming out with authority. But in his next fight, he lost the UFC middleweight championship title to Evan Tanner in 2005. He fought only one more time, a year later when he defeated Scott Smith, but because of injuries, had since stayed out of professional fighting.

After taking twenty minutes of Dave's time to selfishly talk to him about my agenda, I let him go teach his MMA class, though there seemed to be very little teaching going on—at least to my untrained eyes.

"Everyone in the cage," he ordered.

Ten fighters piled into a mini-Octagon that looked to be half the size of a regulation arena. "Three rounds, five minutes," he ordered.

A fighter set a timer while two others circled the cage waiting for it to beep. I'd seen this before. Sparring rounds were something Team Quest was very good at. They would spar with each other for five minutes with gloves and shin pads to avoid leg and hand injuries. Between rounds the fighters got a one-minute rest for a quick drink of water and a new sparring partner. When the timer beeped, the sparring was back on. Whoever was the focus of the training, or the proverbial "man in the middle," got three rounds, each one with a new, fresh opponent. It was designed to emulate a real fight, and it did just that. Only here, something was distinctly different.

The first two fighters started, and immediately I was taken aback. They threw strikes harder than I'd ever seen in practice, barely holding anything back. Even when the spar went to the ground, it was brutal. If I hadn't known better, I would've been convinced I was watching a full-fledged fight. It seemed almost counterproductive to me and bound to cause an injury.

Soon a man named Rick was in the middle. Rick had a fight coming up in less than two weeks in Reno and needed the preparation. Although he started off well in the first round, he found himself in real trouble in the second round. At six-foot-three and around 250 pounds, Rick, a full-time firefighter, was larger than anyone else in the cage, but his size advantage was quickly negated by improper stamina and bad technique. As a heavyweight, Rick had the potential to throw a huge punch and deliver the crowd-pleasing knockout. But he also tired quickly, every fighter's nightmare. It's rare when two heavyweights display any real action after the first round because of their exhaustion. The kryptonite in their game is usually endurance. It's called "gassing out," and it's something every fighter dreads, not just heavyweights, although they're particularly prone to it.

Instead of giving Rick a break for his lack of cardiovascular skills, the others seemed to go after him harder than they might have if he was still fresh. Blood was in the water and the sharks were circling.

In the second round, Rick faced a middleweight named Nathan. The sound of leather smacking against wet flesh is unmistakable; Rick was on the receiving end of a lot of punishment. In desperation, he swung around on Nathan and attempted a spinning backfist, a move that rarely results in success, but the move caught Nathan hard, echoing throughout the gym. Unfortunately, it was low, landing on Nathan's collarbone, which only pissed him off. He came at Rick harder, throwing repeated shots at his head, connecting with most of them. I looked to Dave to see his reaction, which was stoic.

Rick tried to circle away from the aggressive Nathan. But the ordeal continued, and by the end of the round Rick was barely holding on for dear life. As much as he may have wanted to run out of the cage, he still had one round left. And it was with the biggest fish in the tank—Terrell himself.

I thought he might show some mercy and let Rick slide for his last round. In fact the opposite was true. He threw everything in his arsenal at Rick, taking a few swings before closing the distance between them, shooting for his legs and sweeping him off his feet with a thud. It only took a few moments for Terrell to choke Rick out. But if he thought tapping out was going to earn him a break, he was wrong.

"Get up, let's go," Terrell demanded.

"Come on, dude!" the other fighters cheered as he pulled himself up. But Rick was in a bad way. He was panting hard and stood on wobbly legs. His gaze darted around, and his hands hovered in front of his chest, not nearly high enough to protect his head.

Terrell lashed out again, clocking Rick on each side of his face before sweeping him off his feet and slamming him to the canvas. Rick went into survival mode and clinched his arms around Terrell, hoping to keep him smothered and unable to do any more damage. But Terrell was too quick and too strong for the weary firefighter and again choked him out. Rick was relieved beyond words when the final buzzer sounded—as was I. I put away my cell phone, which I had pulled in case someone needed to dial 9-1-1.

Rick's shark tank was over. He collapsed, only to be scolded by Dave. "Walk around. Get water," he ordered. But Rick lay still until two fighters pulled him up. They walked Rick around while David poured cold water on the beaten man's head. He may have taken a serious beating and embarrassed himself in the process, but he was still one of them, and after breaking him down they seemed determined to build him back up again. Almost at once he was showered with praise and criticism.

"You gotta circle more, dude."

"Your kicks are looking better."

Army Rangers are like this. They believe sacrifices in training mean life on the battlefield. Taking care of each other means maintaining a high level of proficiency. An unprepared Ranger is a dead Ranger. And just as important as the individual is his buddy next to him. They go to extraordinary lengths to be better than everyone else by adhering to the highest standards. If that means your feelings get hurt or you break open a blister in the process, all the better.

I could envision David Terrell as not only a Ranger, but a leader of those fine troops. The way he interacted with his fighters—kicking them in the ass or patting them on the back, and knowing the difference between the two—was textbook noncommissioned officer (NCO).

Sergeants are the first line of leadership in the Army. They've been around long enough to know what right looks like, how to avoid wrong, and the importance of making good decisions. They take care of their troops, run faster, farther, and harder than the rest of the platoon, know all the cadences, and will not hesitate to put a boot up someone's ass when they deserve it.

Sergeants are all about action. No matter how brilliant a plan is that some officer schemes up, it's going nowhere without the support of the sergeant at the lowest level who has to execute the commander's vision. General Petraeus came up with a perfect plan to secure Baghdad? Great, but it will fail miserably without the hundreds of sergeants on street corners, checkpoints, and markets enforcing the policy by shaking hands, playing soccer with kids, or smashing in a door.

In the world of professional fighting, the sergeants are the seasoned fighters who have enough experience to give advice without stepping on the trainer's toes. They can corner a fighter and give orders around the gym, but still lack the authority to make decisions that affect someone's career. They motivate the troops and weed out the weak, knowing when to say "good job" or "get your ass up." Dave Terrell is a sergeant at heart. He knows that his fighters will never get better unless pushed to their limits.

While I was in Santa Rosa at Terrell's, Nick Diaz was in Sacramento working on his boxing skills. I was told he'd be in Stockton working on jiu jitsu that night, but again I failed to link up with him, partly because of my own issues. Trying to wrestle an interview out of this guy was like going toe to toe against him and his secret weapon—his schedule. I never did pin him down.

Most fighters sacrifice something to train, whether it's a tangible item like a job, a house, a car, or an intangible one, like a relationship. Most leave something behind to do what they love and put training at the top of their list of priorities. The Diaz brothers sacrifice time and money to spend so many hours stuck in the California highway system. "The Road Warriors" never seemed so fitting a nickname.

SPORTFIGHT & IVAN SALAVERRY

Things may come to those who wait . . . but only the things left by those who hustle.

—Abraham Lincoln

There's a difference between a risk and a gamble. If a risk goes badly, you can recover from it, whereas if a gamble goes south, you're screwed. Crossing the street is risky. Hang gliding over an active volcano is a gamble. Scheduling a major fight on a holiday is a risk, because if it flops, the sponsors who supported it may decide to drop the event like investors dropped Enron.

Sportfight is a small, albeit popular and successful, MMA promotion in Portland, Oregon, started by Matt Lindland and Randy Couture. Their nineteenth installment was titled "Cinco de Mayhem," because it was on May 5, the sacred Mexican holiday marking the ass-whooping the Mexicans put on the French at the Battle of Puebla.

However, the World Boxing Council decided to complicate Lindland's life on this particular Cinco de Mayo by scheduling a massive pay-per-view event—Oscar de la Hoya versus Floyd Mayweather Jr.—for the super-lightweight title. This event was priority number one of the hype machine, touted as "the fight to save boxing" by sports writers who felt threatened by MMA. The event garnered so much attention and enticed such a large fan base to watch it that Sportfight crossed over from risky to an all-in Texas hold 'em gamble. If it failed, Lindland might have to go back to farming full time.

Leading up to the fight, Mike Freeman of CBS Sports wrote a scathing, anger-riddled column calling MMA fans "the barbarians at the gates" and other choice phrases that attacked them on a personal level. Ben Knowles of the International Fight League met this unprovoked attack with a very well-written response that accurately countered every point Freeman made and exposed him as biased toward boxing and uneducated on MMA.

But that didn't end the war of words. Jim Lampley, a longtime boxing commentator for HBO, who was very outspoken about how much he hated MMA, then went on record as saying, "The only reason MMA is popular is because they have white champions." It was a sad day. A sports commentator resorted to the race card to unprofessionally bash another sport.

Ironically, the UFC middleweight champion at the time was Anderson Silva, a long, lean, black fighting machine. Three weeks later another African American, Rampage Jackson, would knock out Chuck Liddell for the UFC's light heavyweight belt. The event surpassed the existing pay-per-view records of any MMA event and earned Jackson an Espy nomination.

As if all this unexpected competition and turmoil wasn't enough, the MMA landscape had just changed, threatening Sportfight's very existence. The UFC bought Pride Fighting Championships and was now firmly in control of the sport. Every big-name fighter was now in the iron grip of Zuffa, LLC, which meant they were owned by Dana White and the Fertita Brothers. In response to this merger, several smaller promotions banded together to ward off the UFC beast. EliteXC, K-1, and Strikeforce pooled their resources in an attempt to solidify their positions and keep Zuffa from putting them out of business. The show of defiance was more symbolic than practical, really a thinly veiled publicity stunt to showcase their upcoming fight card in Los Angeles. Though the threat of Zuffa certainly loomed over their heads, they would have been better off staying quiet.

Under this air of competing demands and unstable conditions, Lindland and Couture bravely pushed Sportfight onward, but with certain trepidation. Lucky for me, I convinced Josh Gross at Sherdog.com to let me cover the event for his website, which turned out to be a better gig than I expected. This was my first glimpse behind the scenes of a professional fight promotion, and it would set the standard for what I would expect to see in the future.

I ran into Matt and asked if he was feeling confident.

"Yeah, mostly," he responded, without any real conviction.

The Rose Garden arena seemed packed, so worry should have been far from his mind. The locals had come out in droves, probably because the conditions leading up to the main event were well known in the Portland area.

The most anticipated fight was a rematch between Enoch Wilson, who had recently been profiled on MSNBC's Warrior Nation TV series, and Travis Bush. On the show, Wilson came across as a likable guy trying to make ends meet by fighting, which greatly increased his marketability as a ticket draw. Just five months earlier, Wilson and Bush had fought a hard battle at Sportfight XVIII, which ended in a rare "draw." These two facts probably contributed to the large crowd that showed up, boxing match be damned.

Taking a seat ringside, I pulled out my laptop and got ready for the action. Being ringside was a whole different world from the Samsung flat screen back in the living room. It's easy to see why seats close to the ring are coveted and expensive despite the not-so-great view of the action. I had thought it was because of the close proximity it provides to the fighters, which many fans value so they can get a glimpse or an autograph of their favorite one. But being ringside puts the fan directly into the action. Every pop of leather hitting flesh is amplified. When Ed Nuno kicked Eddy Ellis in the thigh, the smack was loud enough to make me gasp and wonder how the hell Ellis was still on his feet.

But that's why these guys are who they are. They've learned how to roll their hips when they throw a kick. They know what part of the shin needs to connect to which part of the thigh to cause the most pain. And they know how to set the kick up with a combination, a dip, or a feint so their opponent isn't expecting it. And after all that, it would still take five or six more low leg kicks to make an overall impact on the fight. Leg kicks are like field goals in football; one won't kill you, but added together they can change the tide of a contest.

The notion that the athletes cannot hear fans during a fight is completely untrue. Every voice, and I mean every voice, was audible ringside. Some guy way up in the upper decks yelled, "Kick his ass, Jon!" during a fight just as I happened to look up in his direction. Fighters ignore these cheers, but not out of arrogance. It's just that they're completely absorbed with the rather strenuous task of defeating another man who's trying to kick their ass.

During an exciting undercard fight between Blake Fredericks and

James Birdsley, three strange things occurred. First, Fredericks clamped a solid armbar on Birdsley that certainly looked like it was going to end the fight. Having been on the receiving end of at least three armbars, I knew how much pain Birdsley was in, yet he refused to tap out. Seeing his opponent was hanging tough, Fredericks's corner shouted, "Break it, Blake," several times.

I was surprised by this and instantly looked toward the coach who said it, since I thought it was highly unprofessional to willfully hurt another opponent in that fashion. But I never got a glimpse of the instigator because blocking my view was something I didn't expect—the most massive set of hooters I'd ever been that close too.

In anticipation of the end of the round, the ring girl had prepositioned herself off to my right to climb into the ring and strut her stuff with a "Round 3" card. She was just inches from me and, as I would like to reiterate, was stacked. I looked toward Fredericks's corner only to witness an eclipse of silicone, a blackout of boobs, an obscuration of juggs. Embarrassed and not wanting to miss the end of the fight, I looked away back toward the ring where Birdsley continued to hold on while Fredericks tightened the armbar.

"Break it, Blake!" the shout came again from his corner. I had no choice but to look again. And still they were there. The double Ds from hell.

My transfixion was broken when I heard a shout from the ring. "He bit me!" Fredericks let go of the armbar on Birdsley and scooted away. Sitting in the middle of the ring, he pointed to his thigh, where a stream of blood was trickling down his leg.

"Doc! Get in here!" the referee yelled at a man who had apparently been paying more attention to the ring girl's anatomy. "Is this a bite wound?" he asked. The doctor nodded; the bite mark was clear. Birdsley was disqualified for illegal tactics.

When the MC announced the results to the crowd, the boos were deafening. "He'll never fight here again," I heard a fan yell. "You suck!" another one added. As Birdsley left the ring, he was assaulted by fans who wanted a piece of him. A redneck in a tie-dyed shirt holding a huge beer yelled, "You piece of shit! You ain't no fighter!"

This was strange and funny at the same time. For all the grief MMA fans had endured, for all the terrible things Mike Freeman had said about them, here they were defending their sport in the best way possible—by upholding standards.

Biting is a coward's way to get out of a bad situation and completely unacceptable in a civilized fight. Birdsley was trapped, plain and simple. He had no way out of Fredericks's armbar and chose to hurt him maliciously instead of do the honorable thing and tap out. And for that his name will forever be marred. He'll have a scarlet letter around his neck in every MMA promotion and quite possibly will never fight again.

It's a shame the fight ended this way with just seven seconds left in the second round. Up to this point, the two middleweights had staged an impressive contest. At one point, Birdsley mounted Fredericks's back and for twenty seconds Fredericks walked around the ring trying to get him off. It was an exciting match and could even have been the "fight of the night" were it not for the disqualification.

Sitting ringside I could actually see the sweat and snot being knocked out of men as they connected on each other. We've all seen the super-slow-motion photos of boxing matches where one guy gets hit and sweat seems to explode in all directions. But seeing it up front is different. When Tyson Jeffries connected on Dan Colburtson, the phlegm and sweat that flew off him formed a small, foul cloud that hovered over the ring and held my attention more than the fight itself.

After the Jeffries-Colburtson fight, the judge sitting next to me was no longer leaning on his table. Something had him bothered. "Hey, Ref," he yelled up to the man in the ring. "You got a towel? I got blood on my table here." In the middle of his workstation was a single crimson drop of blood.

I suddenly felt like a kid afraid of cooties and frantically checked to see if any was on me or my laptop. There wasn't, but I still felt the need to strap on a pair of latex gloves before typing again.

Don't ever think a fighter doesn't have a business sense about him. Throughout the night, several fighters changed T-shirts multiple times backstage to accommodate whoever was fighting, just as Nick Diaz had done back at Cesar Gracie's. When Judo Jon Krohn entered the arena to fight Whisper Goodman, his four-man corner crew, most of whom were from Team Quest, wore "Judo Jon" shirts to support him. But when Greg Thompson came out of the dressing room for his fight, several of these same guys were suddenly wearing shirts emblazoned with Thompson's logo. The tactic got their comrade's name more into the public eye and supported him at the same time, and the crew executed it with the precision of a Blue Angels flight team.

The main event was everything it was hyped to be. Travis Bush and Enoch Wilson went at each other like angry mongooses, engaging in an evenly matched fight that brought the crowd to its feet. Bush scored takedowns almost at will, frustrating Wilson, who couldn't get a good shot at his younger and faster opponent. The one time he managed to get on top of Bush, he couldn't maintain it.

In the third round, Wilson nearly fell through the ring ropes onto me. It was becoming clear that cage events are probably safer for journalists than boxing-style rings, providing better protection from airborne bodies—and their fluids.

In the end, Bush was too strong for Wilson and won a unanimous decision as well as the Sportfight lightweight belt, much to the crowd's approval. Although the judges were assigned by the Oregon Athletic Commission and consisted mostly of guys with boxing pedigrees, they knew enough about MMA to render a decision that made sense to the 6,000 fans in attendance. Lucky for them.

Travis Bush hangs out near the ring after winning the Sportfight light-weight title.

With the main event done, the lights came up and a platoon of cleaning staff in yellow shirts descended on the arena, folding chairs, stuffing garbage bags with discarded trash, and shuffling people out. Eleven fights had taken place over three hours, but a small, dedicated group still hadn't had enough. Three hundred-some fans rushed to ring level and lined up to meet Randy Couture and Matt Lindland. On the other side of the ring the night's two headliners, Bush and Wilson, also spoke to fans, signed autographs and laughed with each other about the fight.

"Wait a minute," I said out loud to no one in particular. "Those two guys just fought for fifteen minutes and now they're all chummy like it was a game of shuffleboard?"

I was impressed. Both men still hadn't put a shirt on and Bush even wore his new "Sportfight Lightweight Champion" belt over his shoulder like a medal of honor. He smiled politely and apologized when he failed to sign autographs legibly since he had to hold an ice pack over his swollen left eye. Wilson was in even worse shape with a gash over his right eye that refused to stop bleeding.

You would think these wounds would keep people from wanting to come near the two, but the opposite was true. An autograph was one thing, but an autograph with blood drops from a championship fight was a unique memento, a piece of the fight itself.

I looked around the mostly empty arena and marveled at the approachability of the fighters on all levels. On one side was Couture, a true legend in MMA and probably the biggest name in the business. Near him was Matt Lindland, another giant, gladly shaking hands with people who thanked him for putting on the event. And not too far from them were Wilson and Bush, small potatoes in the overall scheme of MMA, but nonetheless more professional and courteous than any other athletes I'd ever seen.

It made me think of the time I tried to get an autograph from a favorite football player. I'd waited hours to see him only to have him pass by indifferently as I and other fans begged him to take a moment of his time. Looking back on that day, I wondered whether football had grown too big for itself or if MMA was just too young and the days of ignoring fans were still on the horizon. Either way, this was where the future of the sport was really being shaped, by fighters who were willing to take the time to maintain the loyal fan base they'd worked so hard to foster.

With the stars spending time with the fans, I used my press credentials to get backstage, where I saw Tyson Jeffries wandering around aimlessly. Tyson, Team Quest's eighteen-year-old janitor who trained with the team when he wasn't working, had given Dave Colburtson everything he had for one and a half rounds before getting caught in a guillotine choke and tapping out. This was his first professional fight, and although it ended in defeat, he had nothing to be ashamed of.

"Great job, kid." I tried to cheer him up, but got no response. He was crushed at losing, especially in front of 6,000 of his best friends. He wanted to succeed in the sport more than he wanted to see his twenty-first birthday, and this was an unimaginable disaster to the teenager. It's hard to see the logic in "there'll be another day, kid," when you're young and broke and just had your dreams crushed. I sent Tyson off with a pat on his shoulder (the one that held the weight of the world on it) and proceeded to find the locker rooms underneath the stands. While I was consoling Tyson, Enoch Wilson slipped by to get his eye stitched. Enoch was also disappointed, but unlike Jeffries, he knew it was only temporary.

"He's such a cock-strong kid," Enoch said of Travis Bush. "I couldn't get anything going against him. He deserved the win." Admitting defeat is hard. Doing so while someone stitches your eyelid back together takes real guts. When Matt Lindland entered, Enoch's guilt overtook him.

"I'm sorry, dude," he said.

"For what?" Matt responded. "You gave it your all. It was a great fight."

It was, but the bitter sting of loss is never easily discarded. Like most fighters, Enoch was an alpha male who couldn't stand losing and felt he'd let everyone down when he did.

Later, I took a moment to ask Matt about Cesar's theory of the efficiency of jiu jitsu as opposed to wrestling. "He may be right," he said, shrugging his shoulders and glancing off to one side.

"What?"

"He may be right. I've never taken a jiu jitsu lesson in my life. My technique is all centered around wrestling skills. If I entered a straight jiu jitsu tournament I'd probably get my ass handed to me."

"So you think jiu jitsu in general is weak here in Oregon?"

"I'm sure there are good practitioners of it here, but not in my gym," he admitted with the confidence possessed only by those who don't care what others think. "He has his style and we have ours. If his guys won more fights than mine, I might scratch my head and wonder what he's doing better, but we maintain our own, so he can have his opinion."

I was stunned. I expected a resounding, "Hell, no!" from Matt to defend his gym and name, but instead he was simply dismissive of the theory. That's what I get for trying to predict the behavior of a fighter.

Sportfight had been a resounding success. Events like this are the peaks of a fighter's life, the moments where all the training culminates in either sweet celebration or teary self-flagellation, and where promoters either rake in enough for a mortgage or move their families into a double-wide trailer.

But Sportfight was small compared to the behemoth UFC. And I knew there were bigger events out there where the real money changes hands and reputations are made or broken. I needed to see those to investigate the true relationship between money and art form.

* * * * *

A few weeks after Sportfight I spent an afternoon with Ivan Salaverry in Seattle just prior to his return to the Octagon against Terry Martin. Ivan was a UFC veteran who'd been recovering from shoulder surgery and was anxious to get back into the ring against Martin, a scrappy fighter from Chicago.

But Ivan had a few other people to take care of. After dreaming of operating his own gym for years, he and his wife opened a small MMA training facility, which sat literally in the shadow of the Space Needle. Despite the unique eagle tattoo that dominates his right side, Ivan is as classy as Buckingham Palace. If he tells you to go to hell, you feel happy to be on your way. When Ivan smiles, he flashes the work of a talented dentist, and when he speaks it's with the throaty voice of a movie trailer voiceover artist. Despite his Russian moniker, Ivan is as Latino as Juan Paco Miguel Sanchez de Rosa del Portillo Pico de Gallo.

"My father wanted me to have the same initials as him, 'I.S.,' so he came up with Ivan," he said smiling as he reminisced about his old man.

As we spoke, his wife, Brit, worked the front counter while fighters intermittently watched over six-month-old Ivan Junior, who was perched comfortably on a blanket a safe distance from the mats. It was a schizophrenic atmosphere fit for the Twilight Zone. On one side, men pounded heavy bags and each other, while on the other side a couple relaxed with their baby son.

Ivan is a pure gentleman who says what's on his mind while chuckling the way only someone happy with his position in life can. Having served a tour in the Marine Corps and possessing a sharp mind and good business acumen, he has no qualms about calling out an adversary on any subject. He trains his students with intensity, but keeps them laughing with phrases like, "You look like a flounder," "God gave you those legs for a reason," and "What the hell are you doing, Hotrod?"

"You have to have fun." He leaned back against the apron of his newly installed boxing ring. "If you're not having fun then what's the use of this whole thing?"

"So how is getting beaten on by another man in a cage fun?" I asked.

"It's not. But beating on him and showing the world that you can defeat him—that's where the rush comes from." His eyes opened wide like he'd just seen a ghost and he leaned back with a finger pointing to the sky. "That's where guys get addicted to this sport. They feel that rush of conquering their fear, stepping into the unknown and emerging victorious. They feel it once and instantly they're hooked. Next thing you know, they're training like crazy and looking forward to the next fight."

He put an arm behind his head as the waning light of the Pacific sun set through the gym's massive windows. "Everyone has something they love. Some people love flying. Some people love building things with their hands. Some people love to be soldiers." He gestured at me. "And some of us love the feel of raw combat victory." He could have been a successful Marine recruiter. He also could have been a successful organizer for a union, as I was about to find out.

"If you look at how much the UFC made last year versus how much they paid out to their athletes, it amounts to less than 10 percent," he said. "It's horrible what they pay us. We love what we do, but try living off of what the UFC pays to go in there and get punched and kicked."

In fact it may be way less than 10 percent. It's hard to tell because the UFC is only bound by law to release fighters' prize money to the state athletic commissions, who in turn make this public information. As a private company, it's not required to release its profits to the general public. In 2006, MMAWeekly.com estimated the UFC made "over $200 million in pay-per-view buys," and backed it up with strong data. Another source estimated the figure at over $222 million. It was easily the most profitable venture in the pay-per-view arena ever. Revenue from ticket sales in 2006 amounted to over $30 million and advertising revenue for its live TV shows was another $2 million, making the grand total between $232 and $254 million for the year.

Yet the money they paid out to fighters amounted to just over $6 million. This amount, however, only represents the purses fighters received and does not include bonuses, such as "fight of the night," or "best knockout," which can be as much as $40,000 for each recipient. The UFC is not bound to disclose this information and usually doesn't, so the amount they pay fighters is probably higher.

But even if the total was, say, $10 million, this is less than 5 percent of what they made from pay-per-view subscriptions alone. Merchandising and sponsorship money from companies who want to have their logos in the middle of the Octagon aren't even factored in because there's no way to measure them without going through the UFC's accounts. The point of all this is that the UFC makes a disproportionate amount of money compared to what it pays out to the fighters.

But before everyone runs to Dana White's house with pitchforks, there are some other things to consider, like the cost of putting on a UFC show. Estimates range from $500,000 to $1 million to rent out a large events center such as the Mandalay Bay Hotel and Casino in Las Vegas, for a show. That's $10 million a year. Marketing the show on commercials, magazines, and billboards, as well as subscription fees to pay-per-view companies also costs money. And UFC employees have to be paid salaries. And then there's the added cost of a multitude of little things, like medical checks, licensing, referees, supplies, water, microphones, weigh-ins, hotel rooms, transportation, and much more.

All things considered, this still leaves a nice little (okay, a huge) profit. But White and the Fertita siblings didn't get into this sport to preserve an art form that bleeds money. For all their hard work, they're entitled to take home a paycheck at the end of the day. This is America.

Still, the amount fighters receive in prize money seems miniscule after months of training and dedication, and it only leads to frustration among athletes like Ivan. But what can they do?

They could unionize.

Unions are dreaded things to some and saviors to others. But the fact is, most professional sports have one. Unlike federal employees, who are barred from unionizing by law, athletes have the right to form collective bargaining groups, stage walkouts, strike, and use their consolidated powers to negotiate better terms from the promoters who employ them. According to the National Labor Relations Act, it only takes 30 percent of the employees of a company to consent to a union by signing union cards. From there, the group secures funding and, voila, instant collective bargaining tool. Athletes across the sports spectrum have different demands, but the trigger to forming a players' union is usually the same—dissatisfaction with the organizations that control it.

But a union doesn't happen overnight. The NFL Players Association was formed in 1956 by Don Shula and Frank Gifford to advance the rights and salaries of the players. Twelve years and one Supreme Court decision later, it achieved collective-bargaining status, and has negotiated with the team owners over everything from free agency to salary caps to the official start day of the NFL season. Because of the association, players enjoy higher wages, health insurance, and signing bonuses.

The relationship between the Players' Association and the team owners has not always been rosy, though, and the players went on strike in 1982 and 1987. Major League baseball has suffered even worse relations between its players' union and team owners, resulting in three strikes—in 1972, 1981, and 1994.

MMA's closest cousin, boxing, only recently instituted a union for its athletes. In 2003, boxing formed the Joint Association of Boxers (JAB) with support from the International Brotherhood of Teamsters, who also supported the NFL Players Association in the 1950s and 1960s. The

JAB acts as the collective-bargaining representative for the athletes and negotiates with promoters to gain financial support for boxers, both active and retired.

The disproportion of profits made by the UFC versus the prize money it pays out could easily spark a drive to unionize.

"I would absolutely support a union," Ivan said. "We need a guild or an organization that can look out for the fighters and negotiate better salaries. We will never have the paydays or protections that other sports enjoy until we do. I even know who should lead it."

"Who?" I asked.

"Tito," he responded, having clearly put some previous thought into the subject.

Tito, of course, is Tito Ortiz AKA "The Huntington Beach Bad Boy" and one of the most ultrahyped, poster boys of the sport. As a veteran fighter with name recognition, Tito was a good candidate who would be taken seriously. He knew what aspects of the sport could be improved. He also had a bigger revenue base and could afford to stop fighting, unlike the younger athletes.

"The UFC is going to continue to get rich off of us until the fighters get together and put pressure on Dana White. And it doesn't even have to be a huge victory. We don't have to have every demand met. As long as we bind together and show that we're capable of disrupting his operations, it'll be a thorn in his side that he'll have to consider."

He was right, but he was also playing with fire. If MMA athletes were to form a players' association like the JAB, they would certainly gain greater leverage to potentially increase the money and benefits they receive from the promoters. They would also gain the ultimate weapon of a collective body—the strike, which should be used only as a last resort. But there were risks. Promoters can legally fire anyone who goes on strike, although it's unwise because of the huge loss of talent they would be tossing aside for other promotions to snatch up.

A fighters' union could be even more crushing to the sport of MMA as a whole because promoters would have to take measures to protect themselves from the loss of revenue brought on by a strike. Higher prices for tickets and merchandise are just a couple of side effects of a union, since promoters would have to build up insurance capital to weather the storm of a strike. The IFL in particular, as a publicly traded company, would be forced to take protectionist measures that would be felt in the wallets of their investors and fans.

But the fans are the ultimate losers of a strike. Spats between players and associations have caused millions of lost fans that don't see the logic behind strikes and lockouts. Baseball, in particular, has had a rough road to recovery since their last players' strike, and it suffered half-full stadiums for several years in the 1990s as a result. But that's an acceptable risk to Ivan.

"They're not the ones getting punched and kicked in the ring. I don't want the fans or the sport to suffer, but I think we should get what we're worth and right now we're not."

I left Ivan's that night wondering if the situation was really as bad as he'd described, or if fighters were getting more money from sponsors than they let on. Would the athletes ever band together, or would they continue to accept whatever pay they could get for a risky sport? A labor dispute was probably the last thing MMA needed. And hardball union machinations can sometimes lead to thuggish practices. It would be tragic if Tito Ortiz ended up disappearing, like Jimmy Hoffa.

To most people, at least.

JACKSON'S MMA

We few, we happy few, we band of brothers,
For he today who sheds his blood with me shall be my brother.

—William Shakespeare, *"King Henry V"*

No journey through American MMA could be considered complete without a stop in the capital of New Mexico. It was a place I anticipated and dreaded at the same time, like taking out a hot prom date, but going through her dad first.

Jackson's MMA in Albuquerque was world renowned for training some of the best fighters in the sport, like Keith Jardine, Rashad Evans, Diego Sanchez, Nate Marquardt, Duane Ludwig, and Georges St. Pierre.

I was nervous because mixed martial arts was still a relatively small community as sports go, and these guys were the big time. If I botched anything, I would be persona non grata all over the MMA network faster than Tony Soprano's car navigates the McDonald's drive-through.

I figured June in New Mexico should be hot enough to melt the tires on my trusty Land Rover Discovery—affectionately nicknamed "The Disco"—but as I rolled across the barren desert landscape outside of Phoenix, the temperature remained strangely mild. The vise that slowly clamped down on my head failed to trigger the "altitude alert" that most rational people would have recognized. At 5,500 feet above sea level, Albuquerque is a full two hundred feet above the mile-high city, Denver. I'd heard stories of Jackson taking his fighters to run the majestic 10,000-foot Sandia Mountains that eclipsed the city to the east, and I wondered if this range was the secret to his success.

Albuquerque is a city of adobe houses and taupe roadways accented by splashes of turquoise and wild grass. The Rio Grande River runs right through the middle of town before winding its way south and east. It's a city too small to have a global impact, but too big to be discounted as insignificant.

San Mateo Boulevard transits the town with its tattoo parlors and bus stops full of eccentric locals (a nice way to say scary street walkers), but it has less pawn shops and strip bars than Gresham. To the east, a concrete wall separates the street from the neighborhoods, and up and down the road businesses wear wrought iron bars on their windows. I gathered neither the iron bars nor the walls were for aesthetic purposes. As I crossed the famous Route 66 and turned onto Acoma Drive, I found no respite from the less than spectacular neighborhood.

The building that housed the gym was dilapidated, and the alley in which the building was located was only half a rung above a ghetto on the ladder of city zoning. I later learned that this location had been an automobile repair shop before Greg Jackson and his crew bought and renovated it. Despite all the work that had been done, I wondered how it could be a world-class training facility. Then a sign in the entryway put everything into perspective.

Gaidojutsu—Scientific Streetfighting.

It wouldn't have had much credibility if it were in Bel Air.

"Anderson Island?" a voice yelled with a tinge of urgency as I entered the gym. "It's a sign!" Joey Villasenor stood next to Nate Marquardt, gazing directly at me with the deer-in-the-headlights look. "Oh shit! We're gonna lose, bro."

I froze for a second trying to get my bearings, when I realized what had him spooked. I had once been to Anderson Island, Washington, a quaint little dot of land in the southern Puget Sound that was a decent place to take a day trek with the family. On my way back to the ferry, I bought the T-shirt I now had on.

I might as well have been wearing a Notre Dame football jersey in Miami. Joey Villasenor was two weeks away from his showdown with Murilo "Ninja" Rua for the EliteXC light heavyweight belt, and a week after that Nate Marquardt was scheduled to fight Anderson Silva for the UFC middleweight title. They were in the final phases of their preparation when I walked in wearing a shirt with ANDERSON ISLAND, USA splashed across it.

"It's a sign, bro!" Villasenor repeated to Marquardt. "You're gonna lose and so am I because I saw it."

"Don't worry about it," Greg Jackson told him from behind an open door that read DO NOT ENTER in big red letters. "Come on in, boss man."

I entered the forbidden room and he shook my hand. For a guy who trained world-class fighters, Greg was nothing like I'd pictured. He sported a stubble-covered head and beard, weighed in at maybe 160 pounds, and flashed a disarming smile that seemed completely genuine. He quickly made me feel like the most important person in the world, which most would consider a character flaw in a combat sport.

"Is he really that superstitious?" I asked about Joey. "Did I just curse them?"

"Well," Greg said as he plopped down on a La-Z-Boy recliner with a broken footrest. "The closer he gets to a fight, the more he notices those little things. But don't worry about it. It's just him getting nervous."

I felt like the fat kid in gym class who pisses the teacher off so much he makes everyone run laps. So much for making a good first impression.

Born in Washington, D.C., while his father was attending Georgetown University's graduate degree program, Greg Jackson moved to New Mexico at the tender age of three. His pacifist parents had heard tales of the wondrous southwest from his Uncle Pete who'd served in the Peace Corps out west. For Greg, the move turned out to be a lifelong enrollment in the school of hard knocks.

"I was the only white kid in my school, which equated to a lot of after-school beatings," he said. "I would come home all bloodied up and my folks would try to encourage me to be bigger and say, 'violence only begets violence,' which is where I learned that extreme positions and generalities don't work."

Greg's family, including his father, were all champion wrestlers in Indiana (his dad still gets his back when they grapple), so coming from a pedigree of men finely attuned to the combat sports forced Greg to do something that was clearly born into him—fight back.

"There were no good self-defense dojos in New Mexico at the time, so

I created my own style. I saw what the Gracies were doing and knew it was light-years ahead of anything I could read about or find in an instructional video, so I used that as a basis and trained myself."

He called his style Gaidojutsu, but don't read anything into the name. Although gaido is similar to gaijin, the Japanese word meaning "foreigner," and jutsu is similar to jiu jitsu, it's actually just a fabricated word.

"I wanted something that sounded traditional instead of "Advanced American Streetfighting Techniques," so I came up with Gaidojutsu." He never guessed, nor could he, that MMA would soon find him as one of its favorite sons and Gaidojutsu would be as well known as Team Quest's "ground and pound."

Near the gym's entrance was a photo of Greg and his disciples holding black belts embroidered with the word, "Jackson's" down their length. Twenty years ago this would have been discounted as a pretentious farce and "Jackson's MMA" would have been categorized with all the other mystical "eight-animal-super-magic-striking-demon-killing defense systems" that conned people out of their money with promises of teaching mastery of the five-step death strike for a nominal fee. But this was the age of MMA, which meant whoever could walk the walk could talk the talk. As long as Jackson's guys continued to walk into a cage and defeat their opponents, Gaidojutsu—whether it was fabricated or not—was real. For Greg to award black belts with his name on them was no different than the Gracie family laying claim to the belt system of Brazilian jiu jitsu.

Greg's overall approach to fighting was simple—math, science, and beauty. "As long as you understand the properties of physics and geometry, everything falls into place," he said. "Physics in regard to weight distribution and movements, and geometry in regards to the way joints bend. The beauty of it is in the way it's expressed. Some styles of martial arts are impractical but beautiful to watch nonetheless. Tae kwon do, kung fu, capoeira are all impractical in a street fight, but they're fantastic to watch. Gaidojutsu combines the best of all of them to achieve victory. It's an art form, and we are all artists."

If it's an art form, then it would stand to reason that pictures of martial arts masters might be hung up for inspiration, but no portrait of Bruce Lee, Carlos Gracie, or Jigoro Kano graced his walls. Instead, Abraham Lincoln,

George Washington, and a painting of Spartans looking down from a peak were the décor of the day. It turned out that not only physics and geometry but also history lessons were woven into Gaidojutsu.

"I admire Lincoln for his timing and dedication to do what was right and Washington for his tenacity; he never gave up despite so many setbacks. And I really admire Shackelton for his leadership."

Who?

"Earnest Shackelton. He led a polar expedition that went really bad," he said, pointing toward the far wall. On it was a blown-up photograph from the early twentieth century of the ship Endurance, which had run aground on Antarctic ice.

"He was trying to circumnavigate Antarctica by going over the South Pole, but the ship got trapped," Greg continued. "For a year and a half he kept his men alive using unorthodox means, and eventually got every one of them rescued. He was a true leader.

"I also love Sherman's axioms, like 'Always keep your adversary on the horns of a dilemma.' As [General William Tecumseh] Sherman and his Army blazed across the South, they would approach so that he had one or two options of which town to attack. He forced the Confederates to pick one to defend. Then at the last minute he would attack the one that was least fortified."

"So how does this apply to MMA?" I asked.

"Always leave yourself an option," he responded without hesitation. "Make your opponent choose to either defend against one thing or another. Make him defend against a triangle and then catch him in an armbar. Make him think you're pulling guard, but then sweep him instead. It's all math, science, and beauty."

If math, science, and beauty are his friends, they're also messy companions who know nothing about organization. Greg's office and team meeting area were as unkempt as Einstein's wild hair. The inner sanctum was a plethora of boxes, toys, gear, mismatched furniture, cases of soda, clothes, broken dreams, magazines, and two large containers of Nelly's Pimpjuice.

When my first day at Jackson's MMA was done, I was starving. Tyler, one of Greg's students, gave me directions to an area called Nob Hill where

I might find good eats. I pointed the Disco west down Central Drive, where a Mecca of gastrointestinal delights waited—no less than four sushi bars just two miles from the gym. I picked one of them, and the Vegas roll there was little more than a Philadelphia roll cooked tempura style, but the Dragon roll more than made up for it.

* * * * *

Greg Jackson and his incredible stable of fighters are not just riding the wave of the MMA explosion, but creating it and shaping it. At Jackson's one could get an all-encompassing view of the expanding sport. Like legionnaires returned to Rome from all parts of the realm, there were fighters here from nearly every promotion and every weight class.

At one end of the gym Mike Seal, a lean agile kickboxer from Mexico and veteran of no less than eight different promotions, punched a heavy bag. Next to him Damacio Page, who fought in Japan and the United States, sparred with Duane "Bang" Ludwig, a world-class striker and veteran of King of the Cage, K-1, Strikeforce, and the UFC. On the mat was former marine Adam Lynn, who had recently arrived back in town from Arizona. Lynn fought on the Tucson Scorpions IFL team and was enjoying the off-season to work on his ground game and possibly enter some grappling competitions before the next season. Near him, Elite XC light heavyweight contender Joey Villasenor grappled with UFC middleweight contender Nathan Marquardt (I made sure not to wear anything that might spook him). And, of course, the most well-known UFC fighters, Keith Jardine, Rashad Evans, and Diego Sanchez patrolled the gym working on their own skills.

Sanchez and Evans, in particular, were men who helped shape the face of MMA. The explosion of the sport can arguably be traced to the finale of *The Ultimate Fighter*, season one, which Sanchez won when he defeated Kenny Florian in the middleweight division (171–185 pounds). This event, which at one point had a reported 6 million viewers, took the UFC to new levels of popularity. Riding the wave of fame, *The Ultimate Fighter* season two was just as popular, with Rashad Evans winning in the heavyweight division over a much larger Brad Imes. Evans dropped down to light heavyweight (186–205 pounds) and went on to win all of his fights, quite an accomplishment considering the vast amount of talent in the division.

There was also a new paradigm here that I would have to think about. Greg was working punching drills with Julie Kedzie, who had recently defeated Julia Berezikova in St. Petersburg, Russia, on BodogFight's "Clash of Nations," the same event where Matt Lindland lost to Fedor Emelianenko. Earlier in the day, Angela Magana and Nikki Garcia had trained at Jackson's, and Holly Holm, a prominent female boxer, filmed a special for Country Music Television in the gym. I had started this journey to learn why men fight, but I had completely failed to consider the motivations of women to get into the ring and throw down.

"Because I can't dance or sing," Julie said, spitting out her mouthpiece while attempting to brush back sweaty hair from her face. "Seriously, I was always a tomboy. I was athletic, did karate and tae kwon do for years. The strange thing is, I actually don't like violence, and I cringe from guns and gore. I don't like to hurt people, either."

"Why do you do this then?"

"Because it pushes your limits. It tests you to be more."

Okay, I thought, but even strippers aspire to be more or they wouldn't get implants. "Couldn't you get that out of soccer or basketball?" I asked.

"I suppose," she replied, "but I was used to getting hit and was always a bigger frame than most girls, so it was more of a natural fit. It's a love-hate thing for me; sometimes I love fighting, sometimes I hate it."

Though BodogFight and a few minor promotions had accepted women's MMA, the big boys of the sport were still reluctant. UFC president Dana White even went so far as to denounce it altogether.

"I think it's hypocritical to say we want acceptance and equal rights for everyone, but women can't play," Greg said. "The UFC has been fighting for years to gain mainstream acceptance, but as soon as they get it, they say chicks can't play. Maybe it's because my parents were feminist and taught me that women can do anything men can, or maybe I just like doing things people say can't be done, but I'm all for women fighting. Dana [White] says it'll never happen in the UFC, but that's just because he's old school and doesn't think girls should fight. He's chivalrous, but it's inevitable. BodogFight is taking the lead right now, so it's only a matter of time before the UFC responds and does the same."

While we were on the subject of BodogFight and Russia, I asked about Greg's experience over there.

"We met Jean Claude Van Damme," Julie interjected with a hint of sarcasm.

Greg rolled his eyes like there was a story behind the comment, but let it go. "I saw Matt Lindland there," he said, knowing that I'd spent time with Team Quest. "He's a tough guy taking on Fedor like that."

"Do you manage your fighters like he does?"

"Oh, hell, no. I just train them. I don't have time to manage them, too."

When a gym is as popular a training destination as Jackson's is, time is a precious commodity, especially when a wife and two small kids are factored in. Greg's focus was on advancing his art instead of getting involved in the business end of the sport. Nonetheless, I felt the question of unionizing was in order.

"Fighters will never unionize," he said without hesitation. "They're not the right demographic. For every fighter out there unhappy with taking three and three, there's five more willing to step in and do it for them."

Three and three means $3,000 to show up to the fight and $3,000 to win it—two-thirds of what Terrell Owens was fined for missing a Dallas Cowboys team meeting.

Greg had grown up around fighters and had a long history in the combat arts, so his instinct about their character was probably dead on. "But what about all the big names?" I asked. "What if the UFC suddenly got rid of fan favorites, like Rashad, Tito, Rich Franklin, or Randy Couture?"

"They'd make more. They'd be like Doritos. They'd use their deep pockets and hype two mediocre fighters until the public was interested in them and felt they had to watch. Next thing you know, they're operating like it was a speed bump in the road and the guys who unionized are an afterthought."

He had a point. When I'd discussed the possibility of unions, collective bargaining, and strikes with Ivan Salaverry, we'd forgotten to consider the brashness and "do it my way or else" attitude that made Dana White who he is today—one of the shrewdest businessmen in the world. He could do it, too. He could find a whole new generation of young fighters and make them stars until the previous group was all but forgotten. The fact is, the big names of the UFC are like comic book superheroes to fans everywhere, two-dimensional characters created mainly by an incredibly efficient hype machine. Ordinary Joes with striking or grappling skills became stars, and the fans became so emotionally invested in their "lives," that the purchase of a pay-per-view seemed like a bargain at forty dollars. It was like a violent soap opera that they had to know the conclusion to.

Greg also disagreed with Matt Lindland about the importance of acquiring titles. "Belts are important," he admitted. "I'll say out loud that I want to win them all. It's the recognition that this person is the best out there. No one is better at this place or time than this guy."

But is it a reason to fight? Is receiving an object made of leather and imitation gold so important that someone would risk their long-term health to get it? I understood why men who tried out for Special Forces sustained lifelong injuries during the trial period known as Special Forces Assessment and Selection (SFAS—also known as the School for Advanced Suffering). It is a grueling three-week trial by fire that enables those who graduate to go on and earn their Green Berets. It's the entryway into a lifestyle of the Special Operations warrior. So risking lifelong health for one of the Army's Holy Grails is understandable. But is taking the same risk in order to wear a belt around your waist a good enough reason to fight?

Rashad Evans thought so, but he was biased because he'd had a long and comfortable relationship with fighting as a result of family influences. As a kid his brothers would get bored and take him out to beat up the neighborhood kids for entertainment. Evans had cousins that he and his brother would train to fight prior to a family reunion. Despite his sisters' protestations, whenever they brought a boy home, he'd jump him and try to pick a fight.

After high school, Rashad found an outlet for his aggression in wrestling. He was awarded a scholarship to Michigan State, but right away had to overcome the obstacle of stereotypes.

"The recruiter thought I was a gang banger right off the bat," Rashad said as we lounged in the inner sanctum the next day. "The coaches would always say to me, 'Okay, Rashard (they could never get my name right), 'just pretend this guy is trying to move in on your turf back in the hood. Just go out there and treat him like a rival on your turf.' I was always like 'Who the hell do you think I am?'"

Rashad spoke quietly, like someone accustomed to life in a library. He was aware of the world around him, but warily selective of what was worthy of his attention. His vernacular swung effortlessly from blue collar to white and teetered precariously between profound and Ebonic, as did his personality, depending on the audience. He was like the Brooklyn Bridge, with one foot in the affluent offices of Wall Street and the other in the brownstones of Red Hook.

Rashad had dreamed of a career in law enforcement after school. "I wanted to be a cop," he admitted. "But after I graduated the police weren't hiring. So I got a job as a security guard in a hospital to get some basic training in law enforcement until the police lifted their hiring freeze and I could work there."

But without sports in his life, Rashad's fighting ways went unchecked. One fateful night he was knocked unconscious in a bar brawl that resulted in a major head scar. He was at a crossroads and needed guidance. It was time to make a choice—continue down his self-destructive path or find an outlet for all his aggression. MMA was there.

He started training with Matt Torres in Lansing, Michigan, won a Gladiator Challenge tournament, and soon after was thrust into the spotlight on *The Ultimate Fighter*. Winning the show was a huge boost for Rashad, but it also meant a drastic change of lifestyle. He was now in the big leagues and needed world-class training, so he moved temporarily to Albuquerque.

Winning *The Ultimate Fighter* was not all roses and glory. "My whole life has changed," he said. "Before I could train on my own, but now it's an hour of wrestling, and hour of jiu jitsu, rest, eat, an hour of boxing, rest, you know? It's a more disciplined lifestyle that takes some getting used to."

He also had a lot of social adjusting to do, as do all people unaccustomed to fame and recognition. He was never away from the twenty-four-hour lifestyle of a top-ranked fighter, which bothered him.

"When I was a working guy," he said, "I could leave the job and really leave the job. Now it doesn't matter if I'm training or not; I'm always Rashad Evans, UFC fighter. People always want to ask me about fighting, want to know about fighting, want to compare stories about fighting. I can never get away from it."

He paused and looked toward the cage where Nate Marquardt was filming an interview. "But here's the real thing—some people out there want me to be a typical nigger. There are plenty of people who want to see me be a Floyd Mayweather and come out with attitude and talk trash. But I won't, because it's just not me. I can talk shit with my friends because they're my friends and that's the relationship we have. But I would never say anything disrespectful in front of a camera or do something stupid to disrespect who I am."

I had wanted to ask about his recent verbal feud with Tito Ortiz, but Nate finished his interview and it was Rashad's turn to get in front of the camera. On his way to the cage, he and Mike Seal traded acerbic jabs and a few jokes that drew out one of Rashad's greatest strengths—impersonations.

"My defense is impregnable, my skills are formidable, I want to eat your children, praise be to Allah," he said in a perfect Mike Tyson voice that had everyone laughing, but it was the impression of his mother that got everyone going.

"Rashaaad," he said in a high-pitched voice with a lisp. "Rashaaad, why did you hit that boy after he was down? That wasn't nice. Rashaaad, have you got that Bruce Lee video I told you to get? It would help you, you know. Rashaaad, do you know Steven Seagal? He's a bad man."

The man who pulled Rashad away for his interview was Mike Van Arsdale, the strength and conditioning coach of the gym. Mike was a professional fighter who at one point could claim a solid record of eight

Rashad Evans prepares for training.

wins and only one loss to a wicked bad Brazilian. Nicknamed "The Axe Murderer," Wanderlei Silva was undefeated for almost five years at one point, devastating his opponents in the process, including Van Arsdale. But losing to Silva was like having your bus eaten by Godzilla on the way to work; there was nothing you could do about it and therefore the act held no shame.

In 2005, Mike Van Arsdale was considered a contender for the UFC light heavyweight belt. With ripped abs and a boatload of confidence, Van stepped into the Octagon on August 20, 2005, against another contender for the light heavyweight crown, Randy Couture. Van lost by Anaconda choke in the third round, but put up a spirited fight to the end. Unfortunately, though, this is where his career began its swan song. It was the first of four straight losses. His last defeat was to Matt Lindland.

"Matt isn't that good," Van told me as he sat on an exercise bike. "I was beating the hell out of him until his forearm hit me in the neck and reinjured it." Van's neck injury wasn't just an excuse, and he had the surgical scars to prove it. "I told Matt to take me down and end it before I got paralyzed."

Van was that fighter whose glory days were behind him, and he kept the cherished memories mostly to himself unless prodded to tell the stories. He was the guy that got respect in hushed tones because everyone knew he had many fights under his belt, some of which were epic battles. In the Army, this person is a first sergeant.

First sergeants are the top NCOs, right underneath the commander of a company, which normally numbers around 100 troops. They are usually grumpy, older NCOs who stereotypically don't like anyone or anything (especially lieutenants).

But first sergeants really love to be in the middle of things, coaching, mentoring, and taking care of their soldiers. Overall, a first sergeant is happy to have the opportunity to do his job and rarely dotes on material trinkets, like badges for his uniform. They are mission focused and brave beyond comparison.

Van was undeniably the first sergeant of Greg Jackson's gym, and with good reason. Van was once an Army infantryman until the brass learned about his background in MMA and he was diverted to the Army's World Class Athlete Program at Fort Carson, Colorado, after basic training. But

Van puts Joey through a brutal conditioning workout.

the life was unfulfilling, so he decided to attend Officer Candidate School at Fort Benning, Georgia.

"You could see the jaws drop when I walked back into the WCAP with my shiny gold bar on my uniform!"

But the Army life didn't last for Van. "I just didn't feel it in my heart anymore. I was dissatisfied and convinced my wife it was time to get out." He bounced around a few gyms looking for the one that was right before settling in Albuquerque with Greg Jackson.

It was Van who, when guys were hurting or not feeling right, would pull them aside, figure out what was going on and get them back in the game, keeping Greg informed every step of the way. It was Van who cracked jokes and kept the guys laughing when they were stoically bearing a defeat. But most important, it was Van who got things done when everyone was slacking or losing focus. He had his finger on the pulse of the gym, and when a point needed to be made, it was that finger that jabbed chests, accompanied by a firm, "No, this is the way you do it!"

* * * * *

The next morning was the hardest one of Rashad's workweek—the shark tank!

There were a few minor differences between David Terrell's training and this one, but it was basically the same. Jackson's boys called it "Circles," short for "Circle of Death." Here only the two men fighting and Greg himself were allowed in the cage, whereas David Terell let everyone pile in. Jacskon's cage seemed larger too, allowing for more space to execute moves or avoid them.

Despite fatigue and a nasty sunburn from hiking through Chaco Canyon the day prior, Greg had training to do. And like any good leader, he yanked himself up and found some motivation, partly aided by a combat-sized bottle of Rockstar energy drink.

Rashad prepared for his circle by blasting James Brown on the stereo and doing shadow boxing in the ring, marked "Oakdale National Guard Boxing Club" on the floor. I learned later this was George Foreman's ring when he was in his prime; Jackson had bought it thirdhand.

Floyd Sword, a grumpy fighter with a dry sense of humor, prepared to be Rashad's first challenge. "This is a church and that's the choir music," Greg proclaimed as he walked past Floyd, who was absorbed with wrapping his gloves with duct tape and smearing Vaseline on his face.

Rashad moved to the cage and paced it like an impatient animal waiting for its supper while James Brown belted out "Hey! I feel good!" But before the action could start, Greg had one last task to perform.

"Hey, watch this." Holding a giant bullhorn, he climbed the stairs to the gym's second-floor dormitory. Despite the choir music being loud enough to wake the homeless bums on Central Avenue a block away, the fighters in these rooms apparently felt it wasn't time to rise and shine just yet.

Greg did a voice of God as well as any of the best drill sergeants I'd ever heard. "Get up, Mike Seal!" he intoned at a closed door, then pivoted his body ninety degrees to the left to face another closed door. "Let's go in there, Brit!" he demanded of James Zikic, the Cage Rage light heavyweight champion from the UK who was training in New Mexico for a few weeks. He pointed the bullhorn down the hall toward the last closed door and went Latino. "Oye, cabron, vamanos!" And Damacio Page stumbled out a moment later, groggy and blind.

Greg descended and, as he waited for Rashad's sparring partners to get their gear on, danced awkwardly across the gym to James Brown.

"I'm blessed and I know it," he admitted. "I get to do what I love and support my family. It's good. Especially now that I have this!" He lifted the bullhorn to his mouth, pointed it at Joey Villasenor and did his best Austin Powers impersonation. "Yeah, baby. Do I make you horny?"

Joey winced and looked spitefully in the direction of the guy who had brought a bad sign into his gym—me. A few moments later, James Brown faded out and Diego Sanchez ran to the stereo to keep the groove going. "What do you want, Rashad?"

"Anything R&B."

Sanchez threw in a Wu Tang Clan CD. When the music changed, it was as if he'd thrown a high voltage "serious" switch, because the mood turned dark. Floyd Sword threw his mouthpiece in and stepped into the cage, meeting Rashad's wary stare head on.

"Take it easy this first round, Floyd," Greg directed.

"Oh, I'm good, coach. I can go hard," Floyd responded.

Greg paused and looked away, clearly perturbed. "Or don't then. I'm only the trainer here after all," he snapped back.

Greg knew if he let Floyd have his way and go hard at Rashad, he would be letting a soldier disobey him, a clearly insubordinate act, when all the other troops were looking on mere feet away. At the same time, Floyd was a trusted member of his stable and knew his own strengths and weaknesses. If he wasn't prepared to go all out, he wouldn't have bucked Greg in the first place. Good leaders know when to take the advice of subordinates or even let them have their own way. But this wasn't one of those times.

"Look, I want to warm him up this first round. Don't go all out. The last thing we need is one of you getting hurt this close to your fights." This was clearly not a request, and Floyd knew it.

As the two waited for the buzzer to begin the first five-minute round, Rashad's brooding eyes and disdainful scowl burned like a neon sign that read, "Don't fuck with me." At that moment, I almost felt sorry for Tito Ortiz.

As directed, Floyd came out easy against Rashad. They spent an uneventful five minutes doing little more than shadow boxing and grappling for position. The buzzer sounded, and Floyd stepped out, letting "The Dean of Mean," Keith Jardine, in. The buzzer sounded for the start of the next round almost immediately.

"He's good, huh?" Diego Sanchez said as he sat next to me. Sanchez was a welterweight and one of Jackson's first students.

"That break was fast," I muttered.

"Thirty-second rest," Diego responded.

"Not one minute?"

"Nope. Can't get too relaxed."

Jardine went at Rashad harder than Floyd, but still without the intensity I'd seen at Terrell's. Here were some of the most successful fighters in the MMA world preparing one of their best for a major UFC event, and they were taking it easy. Was I missing something?

"Good hook, Rashad," Greg yelled at him, referring to a left hook they'd been working on. Rashad was known for throwing two left jabs and then stepping in with a powerful right. It had taken its toll on several opponents. But Tito Ortiz would see it coming after studying his fight film, and he would certainly be working on a defense. Rashad had to change up the game and add the left hook when Tito wasn't expecting it, so Greg stayed on him to get it down.

Keith's round ended and I was stumped. There had to be something more daunting to challenge Rashad and make him get better.

There was, and its name was Diego Sanchez.

"Time for payback," Diego said as he grabbed his mouthpiece.

"Payback?" I asked.

"Yeah. He kicked my ass when I was getting ready for Koscheck. Now it's my turn."

Sanchez literally leaped into the cage and showed no mercy. He instantly shot in and grabbed Rashad's legs, hoisting him high into the air and bringing him down hard onto the mat despite a thirty-pound weight disadvantage. Rashad scrambled, but Diego remained calm and maintained top control, albeit only for a few moments. Keeping a champion wrestler who outweighs you down is difficult, and at the two-minute mark, Rashad was back on his feet.

Diego continued his assault, snapping a loud kick to Rashad's thigh that echoed throughout the gym. "Oh, shit," someone exclaimed behind me. Not wanting to give the light heavyweight a break, Diego charged in and got another takedown. Rashad defended well and rolled onto Diego's top, but in the process left his neck outstretched just a fraction of a second too long. The crafty Sanchez spotted the mistake and pounced on it, wrapping his arm around Rashad's neck in a deep guillotine choke. He leaned back to finish the move and Rashad had no choice but to tap out.

"Get up. Keep going," Greg ordered after congratulating Diego on his skillful maneuver.

The two moved to the center of the cage and again Diego went for Rashad's legs, getting the takedown. Fatigue and Diego's tenacity were taking their toll. Rashad's defense was crumbling by the minute. Moments later he found some energy and reversed Diego, but he did little with the new advantageous position he found himself in.

"Same effing thing!" Greg mumbled, quickly looking around the gym to make sure there were no children within earshot. Like a computer geek who spots a single flaw in a million lines of code, Greg saw something in Rashad's game and made a mental note to fix it later.

Rashad finally gained side control, but Diego refused to give up and attacked Rashad's arm, securing a kimura. Although named after Masahiko Kimura, who invented it, the move is similar to what big brothers and bullies have done for centuries when they bend an arm up behind the victim's back and yell, "Say uncle!"

The kimura was deep, and it looked as if Rashad might tap a second time when the buzzer sounded and Diego let go.

"Great job, both of you," Greg was quick to say.

After fifteen minutes of work, Rashad stood dripping in sweat. But the sharks were not through with Mr. Evans just yet. Nathan Marquardt, a well-rounded fighter and seven-time King of Pancrase, stepped in.

"Now he's in trouble," someone said.

The buzzer sounded its tortured whine, and Nate moved in, quickly securing a Muay Thai clinch with his hands around the back of Rashad's neck. From here, Nate controlled the fight and delivered knees to Evans's midsection and face at will, though they weren't hard enough to cause much damage. As they worked, Diego Sanchez, sweaty and panting, sat down next to me.

"Looks like you got your payback," I said.

"Yep," he replied. "Felt good, too."

With a thud, Nate took Rashad to the mat and attempted several submissions on his tired foe. He tried an armbar from side control, but Rashad blocked it. He tried to mount him, but was again stymied. When Rashad swept Nate's legs and got on top of him, Nate attempted a triangle choke with his legs around Rashad's head and arm, but Rashad saw it coming and pulled out. Nate finally got out from under Rashad and they both got back to their feet. The two stood in the middle of the cage, one clearly steadier than the other.

The master strategist smiled. "Here's where the mental conditioning starts," Greg said.

As if on cue, Nate charged in and took Rashad's legs out from under him, slamming him hard to the mat. Under better circumstances, Rashad would have immediately defended against being mounted, but it was clear he was not just tired, but fully exhausted. Four fresh fighters had tested him at 5,500 feet above sea level, and his cardiovascular endurance was fading. He struggled to keep Nate off him as Diego yelled.

"Come on, Rashad! Hang tough!"

"This is where you get stronger, Rashad," Greg implored of his fighter, signaling everyone else to join in.

"You can beat him, Rashad!"

"Don't quit, baby!"

Although the shark tank is unforgiving, it is nothing if not fair. Hard work pays off, and Evans's refusal to quit when his body was breaking reaped rewards. With his last bit of energy he reversed Nathan, got to his feet, and shot in for a takedown of his own, slamming Nate onto the mat just as the buzzer sounded.

"Great job!" Greg praised as he unlocked the cage door. "Great circle, Rashad." Others joined in as Rashad's wobbly legs carried him out of the cage and everyone patted his sweaty back. His misery wasn't over yet, though, and an unsmiling Van demanded that he jog around the grappling mats for a while for cardiovascular conditioning.

"Way to go, 'Shad," Diego yelled, and suddenly blew his nose violently on the ground—or actually where I'd just repositioned my leg. Diego's snot rocket suddenly covered it from the knee down. I thought jumping up and shouting, "You blew boogers on my fucking leg!" was probably unwise. Instead I quietly grabbed Diego's sweat towel and wiped my leg off, getting the last laugh—or so I thought. Moments later another fighter—who will remain anonymous—grabbed the phlegm-encrusted towel, wiped his face, and stuffed it into his gym bag.

Frequently booed at fights because of his antagonistic interviews and a verbal feud with Josh Koscheck, Diego was not a crowd favorite. But despite the snot incident, I found myself liking him. He was easy going in the gym and very supportive of his teammates. Diego was another victim of the hype machine that shaped opinions and made heroes or villains out of ordinary people.

Next, Mike Seal, the lanky, boisterous kickboxer from Mexico, leaped into the shark tank for his ordeal. Mike had a fight coming up, so although he's no big name, his training was just as fierce as what Jackson's guys had shelled out to Rashad.

Mike Seal had never graced a UFC Octagon despite twenty-four professional fights. But the dedication he was about to display was no less spectacular than anyone who's worn a championship belt. Over the next twenty minutes, he endured a pounding by Keith Jardine, several near-submissions from James Zikic, a ground-and-pound lesson from Joey Villasenor, a hard body slam and two tapouts from Diego Sanchez, and finally an inescapable choke from Nathan Marquardt, during which he temporarily blacked out. But Seal would find no rest in unconsciousness.

"Get him up, put him back in," Greg demanded as Marquardt and Jardine hoisted Seal's limp body up and revived him. Brotherly love was never so tough.

When his ordeal finally ended, Seal was emotional and left the ring trying to hold back tears. They weren't tears of pain, but rather of disappointment. He'd tapped out twice and got choked out cold, a defeat in anyone's eyes, no matter how high the caliber of opponent. Seal was distraught that he'd done a bad job, but in fact the opposite was true.

Jackson's boys soon pumped him back up and told him how honestly proud they were of him. They had every reason to be. He'd just fought five world-class fighters, all of whom were fresher and more experienced, and he'd given them all he had. He was challenged to show his mettle, his warrior spirit, and came through, however scathed.

In the world of MMA, surviving the shark tank isn't a rite of passage, but leaving everything you have inside of it is. Any decent fighter can go in there and sandbag his way through four or five rounds, conserving energy and avoiding his opponents along the way. But that would not only display laziness and a shallow work ethic, it would also be a fool's errand. The object is to train. The man who dedicates everything until the last buzzer sounds has taught his body to perform and knows the pinnacle of human competition. He has also earned he right to respect himself, as well as perhaps a greater reward—the respect of men of action.

"Everyone in the cage," Greg demanded. The small enclosure was soon full of bodies.

"I will not accept neutral positions!" he snapped. "Grabbing the hips and hanging on is a neutral position. It's not pressing the fight and it will get you nowhere." He showed them what he meant, using Keith Jardine as an example.

"If you get here," he said, grabbing Keith around the hips, "then don't stay here. Drop down and sweep the legs or rise up swinging. But don't stay here. It does no good."

Greg's uncanny ability to spot a flaw and fix it was one of the reasons he was one of the best trainers in the world. He was like a card counter at a casino who knows exactly what cards are missing and will appear next.

An hour later, a clearly exhausted Mike Seal sat in the inner sanctum gazing at the far wall, completely expressionless. He looked like a infantryman with a thousand-yard stare—utterly and completely spent, void of any desire to act or even speak out loud.

"That was the best circle you've ever done, Mike," Greg said to him, snapping him out of his zone. Mike took a swig of water and struggled to get a simple sentence out in response.

"I've shed blood and sweat in here. Now I've shed tears."

* * * * *

For the most part, MMA athletes are very respectful of each other, more so than in just about any other sport. But why? I thought back to Rashad's comments about how people perceive him, wanting him to be more like a common street thug. Sure, the temptation was there to let emotions get the better of him and talk smack to his opponents, but for the most part he didn't. He even showed real concern for Sean Salmon after knocking him out cold with a devastating high kick to the cheek.

In similar fashion, Roger Huerta, after an epic fight with Leonard Garcia that landed on the front page of Sports Illustrated, paraded around the Octagon with Garcia's hand raised high out of respect for him.

The list can go on and on. Sure, there are those exceptions who prefer the old-school ways of using psychological jabs to get under an opponent's skin. The question is, when does a psychological technique turn into silly trash talking?

Diego Sanchez posted a message on Josh Koscheck's website to get into his head before their fight in April 2007, but this was an isolated incident derived from a personal dislike for each other. Sanchez even went so far as to shove Koscheck during the prefight weigh-ins because of the brewing bad blood between the two.

The true master of getting under an opponent's skin, though, is Tito Ortiz. But even his taunting is usually reserved for whoever is next in line to fight him, in an attempt to rattle him and throw off his game plan. Just a few weeks prior to coming to Jackson's MMA, Tito claimed he was going to make Rashad his "nappy-headed ho."

Though naturally reserved, Rashad had heard enough and lashed back at Ortiz. He went on an Albuquerque radio station and said, "I think [Ortiz] is not from Mexico. I think [he] might be from Puerto Rico or Cuba. I think he's frontin' about being Mexican." Even this relatively mild rant he was instantly sorry for. With Diego and Rashad getting into these public altercations, I wondered if their Jedi master condoned the behavior.

"As long as it's strategy and not personal, it's fine," Greg said. "There's tactical value in getting inside someone's head. It's not the Queensbury rules after all. Pushing Koscheck was a calculated risk to get him to do something other than what he did. We wanted him to get angry and throw big punches instead of one-two combos and move away. Unfortunately, it didn't work."

"So behavior designed to illicit a response is acceptable as long as it doesn't cross the line into someone's personal life?"

"Yeah. That sounds about right. You can't put anger into a fight.

Emotion is okay, but not anger. Once someone gets angry, he's lost."

"Aren't most fights born out of anger?" I asked. "I mean, don't you fight someone because you're angry at them?"

"In the street, yes. In here, no."

Nathan Marquardt is only the second man to be awarded a BJJ black belt under Ricardo Murgel. From 1999 to 2005, Nathan dominated the Pancrase circuit in Japan, winning the middleweight championship seven times. In 2005 he was finally lured to the UFC, and after winning all four of his UFC fights, Nathan was now sitting on the precipice of his shot at the big time against Anderson Silva. It would take place on the same night that Rashad was set to face Tito, so it was undeniably going to be a big night for Greg Jackson's MMA.

Unfortunately for Marquardt, he was a virtual unknown to all but the most hardcore of UFC fans. Despite his stellar career, the UFC hype machine had simply overlooked him. Nathan had fallen victim to the pay-per-view blues, a condition that affects many undercard fighters.

On a typical UFC event there are eight to ten fights scheduled, but the pay-per-view portion that fans see at home is limited to three hours. When you factor in the time the UFC spends on short promotional videos of the fighters, commercials announcing its next event, the time it takes to introduce fighters and announce decisions of completed fights, the remaining amount of time to actually air fights is not enough to show all that are scheduled.

The UFC compensates by taping the preliminary fights and then airing the best ones after the main event—if there's enough time left on the three-hour pay-per-view. The next time you watch a UFC, look at the crowds after the main event. The stands will be almost empty because the fight actually took place hours beforehand and is being replayed. It's simply a trick to fill time. You can't blame them for hedging their bets.

Unfortunately, this system means undercard fighters like Nathan are continually left off the show and don't develop much of a fan base or name recognition. They get the pay-per-view blues. So now, as he trained for a title shot that was only weeks away, he was little more than a name on a card that few people recognized, even though he was the main event.

When this happens, another fight will receive more attention and tantalize viewers to watch, especially when there's bad blood involved, like Tito versus Rashad.

Nathan's Brazilian jiu jitsu instructor was also a name few recognized. Ricardo Murgel was not as famous as the Gracie family, but he was no less prominent in BJJ circles. At the age of nineteen, he found the Gracie fighting system and was taught by Joao Alvaro Barreto, a hand-picked disciple of the legendary BJJ grand master, Helio Gracie. From there, Murgel made a life out of training and teaching Brazilian jiu jitsu, achieving the rank of seventh degree black belt and the unwritten title of "frail old man you don't want to fuck with."

On Saturday, I decided to take one of the Marquardt-Murgel BJJ classes. Ricardo dispensed with the "starting off easy" phase that most classes have and took the seminar straight into advanced jiu jitsu moves. I was paired off with Cage Rage champion James Zikic who, like me, had to watch Murgel display a move several times before being able to accomplish it.

When Murgel described a move, Marquardt would assist or stand by waiting to demonstrate. At almost seventy years old, Murgel was not a threatening-looking man, but his technique was undeniable. He demonstrated how Brazilian jiu jitsu has a built-in system to recover from failure.

For example, Murgel and Nate showed how a man on his back can rise up and over an attacker's arm, securing it and bending it behind his back into a kimura. If the defender straightens his arm, which is the correct defense, then the attacker can go for a straight armbar by swinging one of his legs over the defender's head. If this doesn't work, he is still in a good position to secure an omoplata, which puts the entire weight of the attacker onto the defender's shoulder to crush it. If this still doesn't work, the defender is now in a position to take the attacker's back and sink in a rear naked choke.

Before long my partner James was uninterested and moved on to greener pastures. A guy named martin took his place, but Martin had trouble getting the omoplata down, so Nate stepped in and showed him, using me as a "grappling dummy." Nate was stronger than a Tabasco-coated Vicodin, and his technique was smoother than turtle wax. I outweighed him by at least thirty pounds, yet his skill negated that advantage like I was a kindergartner. If my arms weren't already sore from the many armbars and kimuras we'd practiced, they sure as hell were aching when Nate was through with me. In the end, though, it was great training—and besides, surely I'd picked up a move or two that I could use if I were ever picked for a Pros versus Joes challenge.

Like Jake Shields, Nate has the boyish charm of the nice kid next door. He was quiet and void of the pretentious arrogance that a man with 25 professional MMA wins could have. But in the cage, he's pure fighter, with a powerful repertoire of weapons and an intimidating look, only enhanced by his shaved head.

To me, as a victim of male pattern baldness, if you have the ability to grow a full head of hair, the idea of shaving it off is a bit evil. I found it difficult to comprehend why Nate would do it.

"I just didn't want to deal with it," he said. "It gets in the way and I don't want to take the time to groom it. I felt stupid brushing it. It seems kinda vain to me, you know?"

No, I didn't. My hair started thinning when I was twenty-two and I've watched in silent horror as I've had to wash more and more of my forehead every day. Nice guy or not, it was hard not to hate him.

When the class was done, I was filthy. For all the talent in Greg's gym, they couldn't tell you which end of a broom is the one that touches the floor. The remembrance of the Quest essence of Clorox was never so sweet.

My shoulder was killing me. The Motrins still hadn't kicked in when I exited the gym to the distinctive smell of rain weighing down the Albuquerque air. Ominous thunderclouds rumbled a warning very close by. I mounted the Disco and drove toward Shogun Sushi on Central Avenue to fulfill a craving.

At a red light a homeless man stood at a bus stop drenched from the deluge, but not because he got caught in the sudden storm. Apparently he had some personal grooming to accomplish. He smiled wide and ran a comb through his wet hair, seemingly for the first time in a while. Though it was a messy mop, it was still thick and full on his head and he seemed pleased to finally have free water. I laughed until I realized he had more hair than me. Then I hated him too.

* * * * *

Some speculate that the secret to Obiwan Jacksoni's success is the high-altitude training he puts his fighters through, but Greg disagrees. "Altitude training is just a means to an end," he said. "We use it to push them to their limits and beyond, therefore conditioning the mind. The mind is a muscle that has to be exercised. You have to go beyond your limits and prove to yourself that you're capable of more than you think you are." That's a great motivational speech, but did Jackson's guys practice what he preached? I found out the hard way.

Greg trains his fighters at differing altitudes, depending on their schedules and how close they are to a fight. They range from the Sandia Crest at 11,000 feet to lower mountain training at 7,000 feet down to sand dune training at 5,500 feet just outside town. His altitude training has a common theme—no matter which level is executed, they all achieve "torture" rating on the overall scale of suckiness.

One morning toward the end of my stay, Greg rousted the lightweights out of bed early to run the dunes south of Albuquerque. It was clearly an area that no sane person would ever build a house on since several high-tension power lines ran directly over it. The electricity coursing through the wires crackled like a flock of Canadian geese as we stretched underneath them, and I secretly worried it was making us all sterile, but then I remembered Greg had two small children.

We stood at the bottom of a dune and looked up toward the summit—what seemed to be a 150-foot rise. It was early, but the sun was beating down and the temperature was rising.

"What are you gonna do, chief?" Leonard Garcia asked me.

"He's going to take pictures and get the story," Greg said before I could answer. "I'll do some of it with you," I said defiantly.

"Okay, then," Greg replied as if to say, "I gave you an out, dumbass."

"You guys keep stretching out, I'm going to run it once to test it," Greg ordered as he sprinted up the hill. The loose sand gave way beneath his feet as he went up, and once at the top, we could hear his heavy breathing all the way down at our position.

Julie Kedzie carries Angela Magana up the dune.

"Five times up and down!" Greg ordered from the top of the hill. "Go."

The four fighters took off, panting and grunting the whole way. Page made it up first, followed by Garcia, Julie Kedzie, and Angela Magana. Their breath was labored as they made their way back down and their legs wobbled some, but it didn't seem too bad. So on the second sprint up I joined them, and immediately realized the debilitating effect high altitude has on a body. My legs felt like posts and my lungs burned. The loose sand gave back to the dune part of each step I took. It was harder than swimming out to sea against the surf—and a good deal less refreshing.

"Keep it going," Greg prodded as I passed him near the summit. Once there, I had to pause a moment—to enjoy the view, as I told myself.

"That's a whole new level of suck," I told Jackson.

"That's why we do it."

On her third sprint, Julie Kedzie let her true feelings be known. "Fuck!" she yelled as her legs bogged down in the sand.

Greg smiled like a heroin addict feeling the sweet burn of the needle. "Music to my ears. Now we take her past her breaking point and build her back up." He ran down to Julie and motivated her to reach deep and find some inner strength to keep going.

Kedzie gave it her all, but got no love in return. There were standards to keep, and Greg was making sure she did every sprint. Still, she never gave up. Though Page and Garcia lapped her, and I did two sprints in the time it took her to do three, she growled angrily, gnashed her teeth and screamed at herself to keep moving. Anyone who says women lack a warrior spirit needs to meet Julie Kedzie.

As if the five sprints weren't enough, everyone had to complete a buddy climb afterward as well. Garcia jumped on Page's back, and up the hill through the loose sand he went. This was downright murderous, and when it came my turn to participate, I did so with a slight bit of apprehension. But I reached the top, feeling like Rocky Balboa gazing out at Philadelphia. I was tired, nauseous, lightheaded, and proud, all at the same time.

"Good job, buddy," Garcia said as he dismounted my back. In reality, I had it easy. The fighters all had to carry a buddy with a body weight equal to their own. They all weighed 135 to 145 pounds, while I weighed in at 225. So carrying Leonard Garcia up the hill wasn't even comparable to what they were doing.

We left the dunes that morning smoked, but also filled with the privilege of gratification that comes only after thresholds have been breached. The feeling outweighed my fatigue—and I hadn't even done the whole routine. It was the feeling of knowing you'd risen to the occasion, a deep pleasure from confronting adversity and kicking its ass.

It was my last day in Albuquerque and almost time to say goodbye to Greg and his crew. Greg Jackson's camp was the tightest group of people I'd ever met, and that included the many units I had been honored to be a part of in the military. Jackson's troops were a gregarious fraternity of jokesters, renegades, loyalists, dreamers, and doers, but most of all a true band of brothers and sisters.

The success and failure of a group of individuals can usually be traced back to its leader. Good leadership and poor leadership directly affect a unit equally. Just as children are a direct reflection of their parents, fighters are a direct reflection of their training, and the way these guys performed on fight night was indicative of Greg's calculating genius and draconian drive.

Thomas Edison once said, "Genius is 1 percent inspiration and 99 percent perspiration." Greg would call this terminological inexactitude, because in the physical realm of sport an individual relies equally on his mental acumen, veracity, and steadfast resolve in the face of duress. It was basic math, science, and beauty.

Here are some other things Jackson would say:

You're a full contact fighter? Is there a half-contact fighter?

Be good and defend the good name.

What time is it? It's time for love.

The world is an ugly place, you have to find the beauty in it.

Turning the other cheek only gets it hit harder.

The decisions I make don't determine whether or not people die. Dreams yes, people no.

Not long after I left New Mexico, Greg Jackson's fighters experienced a terrible series of losses. Floyd Sword was defeated by Thales Leitas in the first round of his Octagon debut by a well-executed arm-triangle choke. Duane Ludwig lost to Paul Daley at their Strikeforce showdown. Mark Bocek lost to Frank Edgar by TKO in the first round of their fight on the undercard of UFC 73. Also at UFC 73, for all the hype surrounding Rashad Evans and Tito Ortiz's fight, it ended in a less-than-spectacular draw that didn't deliver the fireworks everyone had hoped for.

Joey Villasenor's "signs" proved to be accurate. Nathan Marquardt was defeated by Anderson Silva in the first round of their middleweight championship fight, and Joey lost to Murilo "Ninja" Rua during the EliteXC light heavyweight championship fight. The only bright spots during that time were Leonard Garcia defeating Allan Berubie, and Mike Seal beating Marcos Rodriguez.

Truth be told, Jackson's unlucky streak had started before I got there, when Keith Jardine was knocked out by Houston Alexander at UFC 71. The dark clouds that plagued Jackson's in the summer of 2007 brought a great deal of heartache to the fighters who'd welcomed me into their lives, but thankfully that darkness was only temporary. While I put no faith in reading tealeaves, rolling chicken bones, or omens on souvenir T-shirts, I did feel a little guilty for bringing "Anderson Island" into the gym and possibly placing a psychological hurdle in Joey's mind before his fight.

I still have that shirt though. It's great for workouts.

SITYODTONG

You know more than you think you know, just as you know less than you want to know.

—Oscar Wilde

Mark DellaGrotte's Sityodtong Muay Thai Academy needs a carnival ride sign out front depicting a maximum height:
YOU MUST BE THIS SHORT TO TRAIN HERE
The gym is in the basement under Mark's father's law firm. With its steep, cramped stairway and seven-foot ceilings, it could have been a brothel for degenerate Smurfs and wayward hobbits. You enter through a nondescript, black door on the backside of a building on Broadway, one of the main drags in Somerville, Massachusetts, Harvard University's working-class neighbor, and just a Paul Revere horse ride from downtown Beantown.

When I arrived, the aroma of spicy beef from Gaucho's Brazilian Cuisine hung like a pleasant fog over the block of convenience stores and low-end beauty parlors. Some discarded plastic vodka bottles lay like sleeping drunks in the gutter.

Another world-class gym in the last place I expected to find one. What was it with this trend? Was it the sport's fault? Was the pay so low that they couldn't afford to train in a neighborhood where the number of random shootings was lower than the literacy rate? Or were these guys so devoted to their sport that they just didn't care about outward appearances?

Walking down the steep stairs into the gym reminded me of visiting my big brother's ultra-cool basement bachelor pad when I was ten, only without the black light and crushed-velvet posters. The first test for newcomers like me was to get past Ducati, a big, black, barking, horselike dog that was so named because he ate motorcycles and shit tires. Ducati was from a breed called Cane Corso, which I think is Italian for "demon dog that enjoys shredding man flesh."

"Don't worry about him," Marie DellaGrotte, Mark's wife, said from behind the front desk. "He's harmless."

"Does he have a secret attack word?" I asked avoiding eye contact as I tried to shuffle past him.

"Yeah," she responded. "You'll be fine as long as you don't speak Italian." I was never happier that I had studied Spanish.

The place reeked of Team Quest, which I hadn't noticed while sidestepping the beast. Matt Lindland must have shared disinfecting secrets with Mark because it was clean—incredibly clean. But the humble accommodations seemed not at all befitting the name Mark had built up over the years as a master Muay Thai practitioner.

It was late on a Thursday night and his MMA class packed the place. And by packed I mean there were thirty students. The total square footage couldn't have been much more than a double-wide trailer.

The native New England talent pool made Sityodtong another Petri dish for *The Ultimate Fighter* show. Kenny Florian nearly won the first season, Marcus Davis was on season two, and Jorge Rivera was on season four when Mark was the Muay Thai coach. All three were Sityodtong disciples.

DellaGrotte's walls were thick with memorabilia and photos depicting Mark with everyone from the top man in MMA, Dana White, right down to completely unknown amateurs. On one wall hung three large jerseys from *The Ultimate Fighter*, season four, that were covered in autographs from everyone on the show. That sort of "look at me" braggadocio is sometimes an indicator of a lack of self-confidence that manifests in a need for reinforcement. With his résumé, I couldn't imagine this was the case of Mark DellaGrotte, but I was going to find out over the next week.

"Sawatdee kap," Mark said approaching me with his hands together in a Buddhist gesture.

"Sawami chop," I responded, cluelessly holding out my hand to shake his.

He looked at my outstretched arm and smiled. "We wai here. It's a sign of respect."

"Oh. Sorry."

"Everything is Thai style," he said. "Glad ya could make it. Where'd yah pahk yah cah?

"Uh . . . is that more Thai?"

"This is yah first time in Bahstan, eh? You'll get used to it."

I wanted to walk around and check out the gym, but didn't need to since I could see it all from one spot. I shucked my sandals and strolled forward anyway until—BAM! The steel beam running down the center of the gym was only five feet ten inches off the ground. Unfortunately, I cruise around at six feet even. Luckily, the beam was padded or I'd have a dent in my forehead like Quasimodo.

"Ya gotta watch that," DellaGrotte said.

No shit, I thought rubbing my cranium. Take another cookie from the obvious jar.

DellaGrotte gave me a quick tour, stepping over and around students as they trained. Sityodtong consisted of a boxing ring, an incomplete cage, several heavy bags, and Wal-Mart sized mirrors, like any good facility would, but with terrible lighting. Near the entryway was a small living room with a TV, a kitchenette, and a bedroom that was sectioned off by a sheet thumbtacked onto the wall.

"Who's staying here?" I asked.

"Me," said a voice that sounded like a Maine lobster fisherman. I turned around to see a sweaty Marcus Davis walking toward us.

Sometimes getting your ass kicked is a good thing. After losing a horrible fight against Joe "Daddy" Stevenson on *The Ultimate Fighter* season two, Marcus Davis was unceremoniously discarded by the UFC like several pounds of gelatinous flesh after liposuction. It was the best thing that happened to him.

Davis left the show and went back to New England, where he ate chowder, trained hard, and won five straight fights in smaller promotions. Like an egotistical man who breaks up with a chick only to realize he made a mistake, the UFC took notice and gave Marcus a booty call. He returned to the UFC in 2006 and won five more fights, one of which earned him "fight of the night" honors at UFC 75.

"The guys who won are stuck in a multiyear contract for less than I get for one fight," he told me, sitting back in an uncomfortable wicker chair as tired students walked by cleaning and straightening the gym. "They're making peanuts, but I get to negotiate my paycheck because I'm not stuck like they are. And they won!"

Davis developed name recognition from the show and used it to his advantage like any good capitalist. "I called Randy [Couture] up when I was in Vegas and asked if I could train with him. He was like, 'Yeah, sure.' That never would have happened without the show."

Some people are raised in an environment where fighting is necessary to survive. Others, like Marcus, were simply predisposed to fight, either because of genetic codes or familial tendencies. He came from a family of boxers and fell in line with the profession at an early age, although he was never pressured to fight. His father walked out when he was four, leaving Marcus, his mother, and an older brother to fend for themselves, which had unfortunate side effects.

"My brother was six years older, so he remembered all the bad things my dad did before he left us," Marcus said, nearly shouting. I secretly wondered if he was hard of hearing as his tone grew even louder despite the nearly empty gym. "He kind of took his problems out on me at times and thought it was okay since our dad was like that. I think they call it transference."

By eight Marcus was boxing in amateur fights, a child prodigy with a proclivity for throwing fists instead of dodge balls like his peers. In school, Marcus was never a candidate for induction into the National Honor Society. He was the guy who scored well on junior high school aptitude tests but got poor grades because he wasn't interested in studying. Most wrote him off as a bruiser whose head was in the ring instead of the books.

By sixteen, his volatile ways caught

Marcus Davis runs down Broadway in Summerville.

up with him when the State of Maine placed him in a juvenile correctional facility for grand theft auto and various other infractions. It changed his outlook, but not his activity. A year later, he had a daughter and a job as a bouncer in a Bangor bar along with fellow MMA veteran Tim Sylvia.

With a tendency toward violence when he drank, bar life suited Marcus, but fighting for money, instead of throwing belligerents into the street, was still in his blood. He turned pro boxer at the age of nineteen and spent seven years amassing a 17-1-2 record with twelve knockouts. But just when he reached the pinnacle of his boxing career, boredom set in.

"I just lost interest," he said. "It wasn't enough. I knew there had to be more out there. I wasn't getting tested really in the New England circuit and wanted to do something new."

But before taking on the challenge of becoming an MMA fighter, he had to kick one more bad habit. "I'd get a little crazy when I drank," he said.

Mark DellaGrotte, passing by, raised his eyebrows. "A little? You don't want to know."

"Some people just change completely when they get alcohol in them, and I was one of those guys," he admitted. "So I quit four years ago."

He entered MMA in 2003 as a sober boxer with an overestimated opinion of his own skill set. He tried to keep fights standing up but frequently found himself on his back, with about as much agility in that position as a turtle. After two years in MMA, he was a mediocre 3-3 and had little in his checking account to show for it. Although he was a member of the TUF 2 cast, he wasn't exactly the poster boy for the emerging sport.

Two years and ten straight wins later he was back, his life on the path he had always wanted it to be on.

"I'm living the dream right now. I just bought a house with something like an acre yard. I've never even owned a house!" he said in proud astonishment. "I helped my seventeen-year-old daughter buy a car. And that's all because of MMA."

A large part of making his dreams come true was a result of his UFC 75 throwdown with Paul Taylor. The bout was mediocre through the first round until a kick to the neck woke Davis up. He lashed back and devastated Taylor, earning fight of the night and submission of the night bonuses in the process. In one fight, Marcus earned $12,000 to show up, $12,000 for the win, $40,000 for fight of the night, and $40,000 for submission of the night when he caught Taylor in an armbar. It was a total payout of $104,000, more than he'd ever made from anything in his life. The price for such a fight? The letter R.

"After that fight I kept signing my name Macus. For three weeks I dropped the R from my name and couldn't figure out why. He kicked me stupid."

"With your accent it comes out 'Mah-cus' anyway," I said. He agreed. "So is that your motivation now? Money?"

"Not really. I mean, the money is nice, but I love what I do also. I get depressed after a fight because I know it's going to be so long before I get another one. Then I get antsy and stressed waiting for the phone to ring. I watch fighting, I study fights, I work out just waiting to get the call. Fighting gives me that focus to concentrate and do something with myself."

"So how are you now? You don't have a fight coming up," I said.

"I know. It's killing me. I'm harder to work with than usual. I question everything. When someone says, 'Kick the pad this way,' or 'Throw a punch this way,' I always question it. I ask why instead of just taking it as being true. But here's the thing—I only do that with men. If a woman said it, I'd probably say, 'Yes, ma'am.' You know?" he laughed out loud. "It's probably because I grew up respecting women. My mom raised me and my brother on her own and you should have seen her. I mean, she was the arm wrestling champion of the block, man. She could beat guys with one arm behind her back and a cigarette in her mouth and scold us at the same time!" He imitated her slamming an arm down while smoking a stogie. "Marcus get your bike out of the friggin' yard! Bam! Next!"

Before he headed into the ring to spar, Marie DellaGrotte asked him to sign something. "Don't forget the R," Mark joked.

"Yeah!" he replied enthusiastically. "It'll be a long time before I get kicked like that again," he said, putting on his gloves, climbing into the ring, and shoving his mouthpiece in. "No one's going to catch me in a neck kick again anytime soo—"

Mark kicked him in the neck.

"You plick!"

* * * * *

Somerville had apparently spent its entire annual budget on a solitary green strip of median that ran down the center of town. It was aesthetically pleasing, but left nothing in the public coffers for trash pickup or actual road improvements. Broadway had enough potholes to require full-time four-wheel drive traction. Luckily, my Disco had that covered.

The dominant terrain feature of the area is Winter Hill. On one side sits Tufts University, a nice village of shops, attractive eateries, and huge antique houses with bay windows and widow's walks. Though some of these grand chateaus had fallen into disrepair, they seemed just a new coat of paint away from being touristy bed-and breakfasts.

Sityodtong is not on that side of the hill. It sits on the side where the bus stops are crowded and Dunkin' Donuts is gourmet. There are narrow streets, chain-link fences, and tight rows of chipped and faded houses.

Like so many people in MMA, Mark DellaGrotte is a self-made man. He is also a Bostonian through and through, cheering the Red Sox and damning the Yankees on the same street where his parents grew up and did the same. Influenced by his Uncle Joe, who nearly reached the summit of Mount Everest, he was brought up on tales of adventure. So striking out on a journey of discovery to find himself through the martial arts was a natural choice.

In 1992, he met Guro Guy Chase, who had trained with several martial arts legends, including Dan Inosanto and Karl Gotch, so DellaGrotte could hardly have been influenced by anyone better. He spent the next years on a long and bitter road through multitudes of martial arts. It was under Chase that DellaGrotte opened his first gym, called "Multi-Culture Martial Arts Academy," where fate walked through his door.

A student named Tom told DellaGrotte that he had been to Thailand and professed his expertise on the culture and, more importantly, Muay Thai boxing. Mark was interested in Muay Thai and accompanied Tom on a trip to Pattaya and Kru Yodtong's camp. But Tom turned out to know far less than he had claimed to, which left Mark in a bind. Like Alice falling into the rabbit hole, Mark had to fend for himself in Wonderland.

"I'm actually glad he didn't know as much as he said he did because it forced me to learn it. I had to learn how to say certain words, and I had to learn the ways of Thai people, and I had to learn Thai boxing because he wasn't very talented as a Thai boxer. The camp took a liking to me because I showed skill, and I showed improvement every time I went there."

DellaGrotte brought wins to the camp, which was more important than being able to sweep the floors or hold pads (an art form in itself). After several years with Master Senanan Yodtong, he was appointed as the international conservator of the art in America, which is like the pope making you archbishop. Master Yodtong was arguably the greatest teacher of the sport in Thailand. Being Yodtong's head instructor in the States earned Mark a lot of respect. But with the bigger name came bigger responsibility.

"Maybe two years ago, I was in Thailand and they sprang a fight on me with an hour's notice. I had no clothes, I was at the beach all day, had a sunburn, a belly full of rice," he said, smiling at the comedic misery.

"I came to the camp and there was a big stir-up." He raised his eyebrows and grinned. "They told me a guy from Spain backed out. He had a visa problem and had to leave the country, something stupid like that. Kru Yodtong was promoting the event and it's got to be a white guy versus a Thai guy."

Mark could have refused the fight. He wasn't bound by any contract to take it, and his name wasn't on any posters advertising it. No one would have ever known, right?

"A lot of people were like, 'You're a big Kru now. Why do you do this?'"(Mark earned the title "Kru." It was akin to being called a "Don," a "Monsignor," or a "Supreme Allied Commander.") "It took me eight years or so to build a reputation. I could have lost my reputation and lost heart within thirty seconds of conversation. And that's how the Thais are. If the camp says you fight, then you step up. It's time to go. You say no, you lose face. So I took it."

The result? "It was one of my best performances. I had a third-round knockout by neck kick."

Kru Mark was noticed by Dana White in 2006 and was selected to be the Muay Thai coach on *The Ultimate Fighter* season four. As a result,

Sityodtong was put on the MMA map and fighters came a callin'. Stephen Bonnar, Pete Spratt, and Patrick Cote were regulars at Sityodtong, and just days before my arrival, Murilo "Ninja" Rua had stopped in to work with Mark to improve his striking skills.

With attention came change. As arguably the most influential Muay Thai instructor in the U.S., DellaGrotte's decisions have far-reaching effects that he hadn't foreseen when he opened his first gym in 1992. Had he advised Marcus not to take the Paul Taylor fight, Davis would never have earned such a life-altering paycheck. He was quickly learning that making decisions from the upper rungs of the MMA ladder had second and third order effects on people outside his own little sphere of influence.

Aside from his big-name fighters, he also has up-and-comers who depend on him to make wise decisions in their best interest. Their futures revolve around his ability to make sound judgments. Not everyone could do that and, as the pictures on his wall reminded me, I wasn't entirely convinced of his self-confidence. I'd seen decisiveness in him in the gym, but he also had a humble side. Humility is a virtue, but it can be a killer in the world of business.

Mark had a class to teach, and my forehead had another appointment with a low fucking crossbeam. On the way to his class, he took a minute to walk around the gym and correct the things that didn't need correcting. He lined up five Purell bottles so their labels faced the same direction and pump handles were easily accessible, then adjusted a stone dragon that was slightly askew on the banister. After that he straightened the magazines on the front table, arranged a group of pads into a neat line from largest to smallest, and organized several pairs of shoes that were haphazardly kicked onto the floor.

There are fine lines between tidiness, neat-freakiness, and full-blown obsessive-compulsive disorder. I decided to test which one Mark fell into. I pushed the stone dragon that he had just straightened so it was slightly sideways.

Some dead guy said, "An army marches on its stomach." He was right because something about combat makes me hungry. So with Gaucho's Brazilian cuisine and its cute waitresses only thirty feet away, I headed over there for a quick bite to eat before my beginner Muay Thai class started. But like the clam chowder that nearly sidelined me in San Francisco, spicy beef and rice were not conducive to extreme physical duress. You'd think I would have learned from my first mistake.

Jake, Mark's beginners' instructor, soon had me learning it again. "Screw that foot into the ground like a corkscrew," Jake said, as I threw a leg kick as sloppy as the sauce now sloshing in my belly. "Remember, in Muay Thai you want to throw your hips around until your anchor foot points almost backwards. Make it like a pivot point." It briefs well but doesn't execute easily.

After about fifty loping kicks into the pads he held near his chest, I figured out that my problem was the tae kwon do preprogrammed into my head. I couldn't stop chambering my leg and using power from my knee at the last second—a lesson Master Ahn had drilled into me in Korea. The tae kwon do kick had a snap at the end, while Muay Thai was just a swinging meatstick that took advantage of the mass of the leg to produce more momentum and therefore more damage. Instead of the power coming from the knee, it came from the hip.

But there was a physical problem to my kicks as well. I was a big white guy trying to learn a move meant for small Asian men. Like a neutered dog, I just didn't get it.

"Isn't this counterproductive?" I asked. "I mean, if I miss and spin around like a top, I'll have my back to my opponent and be vulnerable."

"Don't miss then," Jake said. Though he sported a cool name, Jake looked like a nerdy nerd from nerdville. He was far from chiseled, which would probably play to his advantage in a street fight, since his fighting skills were certainly formidable. It was a trend that ran like a vein of gold throughout MMA. Physical appearances were deceiving, and you just never knew who had an ace up his sleeve.

Suddenly, I was double-teamed. Mark's senior instructor, Neil, decided the class dork needed some extra attention. "Try to kick through the target instead of stopping at it," Neil said. I did, and suddenly it made sense as I tried to kick through Jake's thigh pad and into his opposite knee, burping up some Brazilian curry in the process. I threw a few good ones into the pads and fooled Jake enough that he and Neil moved on to another victim, leaving me to practice kicking air.

And the air was no match for my powerful strikes, or possibly my Brazilian beef breath either. Imaginary bad guys were collapsing all around me under the relentless assault of my lethal leg—until I threw a particularly hard one and my anchor leg came off the ground, and I landed like a sack of bricks on the mat facing backward. "I'm okay," I declared, jumping up. But it was too late.

"I've done that a hundred times," Mark said, passing by the ring. "I did that once on the cement in Thailand. Talk about pain." Worse than the pain in my ego? I didn't think so.

When the class transitioned to knee strikes, I got extra "Jake love" again. "Throw your knees farther out," Jake said. "Throwing a knee upward does no good. You have to throw it out and into your opponent's midsection to do damage." I thrust my hips and knees so far out I felt like a member of the adult film industry.

"Keep moving forward as you strike. Muay Thai always moves forward," Jake said. "It's always on the toes and ready to strike." He prowled the ring on his toes to demonstrate, but when I tried it, I looked more like a ballerina with double leg cramps and a bad case of acid reflux.

Despite my poor technique, I saw similarities between Muay Thai and other martial arts styles. The "teep kick" in Muay Thai is similar to the "intercepting way" Bruce Lee philosophized about in his book The Tao of Jeet Kune Do. It's meant to interrupt an attack before it happens by putting a foot into your opponent's midsection as he comes in. The punch combinations are hardly different from regular kickboxing and just about every other martial art form. One art calls it one thing while another calls it something else, but it's basically the same, as Chris Wilson at Team Quest had pointed out.

The workout was miserable, but not overly taxing. I'd certainly been through harder events in my life, but the simple movements seemed more difficult than they should have been. DellaGrotte's crew is nothing if not technical, because they prefer the Muay Chalat form, which emphasizes smooth, technically correct movements, as opposed to Muay Lang, which emphasizes power. Throwing strikes repeatedly to achieve correct form and posture is a different version of hell. It isn't the ass-kicking physical torture

Mark DellaGrotte takes a break during training.

of conditioning drills or the overall crushing pain of a shark tank. But the class provided me with a deep muscular burn in my shoulders and hips and a sense that it would take several years to get this thing right. With the smoothness of ten years behind it Mark could throw an elbow and slice water droplets in the air. Mine was more like that of a panicked polar bear caught in quicksand.

Mark's skills are the reason people show up every day—to learn the traditional ways they don't have the means to learn themselves. He'd been to the place where it all started and came away in the favor of one of the greatest teachers of the sport. As an appointee of Master Yodtong, he had the right to teach hundreds of years' worth of the Thai national sport to the masses in Boston. He knew the difference between Silat, Kali, and Muay Khmer (Cambodian-style boxing). He awarded ceremonial head amulets called Monkgols to his students the same way the Gracies awarded BJJ black belts. The amulets differ in color from white to blue to purple to red (the color of the Kingdom) to gold (the color of Buddha). Brown and black are not used because they are sacrilegious to Buddhism.

After one simple hour of punching and kicking (and taking a few kicks to my own thighs), I better understood a few things. Fighters truly are artists that craft their bodies and minds into human weapons. And the feeling of getting that one punch or kick just right is addictive. For every fifty kicks I threw, maybe four got an "attaboy" from the instructors, which was enough to make me throw fifty more. After dropping the gloves and shin guards and knowing I'd made progress, however small, the need that fighters have to fight became a little clearer.

As we cooled down, Marie DellaGrotte dropped a bowl of fruit in the middle of the sweaty circle and, like a bunch of gorillas, everyone dug in.

"Everything is Thai style here," Mark said, chewing on a slice of mango. "The commands they were giving you, the way we greet each other . . ."

I pointed at a clothesline hung across the west wing of the gym.

"That too, but . . ." his voice lowered, "watch this. . . ." I warily glanced over my back, expecting a bucket of cascading Thai Gatorade to engulf me.

"There's an unspoken pecking order. Right now, all the big dogs are eating, while the new guys are starting the nightly wipe down. In a couple minutes, they'll get the courage to come over and grab a piece of fruit. It's like that in Thailand. You'll see a new kid try to eat before the regulars and get bitched at for it."

A few minutes later, the bowl was half empty and the quieter guys, who had been preparing the mats for the Buddha to walk on, dropped their rags and mops to snatch a piece of fruit.

"I think they picked up on it when I took them all to Thailand. It just sort of happened," Mark said.

With my gut full of Brazilian beef still complaining about the workout, I was more concerned with taking notes than eating, but my hands were shaking too badly to write. I can't imagine the difficulty fighters have signing autographs after a fight. For them it's probably no big deal since the human body is so good at adapting to its surroundings. If MMA continued to enjoy the success it had, fighters would evolve to have clubbed hands, triple jointed legs, edged shins, a thickened neck, and a hardened bowl of cartilage around their nuts. Darwin would be proud.

"Check out this dude's mullet," someone smirked as I tried to convince my hands to work properly. He held up the latest issue of Black Belt magazine, which sported a mulleted fighter who promised to "smash what you know about Kung Fu."

"He looks like one of the guys from American Gladiators, what was his name, the blonde guy with the super mullet?"

"Dynamo?"

"No, it was Blaze."

There is little tolerance in the MMA world for charlatans. Not that the guy on the cover of the magazine didn't have something relevant to teach, but for these guys, the proof was in the arena. Held up for ridicule on Mark's wall was a magazine clipping advertising a barroom brawler who was "chosen by the nastiest special ops division over special ops soldiers to teach them his skills," and—lucky for you—he'll teach the same secrets for seventy dollars. The good book says not to worship false idols. The same advice holds true in MMA.

"You have no idea how many people come in here and want to fight and never come back," Marie DellaGrotte said. "I was at the front door one time and this guy came in straight out of prison, right? Well, you could tell he had some fights in him, but none that were legal, of course. Anyway, I asked him if he wanted to try the beginner class or the trials we put them through to see what kind of skills they have. He says to me, 'I'm here to put you guys on the map.' Can you believe that? I looked straight at him and said, 'Oh, thank God you're here. You're exactly what we need to put us on the map!' I get so tired of it."

It wasn't the first time I'd heard this. MMA is a world where courage

Mark DellaGrotte (center) and his Sityodtong crew. Kenny Florian is to Della-Grotte's right.

conquers, but only after devoting a large portion of one's life to pain and humility. Posers and the faint of heart need not get off the couch.

* * * * *

Sityodtong is not a gathering of rough-hewn men. I found no shredded steroid monkeys striking fear into new students when they showed up. If anything it was overly friendly, affording anyone who wanted to train an affable place to do so. It was a gym diverse with the scrawny and overweight, good hair and bald, glasses and acne scars. There were few tattoos and even fewer muscles. But their deficiency in hulking animals was compensated for with technique, work ethic, and sarcasm. The ring leader in each category was Kenny Florian.

He had just defeated Din Thomas on Spike TV's Ultimate Fight Night and was recovering from a compressed neck as a result. Kenny struck his head on the ground while taking Thomas down in the second round just before finishing him off with strikes. But injury or not, I needed his expertise to either verify or deny one of the core principles of Brazilian jiu jitsu and hopefully improve my own technique in the process.

Helio Gracie had made huge strides in perfecting BJJ because he was forced to compensate for his smaller stature by improving his submission techniques. Likewise, Kenny Florian wasn't blessed with a linebacker's physique, but he was a very talented grappler and the perfect person to teach me how to defeat an opponent of larger size and strength.

"An important thing you want to know is how to get out from a bad position," he said, placing me on the mat and getting into my guard. "When someone has you here, especially if they're bigger and stronger, you need to get out. One of the best ways to do that is the hip sweep."

Kenny walked me through the steps of getting my hips into his chest, trapping an arm, and rolling him over quickly. The cool thing about this move was how it ended up with me on top in the mount. From there I could have done just about anything to Kenny. And, like most BJJ moves, this one has a backup plan.

"If for some reason your opponent blocks the move by dropping his weight down, the guillotine and kimura are right there. In order to block the move, he has to expose a vulnerable area—the arm or the neck."

We then worked the dreaded armbar that I had fallen victim to so many times. But this time, I was on bottom and got to use the move to my advantage instead of being tied into a pretzel.

"You have to make sure you get perpendicular to your opponent or it won't work," Kenny instructed. "You have to trap a hand first. Then you want to push off with one foot and swing it over my head quickly." I did as instructed. "Clamp your legs together and lean back."

I did so lightly, and Kenny quickly tapped out. "You're joking," I said, not believing that so little pressure could cause a tapout. "That little bit was painful enough to tap?"

"It doesn't take much. The elbow is a fragile joint; that's why it's targeted so frequently. It's easy to get control of and put painful pressure on so your adversary quits."

I knew this to be true. I'd been caught in plenty of armbars, but none of them were like the one he showed me from the guard.

Kenny's philosophy on martial arts runs deep. "You have to have an advantage. If Mark and I turned out all the lights in this gym and raced from the front door to the bathroom he would win, because he knows the way there. He knows where all the walls are, the supports, the bags. It wouldn't even be a contest. MMA is the same way. You have to bring someone into your dark room and know the room better than they do. Now, granted he may know that room real well also, [so] I have to have a backup plan to constantly be able to not only move quicker through that room, but also change room to room and keep bringing him into my room as quickly as possible. That's the game. Now the question is, through this big house of techniques of jiu jitsu and Muay Thai and boxing and wrestling that we have, who's going to bring who into what realm, and who's going to move through those rooms quicker. It's constant and it's in flux. Whoever can think quicker wins. There are guys who know those rooms inside and out. You get them on the mat and they practice and they move like poetry in motion. But all of a sudden the lights come in and the ref comes in and the cameras come in and they're like, 'Oh, no!' They freeze up."

After grappling, we lounged on the mats while the younger guys set about scrubbing, mopping, and disinfecting.

Kenny is just who BJJ was meant for—a man underdeveloped in strength, but calm and even brilliant in the world of grappling, where many men panic. Of his seven wins, six were by submission. In 2004, he was a BJJ hobbyist working in a financial translation company, which means he could tell corporate businessmen they were broke in five different languages. That's when Kenny fought MMA veteran Drew Fickett to a decision while Dana White was in the audience and won his attention.

"I think he saw the one thing I have that you can't teach, and that's heart," Kenny said, looking back on that day. "I loved the competition of MMA and still do. Fickett had like twenty MMA fights at the time, and I fought him to a decision because I just wanted to win so badly, you know? So when it was over [Dana] told me about *The Ultimate Fighter* and said I should send in an application." He laughed, remembering the moment. "But I didn't have anything to send, so I mailed one of my instructional DVDs, which probably wasn't smart looking back on it. But it got me on the show."

"Was it everything you thought it would be?"

"It's weird. I never thought the show would even be seen by anyone, let alone be so popular. I mean, it was crazy looking back on how much it took off. It's especially weird when I'm picked to headline a trip to Afghanistan to train troops. We went there for two weeks and trained the troops and signed autographs at the bases. The whole time they wanted to meet me, but I was in awe of them and the things they do."

Kenny had headlined three UFC events: against Sean Sherk, Din Thomas, and Sam Stout. More than well known, he is now one of MMA's poster boys, a hype-machine darling, a dream fighter who easily interacts with people and brings new fans into the sport. And he had managed to arrive at this lofty place despite a major obstacle in a sport based on violence. He looks like a band camp geek who is only a horn-rimmed pair of glasses away from Louis Skolnik in Revenge of the Nerds. He also has a boisterous, nonthreatening sense of humor. On top of all that, his nickname, KenFlo, sounds like an air filter.

But luckily he has 155 pounds of fighting talent and a natural ability to be the center of attention. These served him well on *The Ultimate Fighter*, but like most who had earned MMA celebrity status in the TUF house, he had hated it, though his reasons for doing so were different. "I couldn't wait to get back to Sityodtong, man. I felt my striking skills deteriorating by the day there."

"Even with Chuck Liddell coaching you?" I asked.

"Yeah, they just weren't technical enough for me. Mark is more precise about the strikes and focuses on having correct style instead of trying for that one big knockout punch."

Despite his accomplishments, at the time, Kenny's name wasn't at the top of anyone's list whenever talk of the top lightweights was on the table. Gomi, Sakurai, Stevenson, and Penn were the best in the world in 2007. That was probably fair, since he hadn't been tested against a top contender after his bloody loss to Sherk in the UFC lightweight championship match. Early in the fight, Kenny had delivered one of his patented elbows to Sherk's head, cutting a nasty gash over his right temple. Sherk bled profusely, and the fight was nearly stopped.

"I'm glad they didn't stop the fight because of the cut," he said. "At the time, I didn't know what my capabilities were. I didn't know if I could go the distance with a guy like Sherk. I hadn't been tested for five rounds, so even though I lost, I knew where my limits were after that fight. If they had stopped it for his cut, I don't think the belt would have meant that much to me."

* * * * *

"You're up early," I said to Mark as I entered his basement at the crack of 12:30 the next day.

"I sleep in three-minute rounds," he responded.

Right away I noticed that the dragon on the banister had been straightened again. "What is up with you?" I asked frankly as he lined up a row of Lysol bottles that didn't need lining up. "Why are you so organized?"

He laughed. "My life feels out of order if I come here in the morning and there's something on the floor or the pads are out of order. I believe in the Samurai lifestyle. Everything has an order."

If the Samurai were anything like Mark, then they were the pioneers of obsessive compulsive disorder. He might not be able to admit it or might prefer to call it something else, like perfectionism, but it sure looked like OCD. At first, I thought he was a simple germaphobe because everything was so clean, but that didn't explain the proper placement of every single item in the gym and the nagging desire to do everything in a certain order for a predetermined number of times. Mark should have been nicknamed "The Sanitizer." He was disgusted at the lack of cleaning the mats got on *The Ultimate Fighter* show. I can only imagine him going completely apeshit at Greg Jackson's gym. He was the MMA version of Wade Boggs, a true legend in the annals of OCD.

The cleanliness of Sityodtong, though, added to the charisma of the basement training camp that churned out successful MMA fighters. It felt more like a clubhouse than a gym, only needing a "No Girlz Alowed" sign on the door. The cramped facility lent itself to closeness and a strong, symbiotic relationship between DellaGrotte and his students, fighters, and instructors.

Good pupils adhere to their masters in deference of a recognized higher authority. Poor ones develop an acrimonious love affair with disappointment. The challenge of leadership is to deal with both, to be the guy out front giving the orders and making decisions, the guy who had to put his foot down and choose the hard right over the easy wrong.

"Ninja came in here last week, and he was a good guy," Mark said. "But his translator kept saying, 'Ninja want you to hold the pads this way,' and, 'Ninja like to train a different way.' So finally I dropped the pads and we sparred for a while, and after a few kicks that he couldn't block, he changed his tune. My question to somebody who's difficult to train and somebody who's like that is glove up. Cause if you put the gloves on with me and you get lumped up a little bit, you're going to be a little more receptive to learning. I'm not the fat karate guy in the gi that's telling you how to break the board but can't break the board. I don't tell my fighters to go out and give me ten. I do it with them. There can't be any bullshit, because I'm living the life of the fighter too."

The ability to set an example is an indispensable facet of leadership. Not only is Mark skilled at speaking the one true language fighters understand, which is pain, but he can do it fluently and deliver it with pinpoint accuracy. He'd knocked men down and been flattened himself. In the Army, the equivalent is a captain.

The Army captain is responsible for a great many people. He's arguably the last officer to have a direct impact on the day-to-day lives of soldiers. Although higher-ranking officers make decisions and formulate guidance above him, the captain and his first sergeant are the ones responsible for the training and welfare of the troops at all times. The captain has been around long enough to make well-informed and rational decisions that take all variables into consideration. He develops, analyzes, and chooses courses of action for the benefit of not just himself, but the team as a whole.

In MMA, the captain prepares the fighter, sharpens his skills, identifies strengths and weaknesses in his game, assists in making fight decisions, develops a game plan, and molds his prefight preparation. The captain bears the brunt of responsibility for his grunts. And in MMA, a fighter's record is a direct reflection not only of himself, but the training and personal guidance he's received from his trainers. The trainer is the keeper of the flame, the protector of the art, and the voice of reason that keep fighters in balance.

Like a good captain, Mark didn't waffle when there were choices to be made, and he refused to lead by committee. He supported his instructors like a good commander stands behind his subordinate leaders. Good commanders have to trust that their subordinate leaders are well trained and will do their jobs professionally without having to constantly look over their shoulders.

That's probably not something a true obsessive-compulsive would be able to do, I supposed. So when Mark left to train one of his younger fighters, I knocked the dragon out of alignment again. After all, since he wasn't a true obsessive-compulsive, I could say I wasn't intentionally messing with a mentally ill man.

* * * * *

Everyone has a fighting stance. Tateki Matsuda's was unusually wide and low, like an invisible wrecking ball was dangling on a rope from his scrotum. Tateki was 0-0, a virgin in the professional MMA world and two weeks away from his first fight. He came to America for three years to study in Boston with a deep desire for learning both in the classroom and on the mats.

At twenty-one Tateki Matsuda thought the world was a John Wayne movie. He was a Japanese college student soaking up the pleasures of living in America one capitalist day at a time. Mark and his crew tested his resolve one night. I sympathized with Tateki as he sat on the edge of the shark tank, dangling his feet in the cold water while the predators lurked just feet away. KenFlo, Neil, and Sean adjusted their gear and greased up their gloves, salivating like cowboys about to break a wild bronco. Tateki was calm, showing no emotion as he climbed through the ropes and took up his oddly wide stance.

Like Rashad Evans's training, Tateki's started off light. Neil LeGallo went in first. The two stayed on their feet as Neil stalked Tateki, backing him into a corner repeatedly before throwing a few zingers. Neil was no professional MMA fighter, but his Muay Thai skills were impressive, and Tateki's face surely felt the sting. The round ended uneventfully, but I was sure it would pick up.

After a thirty-second break, KenFlo stepped in, determined to improve a different aspect of the young Japanese student's game. He instantly shot in for Tateki's legs and abruptly introduced his back to the mat. Just a minute into the round, Tateki was mounted by the almost-lightweight champion. He was in trouble as a flurry of punches came down on him. But again, none were very damaging. Why was Kenny holding back?

"Get out of there, Tateki," Mark barked. Two minutes and more yelling later, it was over. Tateki's heart was admirable, but his skills definitely needed sharpening. Although he had been mounted by a world-class grappler, the position had been far from inescapable and his inability to do much more than roll around and cover up had Mark worried.

"You can't stay on the bottom, Tateki," he said, giving him a shot of water in the corner. "Work hard to get out of there next time."

But the "next time" would have to wait a while. Neil reentered the ring with no intentions of testing Tateki's ground game since Kenny had just mauled him on the mat. He stalked Tateki, cutting off his angles and reintroducing him to a corner with no escape. He fired shots at him and forced the youngster to dodge, retaliate, or get hit. But Neil was still holding back. It was half-speed, which boggled me, since this was his prefight training, not a normal training session when a fighter is months away from a contest.

"Jab, combo, knee!" Mark shouted, wanting to see more correct strikes at the right time. They concentrated on Tateki's fundamentals, ensuring he knew what to throw and when to throw it, instead of beating the hell out of him and forcing him to improve through pain. Tateki defended himself—that's all he really could do against Neil's onslaught—with teep kicks, combos, and the occasional knee when he managed to get into the clinch.

When the round ended, Tateki had more energy than I expected after three rounds in the tank. In the other gyms, the fighter was dead on his feet by now, so either Tateki was a specimen of endurance conditioning or he wasn't being tested—not physically at least. One reason for his stamina turned out to be the clock. The rounds were three and a half minutes long, compared to five minutes at Jackson's and Terrell's. But the rests were short—only thirty seconds for a quick squirt of water.

KenFlo reentered the ring and I expected the mouse was about to get eaten by the cat. On the contrary, Tateki had learned from his previous mistakes and got side control on Kenny. For once he was not in a position to be exploited, but he couldn't capitalize on his good fortune of being on top. Kenny was soon in control of the sparring session, but again held back.

I kept expecting the man who rode the pale horse to gallop in with hell following behind, but it never happened. The reason was in the purpose. The focus of the training was Tateki's technique and fundamental ability, not his tolerance for punishment. This was the Thai way of training that DellaGrotte had adopted as his own after spending a lot of time in the kingdom at training camps. Thai boxers fought more frequently than American fighters, which necessitated a training regimen that focused on improvement while minimizing the risk of injury. A Thai boxer who had to sit on the sidelines while healing from an injury lost his sole source of income and possibly his livelihood. At its core, the half-speed training's purpose was to make him more efficient without risking injury. It was a way to train smarter, not necessarily harder.

In between rounds, Mark poured water on Tateki and pulled his hair in a strange Thai voodoo ritual that I didn't even want to ask about. It looked like he was trying to cool him off by separating his scalp from his skull.

And then it happened. Tateki's fifth and final round in the tank was pure punishment. He wasn't forced to face one fighter, but rather two in rapid succession for an agonizing three and a half minutes. Neil came at him first, increasing the speed and ferocity of his strikes, but only for thirty seconds before switching out.

"Change out!" Kenny yelled. Neil peeled off like an F-16 breaking formation, letting Kenny fly at the disoriented Japanese kid with guns blazing. Again he was trapped in a corner with no choice but to slug his way out. The pair finally gave Tateki the pain I had expected, while Mark yelled from outside the ropes.

"Counter! Jab! Knee! Teep! Combo, Tateki!"

When Kenny was done, Neil resumed the attack and vice versa. In a desperation move, Tateki lunged like a kamikaze at Kenny's legs to take him down, but got stuffed and planted back in the corner on his feet where he took a pounding. Despite the increase in intensity, it still wasn't on the level of the other places I'd seen. But given Sityodtong's track record of success, who's to say a physically brutal training session is better?

After practice, Mark declared it was time for a staff meeting. Despite the late hour, his instructors cleaned up and headed to the predetermined meeting place. Before Mark could leave, he had me rediagnosing him with OCD as he went through a closing ritual fit for a write-up in the Journal of Psychiatric Craziness. He started with the water pump switches before moving to the bathroom to make sure the lights were off and no water was running. Then he checked the stove, the refrigerator, the TV, more lights, the pads and other gear, stopped for a moment to complain about the dragon ("How does this thing keep getting like this?"), checked the computer, straightened and tidied things that weren't out of order, set the alarm and locked up. Just when I thought it was over, he reopened the door to test the alarm three times, apparently a pagan ritual to satisfy the god of home security. He then bowed to the gym and said, "Khai Muay kap kum mak kup," to thank it for all the wonderful things it had brought him.

I should have prayed harder to the god of forward thinking because I was sweaty from the night's workout and had failed to bring a change of clothes or even a decent smoking jacket for socializing. Marie DellaGrotte, bless her kind soul, classed me up with a Sityodtong sweatshirt and a matching T-shirt from the gym's stocks.

We occupied the Cheesecake Factory by force, which was quiet when we arrived, but the decibel volume of our ten voices quickly livened the place up. I was sure some patrons wished life had a mute button. Dinner arrived and talk turned to Thailand. Sityodtong makes two or three trips a year to the famed camp that is their namesake. No doubt there were many adventurous tales that might have been told, but the only one I got was the one relating to Mark's first loss—to a giant flying cockroach that he tried to vanquish with a spritz of cologne, only to have the thing mount his face.

Rules, a major concern for this disciplined gym, also got some attention—notably a review of the Chase rule and the Crimson Clause, both of which addressed acceptable social behavior with women of questionable intentions. Kenny introduced a new one: "No member shall drink hot coffee from an open container and fall asleep at the same time while sitting in a tuk-tuk next to an angry fighter." It was unanimously accepted.

As the boisterous meeting adjourned and everyone went their separate ways, I wondered if Sityodtong would be the same if Mark moved his gym to larger quarters, as he was planning to do. The basement, while homey and full of character, had a hard time accommodating the demand for his services. It was a natural time to upgrade to a bigger facility. But maybe there was something about his tiny, underground gym that contributed to his fighters' success. Maybe the close camaraderie was due to the close quarters and that would be lost by moving to a warehouse.

* * * * *

The next day, I strolled around Sityodtong doing the things I enjoyed most—hitting my head on the effing crossbeam and knocking the dragon out of whack. On a back wall I found a poster of *The Ultimate Fighter* season one finale with photos of all the contestants. Of the sixteen fighters, fifteen stared ferociously at the camera with their best "Zoolander Blue Steel" face, except one—Kenny Florian. It was appropriate for how Sityodtong operated—the only smiling face in the middle of a group of snarling pit bulls. Everyone here was easy-going. They got along well and were always polite, courteous, and joking. It was too good. After all, every good story requires a villain to force an ordinary man to become a hero. I decided to find someone mean, even if I had to provoke it out of him.

"Are you ever an asshole?" I asked DellaGrotte.

"Only when I get disrespected. It must be the Italian in me," he replied before walking off to be nice to someone else.

"Are you an asshole?" I asked "Big Drunk" Johnny McDonough just before his class started.

"Assholes don't last here," he said without a second thought. "If you're an asshole, we'll make life hard and weed you out."

I ambled up to Sean Matthews while he watched a student. "Are you an asshole?"

"Do you want me to be?" he replied.

If he had to ask permission to be one, then that would negate the experiment.

"Kenny's a dick before fight time," Keith Florian said as he stretched.

"Tell me more." I walked over to his piece of mat.

"He gets real intense as he gets closer to a fight. He can't eat what he wants to because he's cutting weight. He doesn't want to be around anyone. He gets so focused that he's just a dick."

"I wouldn't say I'm a dick," Kenny said later when I asked him about it. "It's just a natural process, I think. My body knows something big is coming and it starts to change. It starts to prepare for the challenge ahead. I know that something big is looming on the horizon and I start to adapt to meet it."

"Is that why you seem emotional after a fight?" I asked. "Like when you grabbed the microphone and yelled, 'I finish fights!' after beating Alvin Robinson at UFC 73?"

"Yeah, but emotion has no place in a fight. Before it and after it, yes, but not during. You have to put emotion aside and stick to the game plan. Before a fight and after one, emotions are usually pretty high."

And then a light went on.

Was it possible that fighters became different people when they parked their cars and stepped into the arena? Could they put themselves into a mental state that was so removed from their normal being that they actually changed personalities? If so, was this any different than a plea of temporary insanity?

If this was true, one of the answers I was seeking had been uncovered. I had started this journey through MMA to discover why men fight and why the media portray them so differently from who they are in day-to-day life. The answer to the second question was now right in front of me.

Most fighters are interviewed just prior to a fight or just after it. These are the times when they weren't in their right minds. The specter of combat either loomed before them or was still animate inside them from the fight they had just finished. Therefore, they gave interviews that came out full of raw aggression, bathed in the tide of violence that had risen inside them.

The hype machine loves it. It's even more entertaining in a bad-blood fight like Josh Koscheck versus Diego Sanchez. But they'll stoke whatever fires get started in the heat of battle. Regular news journalists are no better. They are supposed to be impartial and unbiased, but take a look at what happens in an election year. It seems everybody loves a fight.

Tuesday nights at Sityodtong mean sparring—a time for the masters to evaluate what the young grasshoppers have learned. The match is two rounds with full gear—gloves, shin guards, and Vaseline—and is supposed to be

Tuesday night sparring at Sityodtong. Little Fedor (left) versus Jimmy the Greek (right).

performed at half to three-quarter speed to avoid injury. That's the concept, at least. When I was there, it was a slobberknocker for gym bragging rights with pride as the prize and peer pressure leaning in over the ropes.

At the behest of Big Drunk Johnny, a crowd gathered around the ring to watch two students, "Little Fedor," and "Jimmy the Greek," spar in a middleweight bout. True to his name, Little Fedor actually looked like a smaller version of the vaunted Russian heavyweight, albeit one who had been put into a dryer and come out at 185 pounds or so.

The air was just as intense as any professional fight, and probably more so since the crowd knew these guys on a personal level. Big Drunk Johnny, who was completely sober, was the impartial referee and became Big John McCarthy when he tried his signature battle cry, "Let's get it on!"

The two bumped gloves, and Fedor came out wanting to do justice to his nickname. He swung for Jimmy's face, but couldn't seem to connect. Recognizing his opponent's game plan, Jimmy shot in for Fedor's legs, but got stuffed. On his feet, Fedor seemed to have the advantage, and Jimmy knew it. He went for a takedown from the clinch and got it. He landed on top of Fedor with a thud on the mats as the crowd went crazy.

Somehow Little Fedor managed to pull guard and get his legs around Jimmy, stopping his attack for the moment. But Jimmy the Greek was crafty—or at least well trained—and "stacked" Little Fedor in the corner. Stacking is a move that comes from freestyle wrestling, where the man in guard stands and puts all of his weight on his opponent, making submissions like armbars and triangles difficult.

"Don't give up, Fedor!" Marie DellaGrotte yelled as Jimmy suddenly pulled a David Copperfield trick out of his jockstrap and rolled both himself and Fedor over and ended up on Fedor's back. It was like some strange Mongolian league, double inverted reverse flea flicker sweep. The crowd went wild. Jimmy dug his hooks in and went for the rear naked choke, struggling to get an arm across Fedor's throat.

"Fedor can't be submitted!" someone yelled.

And he wasn't before the bell saved him.

In round two, Fedor managed to keep the fight standing up by forgoing the "half-speed" rule and throwing nine-tenths punches at Jimmy the Greek that kept him at bay. Big Drunk Johnny could call this a sparring match all he wanted to, but as soon as one of these guys started to lose, it was just a matter of time before he vamped up the speed of the match. Sensing the upswing in effort, Jimmy the Greek went back to his bread and butter and reintroduced Fedor to the blue mats.

Again Jimmy got Fedor's back, and again failed to capitalize because of good submission defense. Fedor had learned something from the first round, because he quickly got the fight back to the feet.

It didn't matter. Jimmy scored another takedown that Fedor was unable to prevent just as the fight ended. The small crowd cheered, truly proud of their compatriots and knowing that next week it could be one of them.

"In the Greek spirit of Alexander the Great . . . Jimmy the Greek wins."

"Woo-Hoo," a tired Jimmy let out as Johnny wrapped a padded Thai kickboxing belt around his waist like it was a real championship belt. It may as well have been. It was one achieved in sweat and pain, making it all the sweeter.

Drunk Johnny was all smiles.

"The one thing about this sport is you can't train stand up half speed and be any good at it," he said. "You have to go at a certain level…that's the sort of thing with having training partners that you're comfortable with because you know you can go hard and you're not going to get knocked out"

Fun? Despite surviving the Muay Thai class, it was still hard for me to grasp the concept of fun and fighting in the same sentence. But I was getting closer.

"Time to clean up," Mark announced as mops and Lysol were distributed.

The students started the night's wipe-down, and even Kenny Florian grabbed a mop and pitched in. Mark walked by the dragon, and stopped.

"Who keeps doing that? You?" he asked looking at me and then straightening it out. "I'm going to super glue that thing down!"

"But then you can't polish the top of the railing," I said.

He paused. "You prick," he said walking away past a picture of himself with Dana White and Rich Franklin.

I stared at the picture, remembering my first impression that he lacked self-confidence because of all of the accolades on his walls that scream out, "Look at me."

But people who lack self-confidence usually lack the courage to be different. You couldn't say that about DellaGrotte. If anything, he was so humble and so focused on being the best MMA trainer he could be that he never realized that he had already achieved his goals. He was so honored to be photographed with other MMA notables that he was confused when someone asked for a picture with him. He embodied an Eisenhower-like humility born of a simple upbringing, and having accomplished more than he thought he would, he wasn't sure where to go next, which meant he'd have to forge his own way.

Sawatdee kap.

THE IFL FINALS

Bite on the bullet old man. And don't ever let them see you're afraid.

—Rudyard Kipling, *"The Light That Failed"*

"You looking for the fighters?" a skinny, goateed barely-more-than-a-teenager asked.

I nodded, looking over his shoulder at the buxom waitresses in tight tank tops and orange shorts scurrying about with massive platters of buffalo wings. He noticed me ogling them and smirked. "They went into the main casino. Ballroom C, I think. Said they needed more room."

That was disappointing. Obviously a small Florida Hooters restaurant full of scantily clad women and spicy chicken wings would be a perfect place to strip professional athletes down to their underwear and take pictures of them glowering at each other, but apparently someone with considerable pull disagreed.

I was late because two pilots had decided to change the plane I was booked on for one that wasn't broken. When I finally landed it was rush hour in Miami, where Spanish is apparently the official language and asking for directions in English is futile. "Where is el highway-o?" didn't get me very far either.

Ballroom C was a half mile walk away through the muggy Miami climate and a casino full of cigar-smoking geriatrics stuffing retirement checks into noisy slot machines. I arrived sweaty and stinking and my ears ringing with jackpot hoopla. Fighters, coaches, photographers, journalists, and fans were here to compare tattoos and witness the required weigh-in before the World Championship Finals of the International Fight League.

I was here to witness the practical application of all the training I'd been observing, but on a bigger scale than Sportfight. The IFL finals are the Super Bowl of MMA team fighting. Actually, the IFL being the only team-fighting version of MMA, it wasn't exactly a stretch for founders Kurt Otto and Gareb Shamus to come up with its ultimate show. But expanding from six teams to twelve after only one year in business had taken vision, a leap of faith, and a very successful consulting team to raise a ton of cash. In 2006, San Francisco money firm Piper Jaffrey passed a very large hat around to some wealthy people and suddenly found it full of $24 million, which was way more than they would have made from a topless car wash.

But their other revenue-raising technique went directly south when the IFL decided to become a publicly traded stock on the Dow Jones Industrials. After bolting out of the gate at seventeen dollars a share during its initial public offering, the stock plummeted to a paltry fifty cents a share and showed no signs of recovering. The reasons for the stock diving so low? Maybe the looming specter of the UFC, the untested MMA team concept, and the initial perception that the IFL consisted of mostly B-rate fighters.

This last point was the other reason I was here. Was this a league of fighters who were unable to make it in the big show or was it a completely different MMA concept forging its own path to a gold mine? The cofounder and commissioner of the league, Kurt Otto, reportedly had a passion for taking care of his fighters, which translated into motivated athletes in the ring. Theoretically, this could compensate for a lower talent level because when a fired-up, B-rate fighter fights an equally aggressive B-rate fighter, it can make for a very entertaining evening. A team's worth of B-rate guys taking on another team of them, well, that could add up to A-rated success.

The 2007 IFL season came down to this night. The league's twelve teams had fought three matches each and the final four had slugged it out a month earlier in a semifinal playoff round. The Quad Cities Silverbacks, coached by Pat Miletich, and Renzo Gracie's New York Pitbulls emerged as the last two teams standing. After a disappointing season, Matt Lindland's Wolfpack failed to make the finals, but "The Law" could still be seen cruising the crowd shaking hands and being his usual congenial self. As an IFL coach, he was here to support the event, but he also came to corner one of his guys, Jake Ellenberger, who was on loan to the Silverbacks as a replacement for the injured Rory Markham.

The day before the event, the fighters are required to go through medical examinations and weigh-ins. It's an eagerly anticipated moment in their lives because it means food—the end to three or four days of fasting to make weight. If a fighter gets on the scales overweight he's unable to compete, plain and simple. It's unprofessional, a monumental letdown for the team, and more embarrassing than getting caught with porn, which has never happened to me.

As usual, the event started late, which was lucky for me since I had to hike a mile to it. When it finally started, Referee Jorge from the Florida State Athletic Commission gave the mandatory rules briefing, dispensing with the easy ones first (no eye-gouging, biting, kicks to the balls, smuggling in a prison shiv, etc.) and then focusing on the more difficult ones.

"We use the same unified MMA rules as most organizations, meaning no knees or kicks to a downed opponent," he said. "But we do not allow elbows to the head. There are no twelve to six elbows, meaning you can't bring the arm from twelve o'clock to six o'clock."

I secretly wondered if this mostly digital-age crowd was completely confused by the clock metaphor. He summed up the brief by repeating for the seventh time that his number one job was the fighters' safety and reminded everyone that if they have to tap out, "be sure to tap strong."

His colleague, Referee Troy, felt Referee Jorge had skipped something and stated, "You always have to improve your position. You can't turtle up and take shots to the head or we'll stop it." He proceeded to cover himself up in a fetal position and say loudly, "No martial art that I know of teaches this as a defense." I guessed he'd never been in a foxhole.

Maurice Smith, the coach of the Seattle Tigersharks who had one fighter participating in a preliminary match, was stymied and assaulted the referees with a barrage of questions, some of which were about as interesting as "Why does Mickey Mouse wear pants and no shirt, but Donald Duck wears a shirt and no pants?" Smith's extended questioning aggravated the fighters, who were desperate to eat something. I swear I saw one look at Smith like a six-foot-three slab of prime rib.

Finally, the weighing-in began. Making weight wasn't especially difficult for anyone, except Bart "Bartimus" Palaszewski, who was just over the limit. All fighters weighed in wearing shorts. After all, this was a family-friendly show broadcast on cable TV. But if a fighter came in overweight, the league graciously granted an immediate do-over—in the buff. The good news for Bart was he was afforded a towel to get nude behind. The bad news was the ring girls were holding it. I don't know which was worse—being weighed naked or having the hottest chicks in the room see your junk when there's no pool in sight to blame the shrinkage on. Bartimus made the weight and handled it professionally—I think. I looked away from the horror so there'd only be 199 people staring at him instead of 200.

With the weigh-ins over, the fighters were allowed to gorge themselves on yummy Powerbars and Rockstars, except for an unlucky few who were forced to pay their penance to the hype machine. One of the sponsors needed a commercial to plug his product and shuffled a group into the next building to conduct filming. I tagged along feeling like an old Woodstock groupie at a Three Days Grace concert.

Like fighters, camera crews are rarely punctual and these guys needed some extra time to set their equipment. When fighters and coaches have idle time, their thoughts frequently turn to reading, comparing investment portfolios, or mischievous banter.

"Yeah, thanks for keeping us at the weigh-in as long as you did. That was great," Bartimus said to Smith. Since exposing himself in front of the ring girls he'd digested only an energy drink and an energy bar, so he was wired like a non-smoker with eight nicotine patches.

"Hey, it's my job to look out for my fighter," Maurice replied.

"But meanwhile all the real fighters are starving and you're sitting there asking questions like you don't already know the answers." Bart mocked him. "Uh, yeah, I got a question. When am I going to shut the fuck up?" Bart's quick tongue and Polish accent made it sound like one word—shuthefukup.

"Hey, when you're a coach looking out for your fighter, you'll do the same, young lad," Maurice said.

Upon his maturity being questioned, Bart dispensed with his niceties. "When were you born? The nineteen seventies, I bet. Go back to disco, dude."

"I was born in the sixties…" Maurice started before Bart cut him off.

"Even worse! You're really old!"

Like a father whose kid has stepped too far over the line, Pat Miletich raised his head from his BlackBerry. "Bart," he said as the room suddenly grew quiet. "Stop."

"He started it!" Bart said like a kid blaming the chocolate ring around his mouth on his brother.

Finally Kurt Otto got in front of the camera and the room's attention shifted.

"And . . . go," the cameraman said.

"Hi, I'm Kurt Otto, commissioner of the IFL. If our fighters want to wear one of these (he points to his championship ring) or earn this (he points to the belt), they have to drink this (he holds up a tub of powdered Muscle Milk)."

For whatever reason, Otto and the crew weren't satisfied and decided to do another take. But the combined patience of the hungry fighters and tired coaches waiting in the wings for their take was lower than George W. Bush's approval ratings.

"If our fighters want to earn this or this . . . I forgot to say my name."

"Yes, you did," someone jeered at Otto.

"Don't fuck it up, boss," another said.

"Keep going," the crew implored, knowing the moment was slipping away.

"I'm Kurt Otto and if our fighters want to wear one of these or . . . dammit, I forgot to say commissioner of the IFL."

For the next several minutes, he was roasted worse than Michael Vick at a PETA convention. Finally he placed his hands over his eyes and implored the crowd to get out so he could concentrate.

The diplomatic Pat Miletich came up with a compromise. "We'll just turn around," he said, and then turned his back to Otto. And everyone did just as Pat said. Turning toward the wall like schoolchildren forced to stand in the corner for farting in class , everyone showed Otto their backs so he could get one more good take. Though funnier than any verbal punishment he'd gotten, the tactic worked. Otto nailed his next take, bringing the torture to an end.

Bartimus (foreground, black hat) and the other fighters fliming the Muscle Milk Commercial.

Now it was the fighters' turn to film and happily their part was simplified. All they had to do was run in and decimate a table full of Muscle Milk products. It was the kind of commercial a fighter dreams of—no lines and gratuitous violence. Plastic drinking bottles and tubs of protein-saturated powdered supplement flew everywhere. They nailed it.

Bartimus and his opponent, Lithuanian Davidius Taurosevicius, leaped onto the table and scarfed up all they could hold while Rory Markham and Fabio Leopoldo joined in. The interesting part of this social dynamic was that Bartimus and Taurosevicius were opponent's in tomorrow's match. In less than twenty four hours they were going to do their best to inflict bodily damage on each other, yet here they were filming a commercial together.

Afterward the same guys who made the mess apparently felt guilty for it, so they all helped clean the place up by loading boxes of Muscle Milk products into their arms and running away quickly. A certain writer made out with a few free goodies too—mostly a handful of Muscle Milk bars. I have more respect for these guys after digesting half of one; as nutritious as they are, it was like eating chalk in the Sahara.

A short while later, I managed to catch Bartimus in a calmer moment. Behind his cool green eyes, he is a fearsome striker with one-punch knockout power. Respected and feared in the league, some even idolized him, perhaps for his ever-changing hair. It changed often, from red and long, to blonde and spiked, to tonight's choice—black and Mohawked.

"I fight because it's a job," he said, shrugging his shoulders as if it required no thought. "Some people want to be graphic designers, some want to be cops, or some . . ."

"Want to be soldiers?" I interjected.

"Right. It's just something I enjoy doing."

"You enjoy the rush or you enjoy hurting people?"

"No, I'm not like that. Some people get a rush from it for competition and I do too, but I think . . . honestly, it's like my own stage out there. When I'm in front of a few thousand screaming fans and they clap or yell or scream when I do something, it's cool. I think part of it is the attention, you know? I think this is what I was meant to do."

If that was true, Bartimus's upbringing did nothing to prepare him for it. His path to the ring was never clear, like Rashad Evans or Nick Diaz, both of whom came from environments ripe for fighting. On the contrary, Bart had shunned trouble as a youth and had never even been in a street fight, which he considered a drawback. His lack of experience with the juvenile penal system was due to fear of what his dad might do to him.

"Pops is a good guy, a good example. I think I stayed straight because I was afraid of how pissed he would be if I did something wrong. Plus I never wanted to disappoint them [my parents], you know?"

"What did your dad do?" I asked.

"He was a businessman. He tried to start an import-export company between here and Poland, but it didn't work out. He ended up getting into construction and brought us all over here when I was thirteen."

"Which do you consider yourself, Polish or American?"

"I'm proud to be Polish, but I consider myself an American now. I'm so grateful for the opportunities this country has given to me. I won't take it for granted, you know? I mean America was built on the backs of immigrants and that's what I am. I'm here to embrace this country and help build it more. I took my citizenship test and passed it so I'm a full-blooded American."

"Is that why you have "We the People" tattooed across your back?"

"Yep. I saw it on the ten-dollar bill and thought it was really cool. I read the Preamble [to the Constitution] and thought it sounded like something I believed in. It's better than my name. I don't like names on your back or belly, and mine's really long."

Responsible parents miss their kids, so it was good to hear Bart talk about his newborn daughter back home. Since this was his first fight since she was born, I was concerned he wouldn't be able to get her out of his mind.

"Oh, man. I miss her so much, you know." He rolled his eyes and looked away proudly. "She's only six weeks old and this is the first time I've been away from her. I miss her enough that I want to call home a lot more. If anything, there's added motivation because now I have a family to support, you know? I got to suck it up and go in there and do what I have to do to support them."

Everyone went to eat, so I did the same, at the Tatu sushi bar. The South Beach roll seemed appropriate for the setting and lived up to its name. It was served with a trendy presentation, but was completely void of any flavor or substance. Luckily Captain Morgan was there to save my palate.

Outside the restaurant, I ran into Jamal Patterson and Delson Heleno of the Pitbulls. They were idly discussing one of their opponents, Chris Batten.

"He's one cut-up dude," Jamal said with a smile. "But that's about it. I watched some tape on him."

"You're not nervous?" I asked.

"Nope." He stretched and threw his arms wide out. "Should I be?"

I shrugged, surprised at his nonchalance. This was supposed to be when fighters were in the final stages of change—transforming from normal human into man-beast. Tonight ought to be a tense and brooding time, the period when they couldn't sleep because their nerves were bunched up like the Gordian knot. This was when there was nothing to do but think about tomorrow and let it drive them crazy. They were now a mere nineteen hours from either receiving or delivering an epic beating in front of a few thousand people. The mood should have been somewhere between, "Jesus, let me do my best," and "By Odin's beard, I will be triumphant!"

I imagined it like the night before an airborne operation, when the thought of jumping out of a high-performance airplane at 130 miles an hour with a ridiculous amount of gear strapped to your body seems suddenly unnatural and concern starts to creep in. You know that in a short amount of time you will test death and trust your future to the engineering ability of man. Even after fifty jumps it's difficult to simply put away the lingering apprehension and act as if everything is Jim Dandy. Some soldiers can do that, but only the ones who haven't experienced enough life to know how utterly disappointing death would be. After all, a little fear is normal. Indifference to it is irresponsible.

Of course, jumping out of a plane and getting into a fight are not really the same thing, but they are both risky and abnormal events that could result in injury or death, no matter how much we try to control the circumstances. Managing the apprehension is usually pretty difficult.

So I expected to see worry and trepidation. But unless you knew better, you'd think Jamal and Delson were lounging a Wednesday night away, unconcerned that anything out of the ordinary was about to happen.

The next day I met Kurt Otto in the hotel's café. Otto smartly drank water while I chugged coffee like a Wall Street Futures trader. "I believe that everybody has a push inside of their chest that says I want to be somebody," he told me just hours before the big event. "I think everybody wants praise and recognition, and the power of praise and recognition is worth so much more than the money you can give anybody. If you reward them psychologically, it's just as important as the money."

Otto started the IFL with his business partner, Gareb Shamus, after watching *The Smashing Machine*, a video about the life of MMA fighter Mark Kerr. Affected by the way Kerr was cast aside, he set out to not only make the sport better, but to enrich the lives of the people he employed, applying the golden rule to his business model: treat others as you want to be treated.

"You can't beat somebody down. You can't emotionally attack them. You can't do those things to a guy who's supposed to be focused on winning. To play games with contracts, you just can't do that because at the end of the day it's just going to backfire in your face."

The night prior, Maurice Smith had boasted about the virtues of working for Otto to me in the elevator. It was a recurring theme throughout the league. Working for Kurt was like working for your retired juvenile court judge grandfather—he's fair but generous and knows how to get the best out of people through irregular means. Smith didn't know me from Adam and could have said anything in that elevator from, "He's a real jackhole and I'm merely his puppet," to "I'm afraid of heights; please call the fire department." Instead, he sang the praises of the commissioner unsolicited when I simply asked how he liked being a coach in the league.

While it wasn't quite like Kru Yodtong's Muay Thai camp taking kids off the street to train them, Otto had created a successful environment for his athletes that had seen only three fighters leave it unhappily: Mike Pyle, Joe Doerkson, and Chris Wilson. To be fair, the IFL had only been in business two years, but three out of sixty-six fighters was less than 5 percent, which sounded like a decent employee satisfaction rate.

But it was easy to be satisfied when you've never fought anywhere else and have money in your pocket for the first time, which was the case for many of the IFL's previously undiscovered fighters, who get more than enough money per fight to pay the bills.

"I don't know the exact figure, but we're in the double digits," Otto said sipping his drink. "Anywhere from thirteen thousand to up to thirty-two thousand because some guys are fighting once or twice or three or four times [a year] so you gotta rack it up. They could get a hundred grand a year, and if you average it over three fights, it's thirty-three grand a fight."

That's good pay when you haven't made a name for yourself, but what does that do to the organization in the long term? If they continue to showcase unknowns, doesn't that become a "Bush League?" Or did they even need to attract a high caliber of fighter in order to stay in business, since the unknowns had proven to be exciting in the ring?

The answer to that may be found in a comparison of college sports and professional sports. College football has had some of the most memorable moments in sports history. Who could forget Doug Flutie's Hail Mary pass, Kordell Stewart's Hail Mary, Miami beating Nebraska for the national championship on a failed two-point attempt, Desmond Howard's Heisman pose, Colorado's fifth down, and California's wild scramble to beat Stanford when the band was on the field. In the last few years, the Bowl

Championship Series has delivered tremendously exciting games, like the 2003 Ohio State–Miami Fiesta Bowl that went into double overtime, and the 2006 Rose Bowl that saw Texas come from behind to beat USC. College basketball is equally fervent with its March Madness and annual last-second buzzer beaters, yet these athletes make no money.

College athletes don't have the luxury of contracts, holdouts, or agents, but they play hard, making the Saturday NCAA football games equally as entertaining as the Sunday NFL games. It's true that the more talented athletes desperately want to break into the pros. They want to eventually make money, and that's why they bust their butts on the field. But the majority of NCAA athletes have no delusions of grandeur and will simply graduate in order to enter the job market. Their motivation for winning is a love of the game and a sincere desire to bring a trophy home to their school. Large paychecks are not a necessary ingredient for spirited contests of skill.

But talent is still talent, and people want what they're worth. It was an indisputable fact that the IFL didn't have the best fighters in the world. If they did, names like Fedor, Rampage, and Gomi would grace their rosters. The IFL was a team-based competition, which in effect shut the door to the best fighters because they weren't attracted to an organization where they weren't the center of attention and didn't receive top billing on posters and parties. Signing these athletes would take mountains of capital.

So the guiding directive for Otto and the IFL was to do the best with what they had—find the undiscovered talent out there, invest in them, and let them dazzle the fans with exciting fights.

Otto looked out the window where a waterfall cascaded over fake rocks into the hotel's pool. "At the end of the day, when you look at the monies that we have, a certain budget goes for fighter compensation, a certain budget goes for coach compensation, a certain budget goes for offices and overhead in Las Vegas and New York, and you have staff compensation, and you have what it costs to produce an event and what it costs for travel, hotels . . . it adds up. It's not like I'm out there flying around on a Lear jet with hookers."

That's too bad. I wouldn't have minded catching him stepping off of a Gulfstream with a bimbo on each arm, but Otto wasn't the type to be splashed across the covers of grocery store tabloids or involved in scandalous affairs. Educated at Pratt Institute in New York City to be an architect, he forewent other lucrative business opportunities to head up the IFL. His Manhattan vocabulary was tinged with a Brooklyn audacity, kind of like a guy who wears suit and moves among the refined, but drops strategic f-bombs on purpose just to frighten them. He was an odd cocktail of entrepreneurship and compassion, of Trump and Gandhi.

"You step back and you look at the money that we've spent building our brand, it's really chicken scratch in the scope of things. You gotta build your brand!" He rapped his hand on the table like a judge's gavel. "You gotta build the engine. The gas is money. The engine is our athletes. The engine is a force that is able to get these guys on TV and is able to get a quality production, create a platform for success."

So what is success? It's a question many people can't answer because they lack the long-term vision to recognize what they set out to accomplish. So many businesses in America fall victim to short-sightedness, the inability to clearly define goals and objectives and know when they've achieved them.

"What I'm trying to accomplish with the big picture—not just here at the Hard Rock in Florida, but I'm talking about globally in mixed martial arts—[is] getting all the countries involved and really determine who's got the best style, really come to the conclusion 'Is ground fighting better than stand-up?' Because one guy versus one guy in an Octagon or cage is not going to tell us the story if ground fighting is better, but if you have five guys versus five guys, and if you're nominally a stand-up team versus nominally a ground team, then you know what? At the end of the night you're going to know if the Miletich Fighting System is better than the Gracie Jiu Jitsu. We're answering questions."

But the other organizations are answering questions as well. The Pride merger, for example, showed how different rule sets affect different styles and overall effectiveness. The debate over who had better fighters, Pride or the UFC, was somewhat answered when the two organizations merged and many of the top dogs found themselves in the Octagon. Far from taking control of the cage as everyone had expected, they were as sketchy as the Detroit Lions in the win column. Brazilian jiu jitsu experts were suddenly vulnerable without being allowed to knee a downed opponent to the head—a critical element of Vale Tudo fights. There were some successes, but the constriction of regulations around them was like cutting off Sampson's hair.

"We have a completely different model," Otto said. "We're a team format. We're on free TV, not pay-per-view at this point. We're not an individual format. They fight in the cage; we don't. We're more for the sport."

I asked a leading question "Do you see yourself as a David going up against a Goliath?"

"No. I'm just competing with myself, you know? I'm competing with trying to convert a big wrestling fan into an MMA fan. I'm competing with getting a kid who's thirteen, fourteen years old, who doesn't understand the sport, to get emotionally attached to it to the point that he joins a school that teaches MMA or decides maybe to not play basketball that year and maybe go out for the wrestling team."

And how do you do that? With approachable, charismatic fighters who are willing to go out and engage the public. The IFL has learned to take advantage of its athletes. When they enter a city for a fight, they conduct a PR full-court press, sending their guys out to meet and greet, sign autographs, take pictures, and shmooze.

But as much as he cares about his fighters, Otto's good nature only goes so far. There are standards. Do something that discredits the league and you're gone faster than the French can wave a white flag.

"Two things are gonna happen. They're either gonna get fined or they're gonna get kicked out of the league. It's that simple." Though they had no formal standing code of conduct, embarrassing the IFL was strictly taboo, like the Army's zero tolerance policy for DUI. The league was riding the wave of the MMA explosion just as much as any other organization, and the point men were their athletes. If any of them did something stupid, like driving under the influence or fighting publicly, their golden ticket was punched and rejected. Stay in line, on the other hand, and you're guaranteed face time with national and local media.

"We constantly have things for our guys to do. They're always doing something, whether it's an appearance or a seminar, or what have you. Matt

Horwich, for example, is working with USA grappling and got a silver medal in Turkey. We don't leave any rock unturned; no matter what city we're in, we're going to go in and invade it and use every one of our resources to come in and reach out to every radio station, every TV network, every journalist and writer and get the word out."

Otto was lucky. At this time, there had been precious few instances of IFL fighters doing something stupid, like failing a drug test, getting into an altercation, or running a dog fighting ring.

"I think that the majority of the guys don't like to talk smack and don't like to talk about the sport in a negative sense and like to be perceived as professional athletes."

Unfortunately, not all professional athletes abided by this code of conduct. And in a sport where it was almost expected because of its aggressive nature, Otto's candor was invigorating.

Otto left the café for a meeting with a group of men who apparently mistook Miami for Montreal. As he led them outside into the sweltering heat in their black suits to discuss something super secret near the hotel's waterfall bar, I found a new table under an air conditioning vent and ordered another coffee, feeling only slightly sorry for them.

"What the hell was that?" Steve Molen asked as Jamal Patterson did his victory dance in the ring.

"Don't worry about it," Scott Holmes from Sherdog.com replied, leaning back in his seat and running his hands through his Grizzly Adams hair.

Molen drew the short straw among the reporters covering tonight's event and had a crappy view of the action. Even worse, his view of the Jumbotron TV at the far end of the arena was eclipsed by the ring's turnbuckle corner. As a result, he had no idea how Patterson had just submitted Chris Batten. For that matter, neither did anyone else.

Patterson shot in for Batten's legs as the fight started, but instead of getting the takedown, he found a baseball bat of an arm wrapped around his neck from the backside in a guillotine choke. Jamal remained calm and pressed his shoulder into Batten's throat, slowly cutting off his oxygen supply until he was sleeping peacefully.

"He's out!" Renzo Gracie yelled from the corner, correctly assessing the situation. Immediately the ref stepped in and confirmed that Chris Batten had grown bored with the confrontation and decided to take a nap.

This fight, along with three others, made up the preliminaries – fights that would have a winner, a loser, and a paycheck, but would probably never be seen on the televised version of the event because their purpose was to give the fans who bought tickets something extra for showing up. These fights were akin to media blackout – they happened, but only in the win-loss column of the participants. This was exactly how Nate Marquardt got overlooked by the hype machine.

I was granted a seat in the press row near the ring apron, close enough to see and hear the action, but fortunately out of range of flying bodily fluids this time. The press area was twice the size of Sportfight's, with every MMA media outlet in attendance. It was amazing to see the sheer number of magazine, radio show, and website representatives there to cover the sport.

There was Sherdog.com, MMA Weekly, The NHB Show, MMA Madness, MMA News, just to name a few. It was the hype machine itself, reaching its tentacle wires out to the world in real time. The public perception of fighters, trainers, coaches, and ring girls was formed at these two rows of tables. Losses could be labeled as flukes or wins dismissed as unimpressive by these individuals.

As the action unfolded I surfed the Internet via the miracle of Wi-Fi to see what they were saying in the "play-by-play results" section of their websites. For the most part, it was consistent and fair. But writers will be fans, and a couple of outlets skewed the results in favor of the fighter they secretly pulled for. It was nothing new and certainly not unique to MMA. If anything, these guys were just catching up to the rest of the sporting world.

Compared to the simple walkway and red glow of Sportfight, the smoky tunnel entrance and full-spectrum of Van Halen-like arena lighting was like going to Roller Coaster World after a visit to the local playground. This wasn't just a fight; it was theater. A few hundred thousand people would eventually see this on TV, including a significant group of shareholders—a crucial demographic for the IFL's financial success. The perception of a big league venue was just as important as having competitive, exciting fights.

Aside from the theatrics, this was a defining moment in the MMA year. The clash of styles—Miletich Fighting Systems versus Gracie Jiu Jitsu—was exactly what Kurt Otto had envisioned for the team fighting concept. The Miletich and Gracie names represented two of the most respected, if not the most respected, fighting systems in the world.

The crowd at the Hard Rock, though not huge, was well-versed in MMA. They clapped when Ryan Schultz got out from under Aaron Riley and on his feet, realizing the fighter had just escaped a near mount. They cheered when Rolles Gracie got Sam Holloway's back, knowing a choke-out was imminent. And they were all over Brad Blackburn when he kneed a downed Travis Cox, knowing it was illegal and potentially malicious. Cox was on the ground and trying to get up when Blackburn brought his knee crashing into his neck and shoulder area. Cox crumbled to the mat while Blackburn backed away to a neutral corner, knowing he'd done wrong. In the early days of no-holds-barred, this would have been cheered, but modern MMA fans simply don't tolerate illegal tactics. Blackburn was booed incessantly for the move, which he later claimed was a half-speed strike and Cox was acting.

The official ruling of that fight was a rare "no contest," meaning it technically never happened. Referee Jorge, who'd clearly described the action as unmanly during the weigh-ins, decided Blackburn had delivered the knee unintentionally, which I still don't understand. Does that mean if I drive my car through a red light, but didn't mean to, I get a do-over?

The Ryan Schultz–Aaron Riley fight displayed more weaponry than an Apache helicopter. The lightweights' use of knees, kicks, punches, takedowns, clinches, submissions, wrestling, jointlocks, and anything else they could think of emphasized the myriad choices available and how this had become a sport of strategy. The days of bar brawlers like the legendary Tank Abbott stepping into the cage and swinging wildly until one of his meat hooks connected were long gone. That style was undisciplined and outdated. Diverse training was now the norm, and the best compliment a fighter could get was to be called "well rounded" instead of "tough."

Schultz, whom a female fan behind me dreamily compared to "Justin Timberlake," had a successful move that he executed on more than one occasion. He would fake a shoot for the legs and when his opponent dipped his hands to block it, he'd come over the top with a looping right hand that had a tremendous amount of velocity behind it. He'd used this move against Savante Young with great success and here employed the tactic against Riley in the second round.

In between preliminary fights, I stole away to the Silverbacks' dressing room to test what I'd learned from Kenny Florian. I wanted to know if the enormity of the moment changed a fighter's attitude the way Kenny described the metamorphosis that happened to him. I found Bartimus, who was less than an hour from fighting, sitting calmly.

"How are you feeling?" I asked.

"Fine," he responded, shrugging.

I wasn't buying it. As both a parent and a leader of soldiers, I'd learned to spot fraying nerves. Bartimus was a veteran of many fights, but the closer he got to game time, the tenser he was. I admired the way he controlled the emotions boiling up inside him, but one thing was certain—he wasn't the same guy I'd met the night prior at the Muscle Milk commercial. If anyone stuck a camera in his face and asked a question now, they wouldn't have gotten a favorable response.

When the main event started, the crowd was still not filling in as expected. A piece of paper circulated through press row with a number—3,470. It was the night's attendance and it was low—really low. Almost twice that number showed up for Sportfight. Then came the reason: the Miami Hurricanes were playing Texas A&M across town and their star players were furloughed from prison, stealing away the eighteen-to-thirty-five male demographic.

But a small crowd doesn't mean they can't be loyal and raucous. Boisterous fans who get behind their team are great. Creative hecklers are even better. Seat-warming fans who don't know what they're watching are annoying. This fight had all three.

"Who should we look for?" The Justin Timberlake woman asked through a thick New York accent. "Who's good?" In the cheap seats, this might be a valid question, but in the front row it's unexpected, especially when they're such expensive tickets. Before I could answer, a heckler stole our attention.

"Hey, Angle, get your sorry ass in there!"

Sitting ringside in a nice suit was WWE wrestler Kurt Angle, an Olympic gold medalist who was rumored to be considering fighting. Given his laundry list of injuries, this was as likely as Tanya Harding signing with the Boston Bruins. Nevertheless, a pair of skinny teenagers felt it was their duty to give him an earful. "You don't have the balls to step into the ring!" one yelled.

Hearing a fan yell something physically impossible, like "rip his ears off!" was amusing. Watching a punk kid start a fight with a man-mountain was concerning, though I secretly wondered if it was all contrived and Angle was moments away from flying off the top ring rope and squashing the loudmouth. My guess is that's what the kids were hoping for.

The distraction momentarily took away from the real fight in the ring. The first match between the Silverbacks and Pitbulls was on, and welterweights Jake Ellenberger and Delson Heleno stalked each other looking for an opportunity to pounce. Ellenberger gave the Brazilian what he deserved, a healthy respect for his ground game. He kept the fight standing, delivering several crisp strikes and denying Heleno's takedown attempts. It was a smart game plan, given Heleno's formidable jiu jitsu. On the ground Heleno would be hard to beat. He was a ripped fireplug of strength and agility who'd spent a lifetime studying Brazilian jiu jitsu instead of English, of which he spoke none. Jake wisely put all his effort into staying out of that world.

In the second round, Jake picked up the pace and took the fight to Heleno, looking to finish him with a knockout as Matt Lindland shouted instructions from his corner. He might have gotten the KO easily, as he was repeatedly connecting, were it not for a takedown late in the round that he simply couldn't sprawl away from. On the ground, Jake held his own at first and even out-wrestled Heleno, proving he belonged in this match despite the oddsmakers giving him little chance. In the opinion of press row, the scrappy kid was winning. But this was MMA, where a tiny lapse in judgment can turn sure victory into depressing defeat. With mere seconds left in the round, Jake got caught in an inescapable armbar. The pain of a correctly executed armbar can only be tolerated for a short amount of time.

"Fifteen seconds!" Matt Lindland yelled to motivate his youngster. But that's an eternity when the elbow feels like it's going to snap. Valiant as he was, Jake had no choice but to tap out.

A woman suddenly shrieked behind me. "Yeah, Delson!" I dove for cover like an IED had just gone off.

"Are you from the city?" the nasally New York Timberlakewoman asked.

"Brazil. But my husband is on the team," the Brazilian woman replied in between jubilant shouts.

The win gave the New York Pitbulls the first score of the team competition. But Pat Miletich and his Silverbacks had been here before, and if anyone could calm the nerves of his fighters and get them back on track, it was Papa Pat.

Next up, billed as the fight of the night, Bartimus Palaszewski versus Davidius Taurosevicius energized the crowd and tested their verbal skills at the same time. Bart strode to the ring like any focused fighter would. His confidence and swagger had a comforting effect on his team because it was expected he would even up the score.

"Davidius brogasha!" the Brazilian woman yelled.

"Go, Tauropalashimeskidavidiusworskovich!" the Timberlakewoman added, apparently refusing to be outdone.

After politely swatting away mosquitoes from each other's heads with their fists, Davidius backed Bartimus into a corner, but left his neck exposed. Bart pounced on the opportunity and wrapped his lanky arm around the neck, attempting a guillotine choke. He leaped upward, wrapped his legs around Davidius's waist and leaned back. The move was risky. If it worked, it was a fight finisher because Davidius would have an unrelenting amount of pressure applied to his neck, cutting the off the blood flow to his brain. Instead, it turned into an "oh, shit!" moment when Bartimus slipped off Davidius's neck and fell to the mat underneath his legs. Like Stalingrad in 1943, this was a bad place to be.

Fighters usually have a backup plan when a move doesn't work, but this one had no such safety valve. With his left hand on Bart's neck to stabilize him, Davidius used his right to pummel his midsection and head as Bart lay trapped against the corner. When the bell sounded to end the round, Bart got to his feet, looking unfazed, except his head was redder than a boiled crawfish.

In round two the lightweights continued their onslaught, and then controversy happened. With Bart standing over the top of him, Davidius managed to get an armbar from underneath. The submission looked solid, but escapable. As Bart began to wrangle free, Referee Jorge suddenly stepped in and stopped the bout, claiming Bartimus had tapped out. Davidius ran around the ring like a circus pony, while the crowd scratched their bewildered heads. No one saw the tapout, and even on the Jumbotron replay, it still was not clear.

"Yeah, Davidius!" the Brazilian shouted.

"Palashewskiminovich was robbed," the New Yorker replied.

"You still suck, Angle!" the slacker declared.

Kurt Otto rushed into the ring to ask Referee Jorge what happened. Although it was weak, Jorge claimed he saw a tapout, which violated his own rule of "tap strong," and Otto had no real choice but to support him. The replay, which every good sports fan uses to pass judgment, disagreed. There was no clear tapout, and the bewildered crowd grumbled unhappily. Otto could do nothing but declare a winner, since the era of video replay still hadn't made it's way into MMA.

At the postfight conference later that night, Bartimus claimed he was pushing on Davidius's buttocks to get him off and was not tapping out. Davidius claimed he felt the arm break and it was a good stoppage by the referee. Robbed or not, the Silverbacks were suddenly down 2-0 with one of their sure wins snatched away. Renzo Gracie was on his way to proving the superiority of BJJ and the effectiveness of the armbar.

"No one's ever come back from that far down," Steve Molen from NHB Radio said in order to panic everyone on press row. "This might be over."

If Kurt Otto wasn't nervous, then he had to be dead inside. As much as he loved his fighters, his marketability was now in peril. His fight of the night had ended prematurely in controversy, and the Pitbulls seemed on their way to an easy victory. It wasn't exactly edge-of-your-seat excitement.

Two mountains of flesh now mounted the ring, hoping to either salvage or finish the night for their teams. Ben "Northstar" Rothwell was the most dominant heavyweight fighter in the IFL, but he stared across the ring at his biggest challenge yet in former UFC heavyweight champion Ricco Rodriguez. Rodriguez wasn't normally an IFL fighter, but when Pitbulls starter Bryan Vettell was injured in training, Gracie offered Rodrigruez the position, and Ricco stepped up to the plate.

Rodriguez was once huge. And I don't mean in a Muscle Beach way either. Ricco was fat. But Rodriguez had lost a load of weight, impressing everyone at the weigh-in. Unfortunately, like so many who have accomplished this, he maintained a flabby bucket of skin where the fat once was.

Within moments, Rodriguez had gotten his arms wrapped around Big Ben's neck, and he squeezed down a guillotine choke. It was the same move Bartimus had attempted to pull on Davidius, but this time with more success. The choke looked tight, and Ricco even looked over at Gracie and mouthed, "I got it," which took a lot of confidence—actually more confidence than was called for, because he didn't have it.

Seconds later, Rothwell was out of the choke and throwing angry, Vaseline-covered leather for the remainder of the round. In the second round, Rothwell refused to learn his lesson and got caught in a second guillotine choke. But again he found a way out of it. The drawback to cinching down a submission like this and not coming away with the finish is that it takes a tremendous amount of energy out of the fighter. By the second half of the round, Ricco was gassed. As a result, his kicks were sloppy and off target—actually more off target than was called for.

"Ooooooohh," the crowd groaned when Ricco's foot caught Rothwell's family directly in the jewels. The fighter on the receiving end of this offense was allotted five minutes to recover by unified MMA regulations, which Ben gladly took while the crowd jeered at Ricco. When the action restarted, Ricco was in trouble; his cardio was giving out on him. He gasped for air and leaned on the ropes trying to catch his breath. But there was a silver lining for Rodriguez. Unlike most MMA organizations, the IFL uses a four-minute round instead of five. The theory is that a shorter round will bring more action and less likelihood of stalling. In practice, this was true of smaller weight classes, but heavyweights will always be heavyweights and will always gas out.

"Agora! Bacci," the Brazilian woman yelled as the round ended.

Not sure if Ricco spoke Portuguese, someone in the crowd gave him advice in English. "Eat him!"

"Why don't you get your fat ass in there, Angle! Maybe you could hang with the tubby tubbies!" the teen shouted, not wanting to be outdone.

Round three was surprisingly déjà vu; Ricco caught Rothwell in a third guillotine choke. Apparently Rothwell's neck was made of the same material as Stretch Armstrong because he slipped free yet again. Ricco was now thoroughly off target with his kicks and once again caught Rothwell with a low nut shot that earned him more boos than ooohs. Late in the round, Rothwell trapped Ricco against the ropes and threw fists at will.

In an Octagon or cage, this might have ended the match because many fighters try to pin their opponents against the cage so they can immobilize them and pound away. But the IFL uses a standard boxing ring with ropes, so if a fighter gets underneath them, the match is restarted in the middle of the ring.

With just a few seconds left, the ref did just that. But then Ricco made a bad decision. Trying to piss Rothwell off and get him to swing his fists wildly, Ricco spit on him. The move had the intended effect of angering Big Ben, but not so much that he lost his focus. It did, however, anger the crowd and Ricco was accosted with verbal lashings from all sides. MMA fans simply won't stand for uncivilized behavior in a fight.

The kid who hated Kurt Angle managed to throw a dig at Ricco and Angle at the same time. "Did you just spit? What is this, the WWE?"

The fight ended in a flurry of hands and bad words, making it clear they were off each other's Christmas card list. It had gone the distance and now was up to the judges. Were the Pitbulls the 2007 IFL champions? Were the Silverbacks still in it? Despite the poor way the fight ended, the crowd was more interested than they had been fifteen minutes ago when it seemed a sweep was unavoidable.

"And your winner . . . Big Ben Rothwell!"

The crowd was back in it, and the Silverbacks night wasn't over just yet. But again, Rothwell's win could just have been delaying the inevitable. The fate of the IFL championships was now in the hands of two middleweights who'd met before.

Ryan McGivern had a score to settle with Fabio Leopoldo. The two had fought earlier in the season, with Fabio coming away with the submission by kneebar despite McGivern winning the early part of the fight. Leopoldo had waited patiently to snatch the victory when the opportunity arose. Now the former Hawkeye wrestler wanted payback.

If McGivern had a weakness, it was his pasty white skin. Here's a note to you pale-face wannabe fighters out there—get a tan. Although Fabio landed only a couple of shots to McGivern's body, his pale skin amplified the redness and made it look worse than it was. In this case, however, it made no difference; the contest didn't go to the judge's subjective opinions, since McGivern literally knocked Fabio senseless, scaring the Brazilian woman who suddenly screeched like an Amazon bird.

"Fabio! Brababoouch agora!"

The referee finally stopped the one-sided contest, pushing McGivern off the hapless Brazilian.

McGivern transformed into a Spartan warrior, shouting his might to the heavens, intoxicated with the glory of victory. The annihilation of Fabio exposed the weakness of Brazilian jiu jitsu. Great strikers can get through a tough defense and stop a ground game before it gets started. McGivern had adapted from his first loss to Fabio and made a conscious effort to keep the fight off the ground this time, despite his own formidable wrestling skills.

Miletich and his Silverbacks, happiness unbound, rushed the ring to congratulate McGivern. The crowd was now fully into the event, cheering wildly. The score was 2-2, and suddenly there was drama in Hollywood.

A quick Muscle Milk commercial on the Jumbotron calmed the crowd somewhat, but when the light heavyweights made their way into the ring, it was back to fever pitch. The whole season now came down to one fight. It was time for a goat and a hero. Would Mighty Casey strike out again, or would there be joy in Muddville? The team rivalry boosted the tension in the crowd. This was more than a rematch or an individual fight with personal pride on the line. This was now a defining moment between two teams representing the best fighting systems in the world.

"Hey, Angle, too bad you're such a pussy. McGivern would kick your ass too!" Not everyone felt the gravity of the moment.

Mike Ciesnelovicz (hereinafter Mike C, typing that name once is plenty) from the Silverbacks had fought Andre Gusmao of the Pitbulls before, losing by TKO. Ryan McGivern had just proven that revenge could be a powerful motivator in beating an opponent you've previously lost to. On the other hand, there's a certain unshakeable confidence when facing someone you've already beaten. As Chuck Liddell said after beating Tito Ortiz the second time, "I'll always have his number."

I would have liked to take this opportunity to wax poetic about this fight and describe in great detail how close it was, how punishing the back-and-forth battling of titans was, and how it came down to the wire like a ninth-inning home run or a Hail Mary pass in the final seconds. In reality, the fight was over before it started.

Instead of coming out firing, Mike C walked on eggshells; it looked like he wanted to avoid losing rather than to actually win. In contrast, Gusmao was light on his feet and connected with hard, crisp shots to Mike's legs and head. In the movies that sort of thing will usually go on for a while until the villain injudiciously calls the hero's sainted mother a whore and the hero comes back in a blaze of adrenalin. But in this case it only went on for a minute, then Gusmao trapped Mike in a Muay Thai clinch and set him up for a devastating knee to the face that sent him to bed early without dinner. Just like that, the drama ended.

The Pitbulls went crazy. The first man over the top rope to bear-hug his hero was Renzo Gracie. His fighters raised him onto their victorious shoulders and his big, toothy grin shined down like a half moon on them as they paraded around the ring. The Brazilian woman in the front row unleashed a torrent of Portuguese until everyone in her row got up and left. Even the Angle-haters vacated without a last taunt.

When the tickertape subsided, the victors were awarded symbolic championship rings big enough to be U joints on a monster truck, since the IFL didn't have the ring sizes for all the fighters and coaches. Although well-intentioned, the huge rings looked cheesy and took away from the event's professional atmosphere.

Gracious in defeat, Pat Miletich made no excuses and bore the brunt of defeat for his guys in the postfight press conference. After showering his men with champagne, Renzo Gracie took a moment to extol the virtues of

BJJ. "When you're on the ground and you're spent and feel dead, you're really alive if you have jiu jitsu."

"What about the bigger picture? The Gracie versus Miletich system?" I asked.

"Every victory is important, but we learn more in defeat. We get better with a defeat. McGivern proved that tonight. He came back on a different level. As far as this win being big for the Gracie family—it's what we've been saying for a hundred years. We've got the best game out there. To fight us you must know jiu jitsu; otherwise you're just a victim."

The IFL Finals had accomplished just what Kurt Otto had envisioned. It answered the question of which fighting style was dominant, at least

Renzo Gracie shows off his huge championship ring.

for this year. Gracie Jiu Jitsu had anchored its place in history just a little bit more. And Kurt Otto was one step closer to realizing his own goal. Was it B-rate competition? Hardly. Maybe there were no mini-Coutures or junior Liddells, and maybe the last bout took less time than it takes to spell "Ciesnelovicz," but the fights provided the same entertainment level as the UFC, with the added drama of team rivalry.

Watching the fighters and trainers congratulate each other on the event, something Otto had said at the café echoed in my head. "I really believe the sport needs us to exist. They need us to be here because if we're not—watch, it's gonna be one big organization and everybody's gonna get screwed." Opinion, but a relevant one. To be fair, I would have to check out the "other" organization's live show when the opportunity presented itself.

I was starving. But it was well past closing time for every restaurant between the Hard Rock and my hotel, and I was too tired to drive around just to find a processed burger. As I entered my room, a complaint rumbled in my hollow stomach. I dropped my keys on the desk right next to two Muscle Milk bars from the day before.

I wasn't that hungry.

AMERICAN TOP TEAM

Nothing in life is more wonderful than faith—the one great moving force which we can neither weigh in the balance nor test in the crucible.

—Sir William Osler

Coconut Creek, Florida, like Pleasant Hill, California, has an appropriate name, as coconut trees line the streets while canals and streams wind lazily through the flat terrain. Driving around, I found it very Florida: You've got your beaches; deep-sea fishing excursions; daiquiris; luminescent colors; overly plasticated women; jogger-eating alligators; and a strip mall with a Brazilian bakery, a "Free Cuba Now" center, and "Delbert's Gator Tail and Moonshine Emporium."

It also has American Top Team. As I stood in the entryway I realized I'd found the sort of gym I'd originally envisioned world-class athletes would train in—before I began finding them in strip malls, basements, and former used-car lots. Here was more square footage than every other gym I had been in put together, all bathed in a clean shine and the smell of the new.

"Hey, I'm Richie," a small, muscular guy said shaking my hand as I continued gawking at the cavernous palace behind him. "Let me show you around."

We walked around what was like a small city of MMA: side-by-side boxing rings, racks of heavy bags, an acre of grappling mats, a separate strength and conditioning area, and even a pro shop. Fifteen feet off the ground two massive movie screens were mounted in the corners and hooked to projectors for students to watch fights. In the back of the gym sat the pot of gold at the end of the MMA rainbow.

"Is that a full-size Octagon?" I asked feeling myself go numb.

"Yeah," Richie said. "We got permission from Dana White to have that here. The Octagon is actually trademarked, so you need permission from the UFC to have one."

"Great Chuck Norris!" I said, and turned around to again take in the red-white-and-blue panorama of MMA-ville.

American Top Team had set out in 2003 with the goal of being the most dominant MMA camp in the world within five years. The money behind the operation was Dan Lambert, and the talent was Ricardo Liborio. The two met in Las Vegas when Murilo Bustamante fought Chuck Liddell and struck up a partnership that was supposed to be temporary. Liborio, or Libo as everyone calls him, was happy training Brazilian Top Team out of Rio de Janeiro, which he helped start. He was making good money from his fighters and had no reason to leave them for American shores. But he also felt there was something about Lambert's drive to establish an MMA gym that made a leap of faith his destiny.

His involvement was only supposed to be for six months, after which time he planned to return to Brazil. But Libo knew Florida and ATT were a good fit for him and held the promise of achieving great things. Several of his students followed Libo from Brazil, including Gesias "JZ" Calvancante. Before long they were putting their stamp on MMA, and American Top Team has been growing and winning ever since.

I walked around the place, its walls covered in accolades of American Top Team champions. There were framed belts and photos of ATT athletes from every major MMA promotion in the world. In one corner I came upon a camera crew set up to film a documentary on Yves Edwards, a scrappy veteran of forty-four MMA fights and one of the pioneers of the lightweight division. Gazillionaire Mark Cuban's HDNet Fights on his fledgling High Definition channel was set to host its second fight card with Edwards taking on the unknown Alonzo Martinez in a couple of weeks. As I'd seen before with Jake Shields, the crew was there to hype him up.

I'd already explored the relationship of fighter and media ad nauseam, but I watched anyway as the crew scurried about trying to get shots of Yves as he trained with the ATT regulars.

Of course I was in for a surprise or I wouldn't be telling you about it.

Libo and his guys didn't resort to the marketing tactics that other gyms had when the crew was close by. No one changed his shirt for the camera, and Libo didn't sacrifice Yves's training in order to get face time for his guys. It seemed American Top Team didn't think it was necessary.

The lack of interest in these tactics seemed to be an indicator of the gym's personality. Every training camp I'd seen had a vibe, a guiding principle, from Team Quest's "hard work pays off" to Jackson's "have fun always" to Sityodtong's "respect your elders." I wasn't sure what it was here yet, but one thing was certain: this place was well funded and established.

When Yves Edwards first stepped into the Octagon in 2001 against Matt Serra, he already had twenty-three professional fights and four years worth of experience under his belt. But by 2004, the UFC was struggling with the lightweight division. There simply weren't enough of the mighty mites, and the best were fighting in Japan. Just before it was disbanded, Edwards had to fight Josh Thompson, his training partner, simply due to the lack of competition. But with money at stake, the two slugged it out in a memorable fight at UFC 49 that ended when Edwards KO'd Thompson with a high kick to his head.

After his filming, I asked Yves about having to injure a friend.

"I don't feel bad about it. We were two of the only 155-pounders at the time, so we knew it was coming. He would have kicked me in the head if I gave him the opportunity."

"Which is easier, fighting a friend or someone you dislike?" I asked.

"It's different. It's easy to get up for a guy you don't like, but it's motivating going into the ring with someone you know everything about too. I knew all of Josh's strengths and weaknesses and he knew mine, so it was real challenging, you know? It's easier to hit someone when you don't like them, but it's more mental when it's someone you do like."

With every major promotion establishing a lightweight division, every gym now had a couple. At ATT there were even two who had previously defeated Edwards: Mike Brown and Jorge Masvidal. Across the gym two other former enemies trained together as well—Wilson Gouveia and Carmelo Marrero.

"Do the cameras ever get old to you?" I asked as Yves threw his gear into a bag.

"Sometimes, but it's part of the process," he said. "We have to get our name out there and keep it out there if we want to be successful. You can't ignore the media or you won't last long."

Yves isn't the type to talk smack on camera. When they'd asked about his opponent a moment ago, he had simply pointed out some flaws and talked about how good his own training was going. On the other hand, it's not as if he didn't get pumped up.

"I get giddy," he confessed. "That's when I know I'm ready to fight. I get it through my head that I'm going to fight and there's nothing anyone can do to stop it, so I start getting happy. I jump around. I smile. I look forward to it like a kid on Christmas."

Just like Jackson's MMA, American Top Team boasted a roster of fighters with global achievements. By an unfortunate circumstance of scheduling, however, some of the big dogs were absent during my stay in Florida. I checked out a massive photo of Gesias "JZ" Calvancante winning the K-1 HEROs tournament in Japan and wondered why he wasn't in the gym.

"He's getting his knee taken care of in Brazil," Richie said as he walked out of his office, read my mind, and answered the question before I could ask it. Two more notable ATT fighters were also absent. Denis Kang, a top-ten middleweight, was in Canada visiting relatives, and Jeff Monson, who once fought Tim Sylvia for the UFC heavyweight title, was in England. Apparently I had caught American Top Team in a lull period. Yves's fight was the only one on the immediate horizon.

Kang and JZ were anomalies of MMA. Both were in the top ten in the world, but their names were anything but common outside of hardcore MMA fans because they fought exclusively in Asia. JZ was a lightweight and Kang a middleweight. For years MMA fans had salivated at the thought of these two moving to the UFC to fight the prospects in Mr. White's organization. With their talent and the marketing power of the UFC behind them, Kang and JZ could have been household names.

"Denis had too much to pass up when he was weighing the choice between Spirit MC and the UFC," Richie said. Spirit MC is the Korean MMA organization that had a firm grip on Kang. "There was too much money on the table for him to walk away from."

I suspected Kang also had an ulterior motive to fight in Asia. His father is Korean and still lives south of the DMZ. His repeated trips to "The Land of the Morning Calm" afforded father-son time, but it came at a cost. If he were to sign a contract with the UFC, Kang would quickly become a recognized name in preparation for a shot at Anderson Silva. The UFC typically tries to hype talented fighters whose names aren't well known. After all, no one is going to purchase a pay-per-view fight when they have to ask, "Who's fighting?"

Rich Franklin is a good example. For five years Franklin amassed a 16-1 record in small shows. The UFC identified him as a possible champion and put him on prime-time TV against one of the biggest names in the sport at the time, Ken Shamrock. The casual fan thought Shamrock was being fed scraps to feast on, until Franklin knocked Shamrock out, launching his name into the stratosphere of MMA. Suddenly the UFC had a recognizable name to put up against Evan Tanner for the middleweight championship. Franklin got his shot just two months later and destroyed Tanner, launching him to superstar status.

Of course, sometimes this strategy can get derailed. When Mirko Cro-Cop came over from Pride Fighting Championships to the UFC, he was one of the top five heavyweights in the world, and it was assumed he would make minced meat out of then-heavyweight champion Randy Couture. Since the U.S. audience didn't know his name, he had to be hyped in a couple of bouts he would surely win. He beat Eddie Sanchez, but then ran into an unexpected right leg of Gabriel Gonzaga and was knocked out cold. Suddenly the UFC's sizeable investment in Cro-Cop was in jeopardy. After losing to Cheick Kongo a few months later, Cro-Cop was a Cro-Not.

Overseas, Kang and JZ were just as big as Rich Franklin, but without the massive hype machine of the UFC in their corner, they were unknowns to the casual MMA fan. Marcus Aurelio and Thiago Alves, though talented fighters, had less success but more name recognition under the powerful UFC banner.

"I hope the UFC is grooming me to be a star someday," Aurelio said lounging in Richie's office a little later. "All I can do is train to be a good fighter and hope the best happens." Aurelio is one of the UFC's imports who came to the U.S. after Pride died. "Maximus," as he is called, felt immense pressure for being one of the few people besides Nick Diaz to beat "The Fireball Kid" Takanori Gomi. Maximus even choked him unconscious, leaving a crumpled Gomi in the middle of the ring as the crowd gasped in disbelief.

"I love Pride and I miss it, but then I love UFC too," he said leaning back in Richie's chair. "The people in the UFC don't like it when the fight goes to ground. There's more pressure to train harder for the UFC crowd because they like it . . . aggressive. They like it to never stop. But that's America, no? Never stop?"

Maximus had learned a lot about American culture in his short time as a citizen.

That night I watched Libo teach a jiu jitsu class in the west wing of the gym. Relaxing on the apron of the boxing ring was Jorge Santiago, one of Libo's Brazilian fighters who had just won the Strikeforce middleweight tournament by knocking out Sean Salmon and Trevor Prangley in the same night. The tournament format, which requires the winner to fight multiple times in one night, is mostly shunned by the MMA world, but Strikeforce, a California-based promotion, opted to give it a try. Put simply, Santiago came, saw, and conquered to win the belt that sat next to him on the ring apron. Anyone not taking Libo's class shook Jorge's hand and took a second to admire his title, the pinnacle of his MMA achievements thus far.

"Now I just need a shot at Shamrock," he said.

"Jorge Santiago, middleweight champion of the world!" Libo shouted and raised his arms high overhead, filling the vast gym with his tremendous voice. Passing by the front desk, I found Cole Miller thumbing through a copy of *Real Fighter* magazine. Cole was in the second stage of his media hype. As a contestant on season five of *The Ultimate Fighter*, he was beyond his UFC initiation phase and had successfully passed the intermediate stage, which was a fight on a Spike TV Ultimate Fight Night card. He was into the next phase of his marketing—full UFC fights against names equal in stature to his own.

I asked him why he'd come down from Georgia to train here. He stopped thumbing through the magazine and looked around. "I can train anything and everything I want to right here," he said. "I used to drive between Macon and Athens to train, but now I just do it all here." I thought of the Diaz brothers and all the driving they did in California and how a facility like this might make them better fighters. But there was more to it for Miller.

"It's a different attitude when you're around guys like these," he said gesturing toward Thiago Alves. "They strive to be the best. Other guys just dream of being more than what they are and don't do anything to get there."

"So why do you fight?" I asked.

"The Octagon is the most peaceful place I've ever been."

"The what?"

"It is. I'm more calm and relaxed than any other place I've ever been when I'm in there. I'm focused. I go in there and just forget about everything. I'm a pretty high-strung guy usually, you know? I can't sleep if I have stress or issues at the house. I can't stand stress in my life. The Octagon takes all that away."

"We're talking about the same place, right? The cage where violent bodily harm happens?"

He chuckled. "I know. When I first started training, it was like the most fun I had had in my life, and in my first fight I was walking into the ring and I wasn't nervous. I was looking back at the crowd wondering if they were feeling the energy coming off of me. It was the most intense feeling I've ever had. It was the coolest thing I've ever felt, and I still get it when I walk into the ring. I love it. It's just the happiest place to be."

"Isn't it unhealthy to have a lack of fear?" I asked. "Don't you become complacent if you're not a little scared?"

"For some people's mind-set it is, but not me."

I'd heard a lot of reasons why men (and women) fight, but I never thought finding a Zen-like peace would be one of them.

* * * * *

"This Brazilian time is bullshit," Carmello Marrero said, sitting on a set of steel bleachers just off of the grappling mats. Noon every Tuesday and Thursday was reserved for professional fighters. It was called Bloqueio, a Brazilian word whose meaning was lost on everyone, but pretty much meant "training time." But now it was 12:20 and only Marrero and Richie Attonito were ready to train. As Marrero's frustration grew, fighters slowly filed in. Around 12:40 all of the pro fighters were finally on the mat wearing headgear and boxing gloves, including one Jorge Masvidal, nicknamed Gamebred.

I'd been told he was a thug. I Googled his name and found two videos of him fighting in the streets of Miami as a ghetto crowd cheers him and his opponent on. His nickname, tattooed across his neck, came from his fascination with pit bulls. Raised by a mother, a half brother, and a variety of cousins on the streets of Miami, he dropped out of school in the ninth grade and got fired from every job he ever had, once even by the half brother who'd raised him. When he got into MMA, his mouth led the way. He talked shit, plain and simple. If anyone was born to be the poster boy for MMA haters, it was Gamebred. From what I'd heard, he was bound to set MMA back a few years if he ever got media exposure for his surefire talent. I was eager to meet him, but it would have to wait until the day's training was complete.

"Okay," Libo's voice boomed out over the gym as he walked onto the mats. "Shadow box, five minutes, go!" His voice was truly impressive. For such a small, soft-spoken guy, he had a Pavarotti-like projection that could rattle dishes in the trailer park across the street.

Bloqueio was more like Team Quest's sparring sessions than the sheer brutality of Terrell's or Jackson's shark tank. Yet it wasn't the technically proficient sparring of Sityodtong either. They started slow and gradually got faster, working on striking skills and then going to grappling. After the first round of shadow boxing, everyone switched partners. "Strike to the takedown!" Libo demanded. "Five minutes. Go!"

Everyone did as commanded, taking turns throwing a combination of punches before shooting in to take his opponent off his feet. Gamebred started getting into his rhythm, showing off his ability to shoot and get the takedown quickly. He had a winning record of 12-2, and from what I'd heard, was primal in the ring, living up to his nickname. But as I watched, he didn't strike me as an overpowering or supremely technical fighter. He was quick and proficient, but not on the "you have to see this guy" level.

The next round was more shadow boxing, but with MMA gloves. Again it was only about three-quarter speed, but Gamebred's hands started to speed up. Finding his range, he peppered Luigi Fiorvanti with shots from all angles.

After three five-minute rounds of striking, it was time for grappling, and the pace picked up. The fighters went a little harder on the ground, working for positions and submissions. I decided to snap a few pictures of Jorge while he grappled, but as soon as he saw the camera, he posed. In the middle of training, with a sweaty partner trying to submit him, he looked at me and gave a thumbs-up, then struck a thinking man's pose, then pointed at the camera—very cool under fire, or else a real attention whore.

"Okay, full speed. Go!" Libo thundered out after a water break to start the next round. Gamebred hooked up with Micah Miller, Cole's younger brother, and the two went to town. Jorge got the quick takedown on Miller, but found himself in guard. He threw a few half-speed shots at Miller's head and tried to break free, only to find himself in a triangle choke. He defended well against that and worked into the side control position just as the timer sounded to end the round and the entire session.

Gamebred leaned up against a padded wall and BSed with the veteran Yves Edwards. I walked over and sat down next to them, expecting his attitude to take up more wall space than my whole body. "How did you get into fighting?" I asked.

He shrugged. "I've been doing this in the yard since I was ten," he said

Jorge "Gamebred" Masvidal poses for the camera while he trains.

with a Latin accent tinted with urban bravado. "Me and my friends would put on the gloves and do boxing or wrestling or something. I had a lot of street fights like any young kid, you know? But shit, I loved it."

The stereotype of a poor kid with no direction, an aversion to school, and a pair of pitbulls was already building in my mind. I pictured him and a band of other kids duking it out on a hot Florida afternoon in a dirt yard dominated by a rusted pickup on blocks.

"What do you get out of it?" I asked.

"I love to compete. I'm real competitive at anything I do. Anything I take pride in, not just fighting, I like to compete at dominoes, chess, anything. Fighting is what I'm good at naturally since I was a kid. It's what I love to do."

I was having a hard time picturing him playing chess in the back of that rusted pickup. "Have you ever tried to hurt somebody?"

"In the ring? Yeah," he said. "I'm gonna try to hurt somebody. I'm not trying to mess with no one's career like break a hand or nothing, but I'm trying to hurt him. I'm trying to make the ref stop it. I'm trying to hurt someone with a right hand or a left hook to the body."

Gamebred's mouth had more of a reputation than his talent. After a fight, he had called out Gilbert Melendez, who had vastly more experience and a vaunted ground game, and claimed he could whip his ass. His confidence in his own superiority could rival Ali's, but in his mind, he was just being himself.

"It's not really that I'm talking smack, they just ask me how I feel and I'm just saying how I feel you know? I just say what's on my mind."

That night I went to west Miami to meet Gamebred at his regular gym, Young Tigers. It was a far cry from the flowered community of Coconut Creek. Above a run-down Latino Mercado the sounds of leather gloves hitting bags emanated from open windows. The smell of sizzling beef hung in the air, and dogs barked from behind chain-link fences down the street.

Gamebred trained at ATT two or three times a week, but he trained here at Young Tigers gym daily. Inside, the space was swathed in sauna-like heat made more oppressive by the low ceilings. It had a ring, several heavy bags wrapped in duct tape, and a few pieces of weightlifting equipment in serious disrepair. Colorful flyers advertising fights were thumbtacked to the wall or hung with scotch tape. I suddenly couldn't knock Gamebred for having an ego after seeing the environment he was raised in. Here an attitude is a necessity, and making it out of this world is certainly a good enough reason to brag.

He was late. Shocking. I hung around while ten kids, none more than twenty-five, boxed and stole sideways hopeful glances at me. With a Canon digital camera dangling from my shoulder they saw the hype machine in their midst.

Gamebred finally arrived, changed, and trained stand-up with Eric Castellanos, the founder of the gym and the man Jorge credited with taking him off the streets and keeping him out of trouble. After training, Jorge sat on a bench press that looked ready to collapse.

"If you had to pick between fighting for nothing and doing something else for a lot of money, which would you take?" I asked.

He dropped a glove and made a scowl. "If you told me I could work at Toys 'R Us for a lot of money, like a million dollars a year versus fighting good enough to where I could just take care of me and my family, I'd take the fighting. Definitely. I love to fight. MMA is the one thing I really know how to do. I mean I could train all day everyday. I'd be the luckiest motherfucker. That's what I love to do; wake up, eat, train, do it again."

It was hard to see beneath the surface of Gamebred. He was not formally educated, a braggart, and came from a broken home where prison visits were as regular as Sunday church. But the mention of taking care of his family hinted that something more than a bling-wearing gangsta resided in him.

I learned that at the age of three, his father had begun an eighteen-year vacation in the Florida State penal system for drug trafficking. I asked him what he thought about the situation that had drastically altered his life.

Jorge looked at the ground for a moment. For the first time I got the impression that he was really contemplating his answer before giving it. "I think he was just looking out for us, you know? I mean it was kind of stupid, but he had a family at home and had to do something to take care of us. He didn't have any choice but to find ways to make money and support us. If he had to break the law to do that, then that's what he had to do."

"Are you determined not to be like him?" I asked.

"Well, I want to make more money than he did so I can take care of him and my mom, you know? I'd like to get rich and pay them back. I think if I can be more responsible and stay out of jail then he'd be happy with that too."

It was odd to hear him talk about responsibility since I'd built him up in my head to be beholden to nothing, except maybe his wallet. Since we were on the subject, I took it a step further.

"You have all these skills you've learned as a fighter. Is there a level of responsibility that comes with that to keep yourself in check or keep your temper in check?"

"Yeah. You gotta keep your temper in check definitely," he said. "But by the same token, I ain't gonna let someone get close to me, you know? I can bleed just like anyone else. If someone starts messing with me, I try to back it down, and if they get too close, that's when I get scared just like anybody else. Someone gets in my face or something I just step back. I know I can kick ass, but the only time I get ready to fight is when I feel threatened, you know?"

Though he hadn't fully embraced the principles of the black belt, mixed martial arts had apparently formed Jorge Masvidal into a man. His upbringing could be a case study in how professional sports lures in the physically gifted, but economically destitute, and then stands idly by as they self-destruct. I expected to find that in him, but I had misjudged him based on limited information. He was deeper than his outward appearances, and I felt bad for stereotyping him.

Jorge Masvidal was not a punk. I knew the sport of MMA had evolved eons since the days of pure brawlers, but I had expected to find at least one dirtbag who lived to break bones and crush dreams. It's a fight after all, not cricket. There had to be a straight-up ghetto thug somewhere in this sport. But in gym after gym I had not found him.

"You're probably looking in the wrong gyms," Richie said as I ranted about it the next day. "No one who runs a professional MMA gym wants an asshole in his place. Those guys get weeded out quickly. When you become a professional fighter it's a lifestyle change. You have to eat right, sleep right, stay out of trouble. Nutrition and cardio and training become your life. It's humbling. The people who are out there starting shit in the streets are usually the ones who came into the gym for one day and never came back. It's that simple."

This professionalism is never more evident than in the chasm that divides MMA fighters and boxers. Boxing had grown out of poor, inner-city gyms where hungry kids fought their way to a better life. Mixed martial arts, on the other hand, has come from not only mixed fighting traditions but mixed economic situations. There are inner-city gyms, strip-mall dojos, and facilities like ATT where jiu jitsu lessons don't come cheap. This is oversimplifying the socioeconomic structure of the two sports, but the generality is fairly consistent.

"It's like being the biggest bad ass in prison," Richie said. "In the joint you have to survive, and showing weakness gets you killed, you know? I think it's the same way in boxing. Your reputation means everything, and being a loudmouth is part of that posturing. But in MMA it's more of a negative thing to talk shit."

Talking with Richie was like talking to an adult with Doogie Howser syndrome. He was a kid both at heart and in physical stature, but a lot smarter. Until he admitted he was forty-four I thought he was thirty—tops. A lightweight with a BJJ black belt, Richie was the man behind the scenes for ATT. As the gym manager he didn't have any say on which fights to take, but had his hand hovering over the panic button and several speed dial numbers. When Din Thomas, an ATT regular, was arrested for hosting illegal amateur fights, Richie convened a committee within the gym to deal with the situation.

"Our first thoughts were, 'Is Din Okay? How can we help?'" he said. "As we found out more we learned it was a technicality more than anything because there were police in the audience at the time who didn't do anything. Our main concern was Din himself."

The line between sparring and amateur fights is drawn when money is charged for admission and fighters are paid. On the night in question, Thomas had taken money at the door of his gym, but it was supposedly for a raffle of gifts that took place that night. The case had holes in it to say the least and Thomas wasn't expected to be found guilty.

Richie's occupation as the unseen guy who makes his bosses' life easier is comparable to the majors of the Army. Majors are staff officers who are either one step below a commander in a battalion (300–700 soldiers) or hopelessly mired in the minutiae of making a larger unit (a brigade or a division) run smoothly. They sprint from meeting to meeting, write memos, and stare at computer screens long after everyone else has gone home. Like Richie, majors mastermind crises in closed-door conferences and supervise the week-to-week events that keep the military machine chugging along. They gather and develop information and package it neatly so commander's can make educated and timely decisions.

Richie and his fellow gym managers are the majors of MMA. They filter out the information that doesn't need to make it to the owners' and trainers' desks. They run websites, interact with the public and the media, brainstorm the marketing value of potential fights, and make or break a career through brilliant or inept business decisions.

"The UFC is a brand," Richie said sitting behind his desk. "Instead of saying you're going to overnight something, you say you're going to FEDEX it. You say MMA to the average guy on the street and they don't know what you mean. But you say UFC and it's like, 'Oh that Matt Hughes guy and the fighting thing, yeah.' It's a brand now. We have to do the same thing to stay in business. We have to build the brand of American Top Team. We have sixteen schools under the ATT name. Not only that, but we have these instructional DVDs we're developing to ensure the quality of our product. People don't necessarily want BJJ now. I mean BJJ is a good basis and it's proven, but what they really want is MMA."

A few blocks away from ATT I found Hakusan sushi bar and decided to give it a try. Thankfully the tiny restaurant employed an authentic sushi chef who knew what he was doing. Hakusan had a fantastic "Pokemon roll" featuring tempura fish and cucumber. Being mere blocks away from the Everglades, I was hoping for alligator tail sushi, but there wasn't any on the menu.

"Why are you here?" the waitress asked, accurately deducing that I was from out of town. I described American Top Team, the mixed martial arts program just down the street. She looked at me confused.

"Have you heard of the UFC?" I asked, testing out Richie's theory.

"Oh, yes. That cage fighting. I like that."

Richie was right.

* * * * *

Thiago Alves got caught. He took a pill that was designed to dehydrate him so he could get below the required weight of 170 pounds the day before fighting Tony DeSouza at UFC 66. The pill worked its magic and Alves blew through DeSouza like crap through a goose, but there was a problem. The drug he took, Spironolactone, was illegal in MMA. It's a powerful diuretic, and when he tested positive for it after the fight, he was slapped with a nine-month suspension and a $2,500 fine by the Nevada State Athletic Commission.

The young Brazilian didn't deny taking it; he simply didn't know it was illegal. Alves's suspension was harsh, but as steep as the penalty was, he was lucky the fight wasn't ruled a no-contest, as Nick Diaz's had been against Takanori Gomi.

The culture of cutting weight is unique to combat sports. Boxing, wrestling, and MMA have weight classes that place maximums on how much a fighter can weigh for a fight. As such, the goal of a fighter is to be the strongest and heaviest person in that class while meeting the limits.

Because of this system, fighters cut down from their normal "walking around weight" to the limit of their weight class around twenty-four hours before the fight when they're required to weigh in.

In between fights, Alves's natural walking around weight is 195–200 pounds, so he has to cut all the way down to 170 the day before a fight to meet the restrictions of the welterweight division. It's a

Thiago "Pitbull" Alves training at American Top Team.

balancing act. Fighters have to know how much they can cut successfully and how much they can recover in order to be at peak performance. They have to measure the size and shape of their bodies and determine which weight class they fit into best. Alves could have fought in the middleweight (185 pounds maximum) division, but he would have given up size and strength to his opponents. He wouldn't have the long reach of middleweight champion Anderson Silva or the heavier frame of Rich Franklin.

It's common in MMA to cut twenty to thirty pounds before a fight and then build it back up in the twenty-four hours between weigh-ins and fight time. The drawback is the loss in energy levels. Cutting weight means eating less. Eating less means lower energy levels, making training for a fight difficult.

A prime example is Paulo Filho. Like Alves, Filho dropped a lot of weight to reach his maximum-allowed 185 pounds the day before a fight with Chael Sonnen at WEC 31. Filho had a hard time recovering from the drastic weight loss, and his performance in the cage suffered because he simply didn't have the energy to fight at his best ability. He looked gassed out in the second round. His striking was sluggish and his ground game was lethargic. He would have lost the fight were it not for a little controversy.

But Filho didn't have much choice. If he fought in the heavier 205-pound division he would have been at a disadvantage because of his short and stocky build. He wouldn't have the size or reach to compete with the likes of Quinton Jackson or Chuck Liddell. Fighters have to choose their weight class carefully, and they frequently change from one to the other. But no matter which one they choose, the specter of cutting weight always plays a part in their decision.

It had been only two weeks since UFC 78, where Thiago Alves had battled Chris Lytle for two hard rounds. The fight had ended after the ring doctor determined a cut over Lytle's eye was too dangerous to let him continue. The fight earned Alves and Lytle "fight of the night" bonuses, but apparently no time off. Alves was already back in the gym helping train others and doing his own strength workouts when I found him.

"Cutting weight sucks," he said after a series of pull-ups. "It's the worst thing ever. Because you need energy to function and you have to eat when you're training hard everyday, and when you're not eating you can't even train hard. And I love to eat man, especially carbohydrates and junk food. Cutting weight sucks but you gotta do it."

"How far out do you start?" I asked.

"Forty-five days. Thirty days you start watching what you're eating, like no carbohydrates at night. That can drop a few pounds, sometimes fifteen pounds. I like to lose fifteen pounds in the last week."

"Fifteen pounds in the last week?" I gasped.

"Yeah. The last five days. You're body gets used to it. You know it's going to be hard, you just get through it. It's the closest thing to death and you think you're gonna die, dried out with no water in your body burning up in the sauna, but it is what it is."

Fluid restriction is the most common form of shedding pounds. As long as you don't replace the fluid you lose through natural processes, you will lose weight. It takes no extra energy to do it, and you can lose up to six pounds in twenty-four hours. But when Thiago Alves was concerned he might not make the weight before UFC 66, he cut corners to drop more water weight and paid the price for it.

"Are you afraid that the suspension is going to tarnish your reputation?" I asked.

He looked to the ceiling for a moment. "Not really. It wasn't intentional and nothing I say is going to change what is already done. I know I'm going to be tested for the rest of my life and I'm cool with that. I did it and I paid for it."

Cutting weight is just one of the many tolls MMA takes on the human body. It's a culture of aches, pains, diets, supplements, oils, balms, rubdowns, energy drinks, and even fingernail polish to keep the nails strong enough not to rip off while grappling. Marcus Aurelio had some sort of voodoo oil that he rubbed on before Bloqueio that consisted of camphor, tiger balm, menthol, and eye of newt in order to get his vein vacillation going.

Perhaps the biggest obstacle fighters face in training is balancing energy levels. If they use too much energy and don't eat the right foods to replace it, they don't perform well in training. They simply go through the moves and fail to improve. Conversely, those who eat too much and fail to burn it off adequately gain weight, and with weight gain usually comes slower reaction time and lower cardiovascular endurance.

Because of their schedule, fighters are caught in a never-ending roller coaster of energy, perpetually trapped between highs and lows. Most train in the morning, take a few hours off, and then train again in the evening. To recover between sessions most have to take over-the-counter supplements and guzzle energy drinks. When that doesn't work, the mentally weak turn to the "S" word—steroids.

But even those who follow the rules can get caught in a bad situation, such as a legal supplement testing positive for a steroid. According to UFC lightweight champion Sean Sherk, this is what happened to him when he tested positive for Nandrolone. The plethora of supplements on the open market make it difficult for the Food and Drug Administration to keep pace and ensure they are safe and free of banned substances. It's entirely plausible that a fighter could unknowingly take a steroid in the form of an over-the-counter supplement, as Sherk contested.

The ironic thing about steroids is they don't seem to help in MMA. The majority of fighters who test positive for an illegal or banned substance do so after they lose a fight. What a bitch it must be to take something that supposedly gives an advantage only to find it didn't and then get caught, fined, and suspended as well. The risk simply isn't worth it to any rational person.

"I'm sporadic when it comes to supplements," Mike Brown, a featherweight veteran of the UFC and Bodog told me that night. "I can't really tell enough of a difference in my performance to swear by them, although I did notice Creatine made my muscles noticeably larger when I was lifting weights. The problem with that is bigger muscles aren't necessarily good, especially for me because I have to stay under 145 pounds."

"So what's the advantage to taking them?" I asked.

"A lot of guys use them to get rid of soreness between workouts. Like when your body says 'no more,' but you have to get going. Some guys think those little magic pills that you get at GNC can get you going when you're tired."

"Do you take them?"

"Some, but I'm more of a caffeine junkie. I drink coffee like crazy instead of those energy drinks. . .Now my roommate, Benji Radach, he's into all that stuff. We have a refrigerator full of supplements and a kitchen stacked to the roof with it. He makes the protein shakes, pops the pills, takes the vitamins, all that stuff. He even does powdered greens. I think he calls it Ambertose. He swears by it. Says it will cure anything."

Benji Radach, an IFL fighter, is a member of the Los Angeles Anacondas squad, but trains at American Top Team most of the time. Benji had recovered from several injuries to get where he was so if anyone knew about man-made methods to improve the body, it was him.

Mike is a product of the combat lifestyle. He was sitting behind the front desk of ATT and working as the gym's part-time receptionist until his torn biceps could heal properly. Injury is the mortal enemy of the professional fighter. No matter how talented the athlete, a shoulder separation, a torn MCL, or a bulging disk can instantly derail his career. A single injury can mean the loss of a substantial amount of income, as Rich Franklin found out when he tore a meniscus muscle in his knee and had to pull out of UFC 82 where he was supposed to headline against Travis Lutter. The lost revenue from that nagging little injury was in the hundreds of thousands of dollars.

Another killer is infection, more specifically staphylococcus, or staph as everyone calls it, a bacteria that's incredibly resilient and easy to transfer. Several fighters have had run-ins with staph, including Forrest Griffin, Diego Sanchez, Nick Diaz, and Kevin Randleman, who has a permanent hole in his side from a nasty bout with the flesh-eating bacteria. The biggest problem with staph is that it's highly contagious. Once a fighter is diagnosed with it, he has to quarantine himself in order to spare the rest of his gym mates from infection.

All these health issues are compounded by fighters' difficulty in getting health insurance.

Wilson Gouveia lamented to me about how he had been turned down three times because of his job description of professional fighter, even though football is more dangerous. He ended up having to fly to Brazil for surgery to repair a broken nose because it was cheaper than in the States. I had to agree with him. Statistically MMA isn't even in the top twenty most dangerous sports, but the lingering brutal image of early MMA fighters and their multitude of injuries prevails in many minds. Wilson suddenly brought up an issue I'd already explored. "I got a family to support now. I think we need to get together and make like a union or something."

I made a mental note to introduce him to Ivan Salaverry.

* * * * *

"Man I'm so fat," Libo said looking at a picture of himself in Richie's office after Bloqueio on Thursday.

"The camera adds ten pounds," Richie replied to ease his boss' mind.

"How many cameras were there?" Primo jabbed. Primo was the gym's marketing manager and not one to practice restraint when there was an opportunity to fuck with someone.

"Let's get lunch," Libo said as if resigning himself to his new weight. He was far from fat, but his former washboard stomach was covered over by a load of laundry, so it was easy to understand his distress.

Richie, Libo, and I piled into his SUV and drove down the street to a place called The Ale House. I was surprised he wanted to have lunch at a typical American bar and grill since there were so many Latin restaurants in the area, but it turned out Libo was as Americanized as Arnold Schwarzenegger.

"Some of the guys came here to America six years ago," he said sliding into a booth as eighties tunes blasted through the restaurant. "They got married and they got a family. Their kids are American. I got married to an American woman. I have an American kid. It's who we are now. When I came over here a lot of guys at Brazilian Top Team wanted to be with a strong team so they came with me."

My thoughts turned to the IFL and why ATT didn't have a team in the league.

"They approached us, but they wanted to put it in a different name," Libo said. "They wanted to call it Miami Barracudas or something like that."

I was surprised. "Is the American Top Team name that important? That you wouldn't field an IFL team because of it? That's a major business decision," I said.

"We have enough guys right now . . . in all the right places," Libo said. "Our main guys are fighting in the big places. If we go to the IFL, it's a good idea, but they have to accept us as American Top Team. That's number one. Number two, it was better for us to have our guys fighting around the world for titles in other organizations than to have our top guys in one league. We want to be the best team in the world. It would be a good idea to be in the IFL if we had a chance to do what we wanted to do."

Along with co-owner Dan Lambert, Libo was the decision maker at ATT. He was like a colonel in the Army. A colonel commands a large organization and interacts with the highest-ranking people on a daily basis. Colonels are usually in their mid-forties and command brigades, the central maneuver unit on the battlefield. When a situation arises, a colonel has usually seen it before and can whip out a solution based on past experiences.

Libo, Matt Lindland, Greg Jackson, and Pat Miletich were the colonels of MMA, but not solely because of their vast experiences. Each of them had multiple fighters in multiple promotions, and when they made a decision it sent shockwaves through the entire sport. If Libo were to decide that Denis Kang or JZ would be better off fighting in the UFC instead of K-1, it would have repercussions for their divisions on two continents. Likewise Thiago Alves or Marcus Aurelio leaving the UFC would open the doors for other fighters, trainers, and camps to get the big break they needed to fulfill their Octagon dreams. And Libo's decision not to field an IFL team affected the bottom line of Kurt Otto's league.

As we talked it became evident that Libo and Richie's view of the team concept differed from that of other gyms. At ATT everyone subordinates their own interests for the greater good of the team. As I had noted during Yves's filming, no one scrambled to get their face or their name in front of the camera, unlike every other place I'd been. I asked him about that.

Libo leaned back in the booth and propped his arm up on the railing. When his voice isn't booming commands, he speaks softly and smiles as easily as he breathes. "People don't understand that we have to try to make money, but at the same time it's . . . man . . . it's a family. Those guys are gonna stop it one day. They're gonna stop fighting and what are they gonna do without MMA, work at a car wash? Hell no. We're gonna help them open a school and make some money, show them the business end, or be an instructor for somebody."

For years and years Ricardo Liborio had been a banker in Brazil, making good money in a reliable job. He was financially secure and therefore had no impetus to take a leap of faith into the unknown, a terrifying prospect that few can find the courage for. Those who can don't do it without passion. Libo didn't just teach a class and retreat to his office to count his money. He had a passion for teaching his art, and helping his pupils grow on a personal level the way Greg Jackson and Mark DellaGrotte did. And anyone who knew him could bear witness to that.

* * * * *

It was a quiet Thursday night and I wasn't planning on grappling when a gi suddenly fell into my lap.

"Come on, let's train," Libo said. I looked at the dirty, used gi that had a bloodstain on the inside left shoulder and shrugged. There didn't seem to be much choice in the matter.

If you've never worn a gi, they suck. It's the common uniform for martial arts students, consisting of heavy cotton pants and an equally weighty top tied together by a belt. They're thick and even more uncomfortable than the Army battle dress uniform, which most people incorrectly call "fatigues" or "camies." This particular gi, I was soon to discover, was stiffer than a ski boot and twice as warm.

Forty students slowly gathered around the mats, stretching before class in their trendy blue gi's with cool patches. I plopped down and did the same when I suddenly noticed my grotesquely long toenails—considered bad grappling etiquette since they cause scratches and cuts. I tried to quickly rip them off without grossing everyone out.

After stretching the class started promptly late. The first technique was a throw that looked more like a judo-style hip toss than jiu jitsu. I partnered up with a guy named Angel, mostly because he had a white belt so I assumed he had as much experience as me.

So much for assuming.

Although I was larger, Angel threw me over his shoulder and slammed me down on the mat hard enough to make my balls hang lower. I knew how to fall correctly, but since it was his first throw, he put everything he had behind it and WHAM! We worked the throw until I felt old.

The next technique was a sweep from the mount into an armbar.

Angel paired off with someone more his size, and I got partnered with a twenty-something named Jason. I was happy not to be repeatedly thrown to the mat, but this one had its own brand of discomfort. In MMA, when a man is mounted, it's time to rain down hell. But this was strict grappling with no strikes, so gaining a submission was the goal. From the mount we worked on a move where the top man isolates an arm, bends it behind his opponent's back, and steps over his opponent. The attacker ends up sitting on his opponent's head with the bent arm in a painful jointlock. The misery of this move is made all the worse by the inevitable nutsack in the face. It seemed like jiu jitsu's way of saying, "you're my bitch now." I suddenly wanted to go back to working throws.

After practicing this move way too many times for my liking, Ricardo announced through his natural megaphone that it was time for open grappling.

Jason and I paired off again. I'd been here before and trained in world-class gyms so I thought I could show Jason a thing or two.

We started out on our knees, which is the big difference between jiu jitsu and wrestling. Wrestlers start in a standing position and have to find ways of taking their opponents off of their feet, but in jiu jitsu the knees are the common starting position. The gi is frequently used as a point of control so Jason and I reached and grabbed for a collar or a sleeve to gain an advantage.

Jason went for my collar and I managed to get his sleeve in the process. Both of us looked for ways to use the grip, but couldn't. I tried to get his weight going backward and he tried to use my collar to pull me to one side. I used his sleeve to pull him quickly toward me and tried to get his back. But he instantly turned and ended up on top of me in side control. Just like that, I was in trouble. Moments later I was mounted and in real trouble, and the thick, heat-conserving gi was not helping. Picture yourself in a locked car . . . in July . . . at noon . . . in the tropics. Now picture a man sitting on you.

I used my relative size advantage over Jason to wriggle out of the mount, but then got caught in a head-arm-triangle-strangulation-heat-stress-choke. Actually it was an Anaconda choke, but half the reason I tapped was because I simply couldn't breathe.

"Good job," I panted as the five-minute timer finally sounded. "You have a lot of skill for a white belt."

"I wrestled for years," he replied.

Suddenly I didn't feel so bad for getting tapped out.

"Get a drink of water and a new partner," Ricardo shouted.

The next five-minute round I grappled with Bob, a sixty–something-year-old whose hair matched his white gi. I wanted to be a smart ass and ask how the weather at Woodstock was, but the brown belt around his waist made me think better of it. He was the highest-ranking guy in the class, so I opted to show respect. It's well known that the elderly enjoy giving charity, and Bob did just that.

"Tap, tap!" I actually heard myself say out loud when he put me into yet another painful armbar.

"Don't leave it out there so far," Bob advised. Apparently I had a habit of leaving my arm exposed. Bob either felt sorry for me or his high-fiber diet started to fail him because he suddenly slowed to half speed and started talking me through ways to submit him. He was like a blackjack dealer who tells you when to hit and reminded me of Ricardo Murgel back at Jackson's MMA—a nonthreatening older guy who could whip your ass if he wanted to.

I was basting like a Thanskgiving turkey in my own sweat inside my gi. Thankfully Ricardo declared we would only have one more round. I mustered up all the strength I had left and partnered up with a green belt named Jeff. Jeff employed a tactic I'd once seen Royce Gracie use. He immediately pulled me into his guard and worked for a collar choke. Fortunately, I saw it coming and managed to get side control. A minute later I isolated an arm and cranked down on a kimura.

Come on! Tap! I thought to myself. I wanted the submission and tightened the hold. But Jeff was tough and rolled away from me to alleviate the pressure on his elbow joint. I moved with him, hungering for the submission. It may have been a friendly jiu jitsu class, but I'd been submitted and manhandled so much over the last ten months ,that I had to feel him tap. I had to win. When it finally happened, I let go and a wave of relief washed over me.

"You okay?" I asked.

"Sure," he responded. "Give me a minute to get the blood flowing into it again." I fought the urge to run around the gym screaming. I'd felt the elation of victory in sports before—football, basketball, baseball—but this was a combat sport and an individual effort. I had gone one-on-one with a more proficient athlete and succeeded in making him quit. It was addictive. I wanted more.

But some smart dead guy said, "Be careful what you wish for, you may get it." There was still two minutes left in the round and near the end of it, Jeff caught me in—you guessed it—an armbar.

When the timer sounded, I was definitely done. Fifteen minutes of grappling in a gi had absolutely smoked my bag.

A tradition at American Top Team was hand shaking. After the class bowed to Libo, everyone walked by and shook his hand, then shook the hands of every student that was senior to him. Since I was the new guy, I shook forty-plus hands while standing on shaky legs. I bowed to the mat before leaving it and ran a hand across two quickly forming rashes on my face from gi-burn.

"You did good," Ricardo said. "Keep the gi. Wear it when you train here again."

I can now say I was awarded a BJJ white belt by Ricardo Liborio.

As I walked toward the locker room I took a moment to look at a huge poster of Marcus Aurelio in the Pride ring; his arms are held high as an unconscious Takanori Gomi lies on the mat behind him. Though it paled in comparison, after the tapout I'd earned on Big Jeff, I knew how he felt, and I was another step closer to understanding the fighter as a person.

I'm only smiling on the outside. Ricardo Liborio and me after the BJJ class from hell.

ALL ARMY COMBATIVES TOURNAMENT:
THE FAVORITE, THE UNDERDOGS, THE GODFATHER AND THE SEAL

Americans play to win at all times. I wouldn't give a hoot and hell for a man who lost and laughed.

—General George S. Patton Jr.

"Let's walk down there and fuck them all."

It's the punch line to an old joke that advocates taking a bold attitude when staking a claim. Lieutenant Colonel Kevin Petit laughed like he was kidding when he said it, but he wasn't. His chances of winning the team competition weren't great, but like any good competitor he wanted to take home a trophy anyway. The punch line, told without the joke attached, was a rare flash of audacity from a normally reserved officer who'd been taught tact and discipline from his earliest days as a cadet.

When it comes to attitude, there is a fundamental difference between professional athletes and combat soldiers. Athletes get paid exorbitant amounts of money to do what seems like a privilege to the layman, so animosity toward an egotistical player who doesn't show thankfulness is par for the course. One only needs to compare the respect a reserved Tom Brady gets versus a loudmouth like Terrell Owens to recognize the detrimental effect cockiness has on a career in professional sports.

But combat soldiers are the opposite. An ego in battle is as necessary as crust on a pie for the most basic of reasons. If a U.S. Army paratrooper is going to strap a hundred pounds of gear to himself and jump out of a plane at 130 miles an hour, hit the ground, and kill every bad guy in sight, then he better be convinced that he's an indestructible Tyrannosaurus Rex walking the earth looking for tasty morsels of terrorist food. Self-confidence is crucial in modern warfare.

The post-9/11 nonlinear battlefield has changed the way we fight and, more important, who fights. In the war on terrorism, a soldier doesn't have to be a paratrooper, a Ranger, or a Green Beret to have an up-close and personal relationship with a jihadi. When a basic Humvee mechanic goes out into Baghdad to pick up a broken-down vehicle, he has to be a highly skilled combat soldier. He has to know that if bullets start flying, he is the best-trained, best-equipped, and best-motivated weapon on the battlefield. Far from being a bad thing, an ego during an ambush is the difference between going back to the Forward Operating Base and becoming pink mist.

With two combat tours under his belt, Lieutenant Colonel Petit had earned the right to be cocky, but he kept it in check. His surly side wanted to shout out, "Bring your best, motherfuckers!" but his reasonable side kept it buried, only to germinate under the surface. He walked a tightrope of emotion for several reasons. His Screaming Eagles Combatives Team was the underdog of the 2007 All-Army Combatives Tournament, a handicap that only slightly fazed them. The powerhouse Fort Bragg team was favored to repeat as champions and came in with a stronger group than last year. They had a full roster of fourteen fighters compared to only twelve that Petit could muster up, including one woman.

The problem was the war. As the Screaming Eagles Fight Club sat in Fort Benning, Georgia, preparing for the tournament, the entire 101st Airborne Division was deploying from Fort Campbell, Kentucky, to Iraq. The team was lucky. Most of them were from the Second (Strike) Brigade and were late in the deployment order. The First (Bastogne) Brigade and Third (Rakassan) Brigade had left the weeks prior to the tournament. But Second Brigade was the short stack at the poker table and got to deploy last, though it was still a close call. The tournament was being held on Saturday and Sunday, and the team had to deploy on Tuesday. Win or lose, they were on a plane to the giant sandbox just forty-eight hours after the trophies were handed out.

"This is a great thing, but in the end my focus is on beating al Qaeda, not Fort Bragg," Petit said, drinking a Corona on the Friday night before the competition. His coaches, Ze Mario Esfiha and John "The Saint" Renken, huddled around the brackets getting their first look at the fixtures. Their initial matchups looked good, despite the small pool of fighters they brought.

The dichotomy of the situation was etched all over Petit's forty-plus-year-old face. He had a team to lead to victory this weekend at Fort Benning and a battalion to lead into combat back at Fort Campbell. His focus was split. He didn't have anything to prove and could have blown off the tournament altogether in favor of predeployment preparation. But combatives represented a microcosm of what he hoped to accomplish with his own troops.

"It's the inoculation of fear," he said as his fighters debated their first bouts behind him. "Guys who constantly do dangerous things will eventually reach a point where their cup is full and they just can't do it anymore. In the nineties, the 'full line' was a quantifiable number. I think it was sixteen forcible entries through a hostile door before you were pulled out of the line. Infantrymen today go out on patrol at such a high frequency that they get saturated and become too worked up to be any good because they're too scared. It's inevitable. It happens to everyone. By getting into the ring, they can put off that saturation point a little. Combatives shows them that there's nothing to be afraid of. We gotta do something to get our troops tougher—softball ain't cutting it."

Asking Petit why he fought was a waste of time. Soldiers like him fight because it means the difference between life and death on the battlefield. An unprepared soldier is a dead one. Combatives, the preferred term for modern-day hand-to-hand, is a fallback in the event that a soldier's weapon jams, he can't get to it, or he is taken by surprise in a tight environment, such as a market or a house. All soldiers are required to train on combatives, and this tournament is their opportunity to showcase the competition side of what they've learned against each other. Unit pride is on the line. Most of them aren't UFC material, but they're just as desperate to prove their worth as any sport fighter trying to break into the big leagues.

That's what I was here to see. Overall, it was the same concept as MMA—unarmed combat between two competitors. But these fighters are trained with a different overall goal in mind: kill the enemy. In MMA, the fighters strive to submit or knock out the man standing opposite them. But in combat, the winner is usually walking away from a corpse.

In order to survive, the soldier must apply what he's learned in class and in training to the battlefield. But lethal force is not always the answer. Escalating the conflict from deterrence through takedown and submission is preferred if possible. If a soldier doesn't have to kill someone, he needs options and an adaptable, easy-to-learn system to apply them when the situation warrants.

Petit tossed his Corona bottle, burped, and rapped his old friend Matt Larsen on the back hard before leaving.

Larsen was the man who gave the soldier those options. A former Army Ranger, Larsen's place in history was sealed in stone in 1996 when LTC Stan McChrystal decided combatives were a good thing. McChrystal had hand-picked then Sergeant First Class Larsen to put together a program for the Second Ranger Battalion. That program blossomed into an Army-wide curriculum with Larsen at the helm. Eleven years later, the Modern Army Combatives Program (MACP) could claim over 500 lives saved from effective hand-to-hand training. It was a "train the trainer" system designed to teach soldiers the best methods for engaging with and defeating an enemy at very close range when a weapon couldn't be utilized. After completing the course at Fort Benning, graduates were qualified to go back to their units and train them in turn.

I always cringe when I hear an MMA fighter say, "When I go in the ring, it's war. It's kill or be killed." They don't realize how ludicrous the statement is to soldiers who have lived through the reality of that situation. Troops inhabit a world where perfection is the standard and hope is not a method. If they fuck up, someone dies, possibly themselves.

In this context, Larsen and his crew, all of whom he required to fight in MMA promotions, trained the Army. One wall of their shared common area was covered in pictures of them with various MMA fighters and Gracie family members. Occupying a spot of honor dead center on the wall was an autographed picture of "karate master" George Dillman knocking a man unconscious with a single touch. A handwritten (and misspelled) message accompanied the picture that said "Matt—You're waisting the Army's time by teaching ground fighting." Like the magazine clipping at Sityodtong, it was the joke of the office.

"I wonder what he'd think of us now," Larsen said, looking at it. He took pride in the fact that he'd interviewed soldiers and written After Action Reviews (AARs) almost every time there was a hand-to-hand engagement in combat. Learning from success and mistakes was one of the strengths of the U.S. Army, not just on the macro level of brigade and battalion tactics, but right down to the "Joe Snuffy in the field" individual level. Larsen's dedication to the constantly evolving world of martial arts was inspiring. He could tell you the histories and subtle nuances of every martial art out there. He was the Godfather of Army hand-to-hand combat and was singly responsible for the massive strides it had made in the age of MMA. And he was about to put on the biggest show of the year.

*   *   *   *   *

Fort Benning is the home of the infantry. For the millions of soldiers who have passed through its front gate, the memories of the "armpit of the earth" are usually associated with pain—and life-altering images. Sand Hill, The Darby Queen, McKenna Range, the thirty-four-foot towers, Victory Drive, and Camp Rogers are just a few.

On the morning of the first day of competition, at 0800 hours, the hundreds of competitors gathered bleary-eyed and caffeinated at the gym. Among them, "the favorite," Staff Sergeant Tim Kennedy, looked as unkempt as Shaggy, if not Scooby-Do. He was one of the "longhairs" of the Army, as members of his Special Forces unit were afforded relaxed grooming standards.

Fort Benning's main physical fitness center, named for the only Medal of Honor recipient during combat in Iraq, Sergeant First Class Paul R. Smith, is the grandest gym in the entire U.S. Army. A boxing-style ring was set up by Larsen's men in the center of the basketball courts and was flanked by four massive yellow-and-black grappling mats. There were enough bleacher seats for about 1,500 fans.

The field of athletes was vast. I'd seen a couple of large MMA gyms that were home to many fighters, but this was on a different scale. Over 200 soldiers from twenty-nine installations around the Army were in attendance.

Matt Larsen lays down the tournament rules. The Screaming Eagles are seated to the left.

From Guam to Germany to Korea to all points stateside, the tournament was a prestigious event for those who enjoyed competition of a combative nature, which included just about every G.I.

The Godfather explained the rules of round one, most of which went in two hundred ears and out two hundred more. Since the initial round was pure grappling based on scoring, the rules were critical, but not a single light heavyweight was listening—they were too busy sizing Kennedy up. He'd won this tournament the previous two years and they wanted what he had. Sensing many were gunning for him, his nerves started to show.

"I don't like it," he admitted. "I like being the underdog or the unknown like when I fought in the IFL. No one knew me there, but everyone knows me here."

Kennedy had fought twice as a replacement on the Chicago Red Bears team and had won both times. As such, he had no chance of going incognito. Beating him could put someone's name on a small list of who's who in military combatives, so he had a huge target on his back as well as a few cameras on his face. ESPN had passed up the chance to cover the tournament, leaving it to the ever-faithful Military Channel and Army Times as well as one writer representing *Real Fighter* magazine . . . that would be me.

Kennedy wasn't the best in the Army by luck. He'd trained with Chuck Liddell at John Hackleman's "Pit" in San Luis Obispo before life caught up with him. He graduated from Columbia University in New York City and enlisted in the Army after 9/11, going straight into the 18 X-Ray Special Forces program. He was one of those guys who was bound to succeed at whatever he did as long as he could keep his head out of his ass. But like all young men, it would eventually find its way up there at some point.

"I joined up because I was a stupid party head with no direction in life after college," Kennedy said. "I had two daughters born two weeks apart by two different women and didn't know what I was doing with myself. I knew I wanted to be in Special Forces, but it took a while for the 18 X-Ray program to get going."

Before 9/11, any soldier wanting to be in Special Forces had to complete an initial enlistment of about four years before he could even try out. Special Forces consisted of more mature soldiers with experience in the infantry or elsewhere, and kids straight off the street were seen as unfit for the types of missions they performed. But after 9/11, the Army couldn't afford to keep shutting candidates out because of their age and finally established the 18 X-Ray program so guys like Kennedy could enter the service and go straight into Special Forces training.

Beside Kennedy was his training partner from Fort Bragg, who made it very clear where his loyalties were. Anyone not absorbed in sizing up Kennedy was bemused by the blue sweatshirt next to him that had NAVY SEAL emblazoned across it in bright yellow letters, which stood out like Ozzy Osbourne at an AA meeting. It shouted, "Fuck you. Come get me" in no uncertain terms, so I expected the guy wearing it to be cocky.

But of course he wasn't. Like Petit, he was quiet, humble, and even shy. He was SO1 Dale Wooden, and he was the lone Navy representative in the tournament. The rules clearly stated, "Anyone assigned to an Army unit is eligible to compete," which Woody, as everyone called him, used to his advantage. He was assigned to the Army's Special Warfare School at Fort Bragg, North Carolina, as a medical instructor. He took second in last year's middleweight division; a disappointment he wished to avenge.

Kennedy and Woody stood listening to the Godfather give his rules briefing while the Screaming Eagles huddled together in the bleachers looking confident, hungry, and nauseous all at the same time. In the center of the group sat Captain Lauren Shaw like a little sister to eleven brothers, all warily watching over her. A former softball player educated at West Point, she claimed she needed the competition of MMA as a stress reliever after graduating and coming onto active duty. But there was a catch— Larsen believed in equal rights and wasn't about to change his rules for women just because they wanted to fight. Females could compete in the tournament, but they had to fight like men. The apprehension on Shaw's face was almost matched by the curiosity on everyone else's at her presence at an exclusively male event.

The rules brief was over. The months of anticipation were about to end. But the Godfather had one last word of warning.

"We have troops deploying in a few days," he said, raising his voice to wake up anyone zoning off. "Hurting someone only screws your buddy over. Don't make a stupid mistake and damage someone on purpose." Only here would a plea not to hurt someone during a fight be heeded.

Petit and his Screaming Eagles got their chance to make a good start with Corporal Travis Weiner in bout thirty-three. With a couple of quick takedowns, Weiner was up 8-0, but he couldn't capitalize once he got his opponent off his feet. Moments later he found himself mounted, making the score 8-6.

"His cardio is good. He'll be okay," Coach Renken said to reassure himself, since no one was within earshot but me. If the first bout was symbolic of the team's overall chances, their bid to beat Fort Bragg was already slipping away. But then "Oscar Meyer" Weiner took control and secured an armbar with twenty-three seconds left in the match. The Screaming Eagles were off to a good start. But minutes later the momentum stalled on the team's first head-to-head meeting with Fort Bragg.

Senior Airman Josh Landsburg was one of only a few Air Force contestants in the tournament. Like Woody he was allowed to compete because he was assigned to an Army unit at Fort Campbell. Landsburg was an ETAC (Enlisted Tactical Air Controller) whose main weapon on the battlefield was a radio. His unique ability in combat was to speak the language of Close Air Support (CAS) so troops in a fight had top cover from aircraft overhead. In his first match, Landsburg had top cover of his own in the form of Renken and Esfiha screaming instructions at him, even if he refused to listen.

"Secure the position, Josh!" they implored to no avail. Josh spent ten minutes dominating his opponent but failed to score a single point because he never stabilized a position. It's one thing to get a reverse, but another to hold on to the position for more than a second in order to show the judges it wasn't a fluke. Josh repeatedly got taken down and scored on, but always found a way out. But instead of gaining a dominant position and holding it long enough to score, he went for fight-ending submissions and ended up getting shut out 7-0. As time expired on Josh, a soldier from Fort Bragg raised his arm in triumph on the next mat after a convincing win. It was a double-whammy of bad omens for the Screaming Eagles.

But then the wins rolled in. For nine and a half minutes Lieutenant Colonel Petit, nearly the oldest competitor in the tournament, put on a grappling clinic before getting caught in an armbar. Ahead on points, the wily veteran spent an agonizing thirty seconds withstanding the pain as his coaches and team screamed at him to hold on until time expired. If motivation had a physical form, it was this performance from the old man. Not only were the points from the win significant, but the inspiration it provided his younger soldiers was indispensable.

"I felt my fingers getting tingly," he said as he stumbled toward the team's encampment area in the bleachers.

Then Weiner won again, followed by Private First Class Grover Gebhardt and Specialist Fourth Class Derek Lehman. Private Eric Geyer then submitted a soldier from Fort Hood with an armbar, giving the Eagles their fifth straight win and an air of hope that provided a little pep in their step and some pride in their stride. Geyer was a model of citizenry, even if it was for a slightly selfish reason. He enlisted in the National Guard outside of Fort Campbell specifically to be on the combatives team and come to this tournament. A competition is hardly a reason to devote three years of one's life to enlist, especially since the frequency of National Guard deployments had increased so dramatically since 9/11. I suspected Geyer had an ulterior motive to join up, but he wasn't letting on to what it was. Left to my own devices, I surmised that Geyer had a yearning to serve in something bigger than himself and felt a true loyalty to his country that demanded sacrifice.

Unfortunately, that's not a cool thing to admit among American youth, so he used the tournament as an excuse to join up.

On mat three, drama built to a fever pitch. Captain Lauren Shaw was ahead on points against her male opponent. Suddenly the small crowd, which had been quiet all morning, took interest. She was instantly the darling of the tournament and the crowd favorite. At least a hundred fans watched her every move, and twenty amateur coaches came out of the woodwork to shout instructions over Renken's.

When the buzzer signaled her victory, the crowd erupted. Shaw was near tears and wobbly as she picked up a slip of paper from the judges making her win official. She stumbled away from a riot of congratulations and was ushered in front of a camera for the biggest interview of her life. Unlike professional fighters who rehearsed this moment a hundred times in front of a bathroom mirror, Shaw was unsure and stumbled on her words, still lightheaded from the ordeal.

The overkill of attention was strange. She had more people behind her than anyone else, including the favorite, Tim Kennedy. Maybe it was the Cinderella factor—the denied, unprepossessing one taking the prize. A glass slipper might fit a woman's foot easier, but she was a soldier, like everyone else competing here. Did her gender make her that much more of a beloved underdog? Or did the crowd just want to see a guy get his ass beaten by a woman for the entertainment value?

I actually thought all the attention was counterproductive because it proved that she wasn't really considered an equal to the men. Tomboys like Shaw had fought hard for fair treatment both inside and outside the military. The crowd's disproportionate support for her was solely because she was different, which negated all the progress women had made in male-dominated environments. If she were truly seen as equal, golf claps and occasional looks from the bleachers would have been all the attention she got.

But the fans wanted to see her win, not because they adored Lauren Shaw as a person, but because she wasn't viewed as on a level playing field with the men. It could have been any woman against any man and the crowd would have gotten behind the woman like David taking on Goliath. Americans love an underdog, and the outpouring of support for Shaw proved she was seen as just that—an inferior. I'm sure some of the fans wanted to see her succeed because she'd worked hard and deserved a shot at victory. But I suspect that most just cheered because they wanted to see "the little train that could" climb a seemingly impossible mountain.

The Godfather watched the drama around Shaw with interest from his vantage point in the center of the mats. His fights didn't have to bring the crowd to the edge of their seats, but a little excitement always generated interest. Interest generated popularity. Popularity generated money, and money kept the program going. There was nothing wrong with a little drama, even in the usually staid Army with its distaste for anything trendy or flashy.

As Shaw took a seat in the Screaming Eagles encampment, First Sergeant Mike Lamkins was hopeful. "I think we're up on points," he said, looking over his chicken-scratch notebook. "We've had just as many bouts as the other teams and no one's scored more than we have." But there was still a long way to go.

As expected, the favorite breezed through the grappling rounds, dispensing his opponents in 41 seconds, 1 minute, and 2 minutes. After each win, sweaty and well-spoken, he was interviewed by The Military Channel. He was clearly in a different league than the average troop, but he was getting cautious, too. As the matches went on, he took more time to secure the win, not wanting to do something stupid and get bounced early.

The favorite, Tim Kennedy, gets interviewed after winning a match.

"I like to build a point lead before going for the kill," he said, lounging in a frumpy sweatshirt in the bleachers with his new wife of two weeks and his dad. "It may not be the way some people like to do it, but I just want to hedge my bets, you know?"

It was smart, no matter what anyone else thought. There was no need to go balls-out and rush into fights just to get caught in a submission because he was overconfident. He hadn't won this tournament twice by being reckless.

Although a member of the greatest fighting force on the planet, Kennedy got no love from the Army when it came to MMA. Fighting is commercial, something the Army has always taken pride in not being. The typical Army attitude is, "Civilians focus on profits. Soldiers focus on fighting." The two are completely different cultures, and even when it comes to unarmed combat, a shared interest, the Army and the private sector don't see eye to eye.

Although the Army Racing Team received $17 million in 2007 to plaster the black-and-gold ARMY across a slew of cars, reaching out to the NASCAR demographic and possible recruits, there is still resistance to MMA. If the Army were to sponsor a fight team, it would cost a fraction of the money the racing team received. What better way to recruit soldiers than having ARMY emblazoned across an up-and-coming fighter like Matt Horwich or Jake Shields. Even better, what if the Army sponsored a team taken from the ranks, like Staff Sergeant Tim Kennedy?

Kennedy leaned back and contemplated this possibility. "Could you imagine it?" he asked. "We spend millions to sponsor a racing team. Just one million could sponsor a champion fight team. Not even that. A half million could dramatically improve the lives of ten or fifteen people." In a perfect world, the most powerful fighting force would field the most powerful fighters in MMA.

Kennedy's friend, Woody the SEAL, also blew through his competition in the grappling round. It was a by-product of training with Kennedy that Woody readily admitted to. "My game has definitely improved since I started working with Tim," he said as Kennedy rolled his eyes, not wanting the credit.

"He doesn't need me," Kennedy replied. "He's good enough on his own."

Woody's fourth grappling win, which got him into the Pankration round, was by no submission I'd ever heard of.

"It was the weirdest thing. His toes got caught in my uniform," he said. "I leaned back and they cranked over and he tapped out. I wasn't sure what was going on for a second because I didn't think I had a submission hold on him, but he was tapping away. I hate winning that way. It kind of sucks for him, you know?"

Around the Paul R. Smith Fitness Center, the Godfather cruised the crowd and hobnobbed with the brass, his hands always on a cell phone or in his pockets. He only loosely controlled the action, letting his subordinates do the majority of the work. It was a testament to their steadfast reliability that Larsen could sit comfortably and chat, knowing that twenty NCOs were taking care of everything and demanding his time only when something was seriously awry. But even the most confident and relaxed of leaders never truly lets his guard down, and Larsen's eyes covertly glanced from mat to mat as we talked.

"I have to make better fighters," he said as the grappling bouts continued around us. "That's my number one goal. Everything we do is focused on making the average soldier a better fighter."

"Do you find yourself changing based on actual fights in the field?" I asked.

"Absolutely. I find out about most engagements. We do an After Action Review and see what we can apply to what we teach here. Evolutionary pressures are eventual on every art form."

"How do you mean?"

"Well, Sambo, for example, never allowed chokes in their competitions. They train on chokes, but since they're not allowed in competitions, their context is lost. If you can't choke a guy, then why would you take his back? If no one ever takes the back then you soon lose the ability to defend against it. That's why Sambo fighters in the early days of MMA fell victim to chokes from the back mount. But now that MMA has come along, they see that chokeholds work and they've changed."

I thought of Cesar Gracie and how he'd modified his family's Brazilian jiu jitsu by incorporating Sambo and leglocks. Attacking the legs was considered by most to be unmanly and was disdained in most BJJ competitions.

"Every martial art evolves," Larsen said, gesturing his hands as if they wrapped around a crystal ball. "Some will simply evolve away from combat reality. All the crazy martial arts that you see started out as ways to learn to fight. As the need for effectiveness went away, and let's face it there is very little need for the average McDojo to teach real fighting skills, evolutionary pressures changed them over time into the nonsense that we see today. We, at the dawn of a new fighting system, have to be smart enough to understand these pressures for what they are and make decisions based on that knowledge. Is there any doubt that boxing, wrestling, judo, karate, etcetera, all started out as ways to train fighters? What changed them over time into what they have become? Every decision made in their history affected their evolution."

He stole a quick glance toward one of the mats, checking up on his subordinates.

"You know, we get one or two examples every week of some soldier applying some classic submission technique on a bad guy. We had a soldier on a checkpoint in Iraq who had a man rush him. It was too late to go for his weapon so he resorted back to what he knew. He grabbed the man and applied a kimura and subdued him until he could get help. That's an example of applying what works. As warfare changes, we have to change as well and figure out what works and what doesn't."

Something that works for Larsen is discipline, as I witnessed firsthand. At the end of a grappling match, a soldier jumped up off the mat thinking he'd won. But upon gazing at the scoreboard and seeing he was down on points, he decided to take his angst out on the ref. "You got a lot to learn about scoring a match," I heard him shout, pointing a finger in the ref's face. There were a few other comments made as he exited the mat in a huff, but nothing like the ones he would receive from Larsen.

Within moments, he was ejected from the tournament and all the points he'd earned were erased from his team totals. He was out, and so was any record of him competing. It was as if he'd never been at Fort Benning that weekend. However disorderly the tournament appeared to the casual observer with fighters, coaches, and fans bustling about like a beehive, underneath there was quiet discipline and meticulous order. Here the Godfather's word was law.

In the front portion of the gym, the Family Readiness Group from the Second Battalion, Twenty-ninth Infantry Regiment was making money. Family Readiness Groups are organized groups of family members who stick together and provide each other support while their husbands or wives are deployed. These groups are an integral part of the Army, but since the Army can't use any official money to support them. FRGs get by solely on the funds they raise themselves. On this weekend, the 2-29 Infantry Battalion's FRG was raising a bunch. With no arena-style food stands or pricey vendors, a group of wives and family members set up a simple snack stand with dollar empanadas and dollar-fifty chili dogs that made a killing. Everything was made fresh by soldiers' wives and sold faster than Wal-Mart laptops on Black Friday, making them a pretty penny in the process.

Suddenly, the Screaming Eagles' good luck came to a screeching halt. Just as their wins came in bunches, their losses stacked up, and the team hit skid row. Lieutenant Leo Alvarez and Specialist Jeff Green tapped out. Gebhardt won again, but then Matthews tapped out and Shaw's bid for tournament darling was crushed when she was overpowered and submitted by armbar. Private Geyer gassed halfway through his match. I wasn't sure if

The glass slipper cracks when Captain Lauren Shaw loses.

it was his vitriol or his cardio, but one of them suddenly didn't show up.

If that wasn't enough, the most freakish occurrence happened next. Weiner and Ramsey, on adjacent mats, were choked unconscious at the same time by the same choke, a cross-collar. It was weirder than Marie DellaGrotte's birthday trick and stunned the crowd. Each one had to be revived, and both twitched worse than a nerve agent victim when they woke up.

On top of all that, the team suffered a fratricide, also known as friendly fire. Lieutenant Colonel Petit and Private First Class Gary Tate had won all of their matches, and because of the way the brackets were set up, they had to face off against each other. Ironically, Tate was a member of Petit's unit, the First Squadron of the Seventy-fifth Cavalry Regiment. The cavalry was unique in that they referred to themselves as squadrons and troops instead of battalions and companies like the rest of the Army. Known as the Widowmakers, 1-75 Cav was Second Brigade's Reconnaissance, Surveillance, Targeting and Acquisition (RSTA) unit, which was a lengthy Army term meaning, "guys who go out and find the bad guys so the brigade can kill them."

Since both are members of 1-75 Cav, the direct relationship of rank between Petit and Tate only added fuel to the fire for both, but it also presented an ethical question. If this were the second or third round of the tournament where strikes are legal, would Petit be okay with hitting his own soldier? Would it even be legal? The Uniform Code of Military Justice imposes severe penalties against officers who strike soldiers, and when the situation is reversed, prison time is imposed on troops who hit officers. The tournament circumnavigated the UCMJ by being an approved exhibition sporting event, but the moral question remained for the officers.

"Could you hit your own soldier?" I asked.

"Oh, sure," Petit said without hesitating. "That's the name of the game. He knows it. I know it. If he whips my ass, then good on him. If I do it to him, then he knew the risk."

There were obvious incentives for each one to win this bout. The private wanted to beat the old man so he could boast about how he took him down. The old man wanted to win so he didn't have to hear about how he lost to one of his troops for the next year in Iraq. The bragging rights of this match were huge, but in the bigger picture, it didn't really matter who won or lost. Either way, the Screaming Eagles were going to lose someone from the winner's bracket, which only hurt their chances of beating Fort Bragg. Since this was a double-elimination tournament, every soldier had two chances to get into the final four. There was a winner's bracket for those who stayed undefeated and a loser's bracket for those who lost one match. Lose two times and your weekend was over.

After ten minutes, Petit was sent to the loser's bracket by his own troop. Tate smoked the old man 21-0 and moved himself up the ladder while the Screaming Eagles' team leader was one loss away from retirement.

In one of the last grappling matches of the day, their glass slipper cracked. Captain Shaw had her arm cranked back in a painful kimura that she withstood for a full minute, rolling twice to get out of the submission. But no matter how tough she was, a tight kimura is still a tight kimura, and she reluctantly tapped out. "I didn't expect to get much further, to be honest," she said later, her shoulders slumped forward. "I mean I trained hard and hoped I could win more for the team, but I was realistic. I knew I had a mountain to climb."

But then there was hope. Specialist Derek Lehman won by a weird knee crank that accidentally injured his opponent's ankle and forced him to tap out. Petit and Ramsey won at the same time on adjacent mats. Despite being choked unconscious, Weiner came on strong and won two more bouts. Senior Airman Landsburg won a nail-biter by getting a takedown with ten seconds left to make the score 3-2. But Geyer's dreams ended in his fifth bout. He started off strong, taking a 4-0 lead, but couldn't secure a kneebar and reinjured his elbow, resulting in a lopsided loss.

"We got two still in the winner's bracket and five in the loser's bracket," the first sergeant said. "We might still be in it."

In the team's encampment, Geyer iced his elbow and threw on a raggedy baseball cap adorned with a worn American flag. "The rumor is we're close to first," he said, glancing at Shaw. "We're beaten up, but we're good, right, ma'am?"

She nodded, trying to show strength. She could play it off like her performance was par for the course, but she was a competitor of the highest nature. Her desire to succeed was the same driving force behind most dedicated athletes, and I could see the loss disrupted her very being.

Some people have a sincerely hard time adjusting to defeat; they get so totally absorbed in climbing toward a goal that they are unprepared for the fall when it happens. They're the ones whose standard is impeccable precision. They're also the ones who make great military leaders. If there's one walk of life that demands perfection, it's war.

Besides the weight of the world on Shaw's shoulders, the physical toll on the team was apparent. Each fighter had competed in at least three bouts, and those who were still in it had fought five times. And this was just the end of round one. The Pankration round, with hand and leg strikes, was still to come.

The medic station was busy and in short supply of ice. By my count, the tournament had suffered at least two twisted ankles, three banged up elbows, and two rib injuries. Several troops walked around with raspberried faces and ice-packed necks like a China Beach triage. The medical treatment was thorough and for good reason. TBI (Traumatic Brain Injury) was a real concern, and not because Larsen was afraid of someone receiving one. Most of the soldiers competing had at least one tour of combat and could have a lingering or undiagnosed brain injury. Having one aggravated by the stress of hand-to-hand combat was something the Godfather wouldn't risk, so there was a good reason for the robust medical staff on hand.

Around 3:00 p.m., the remaining competitors laced up shin guards and prepared for round two—Pankration. It is a Greek word meaning "all powers," and can be loosely translated to have the same meaning as the Brazilian phrase "vale tudo," or "anything goes."

Without skipping a beat from the grappling round, Kennedy earned a bye for his first Pankration fight and breezed through the second one, but not without a little controversy. Kennedy delivered a barrage of unanswered strikes to his opponent, prompting the referee to stop the match. But when the other fighter jumped to his feet, seemingly unfazed, the question of an early stoppage emerged. Was Kennedy getting a free ride because of his reputation?

His opponent was infuriated, and with good reason. He'd spent all day winning five grappling matches just to earn his shot at Kennedy, only to have it stopped when he was blitzkrieged into the loser's bracket. The stoppage probably saved the guy from the inevitable, but that didn't console his shattered dreams, which were dashed before he could even mark up the favorite's face with a decent shot.

At this point in the tournament, every match winner got a little camera time with The Military Channel, but only Kennedy got the sprinter treatment, with the crew running over at breakneck speed from the other side of the gym. If one electrical cord been in their path, someone would have found a microphone up their ass.

His father was proud. "We didn't want him to fight and tried to draw the line at making money off of it," Mike Kennedy said. "We told him we didn't want him to go pro, but what can you do? If he wants to fight, he wants to fight." He shrugged his shoulders and looked away like it was an argument he knew he would lose.

The issue of going pro or not was being exacerbated by a policy that had been enacted by Kennedy's chain of command. The policy barred special operations soldiers from competing in professional MMA bouts. Even while he was cruising through the tournament, a life-altering decision loomed in the future. He faced the possibility of having to choose between the two things he loved—the Army and MMA. "The funny thing is," his dad continued, "he likes being in Iraq as much as he likes being in the ring. If this memo is real, he's going to have a hard time deciding."

On mat number two there was trouble. Woody was losing his first Pankration match, and Kennedy ran from the bleachers to support him. Woody was as hard as woodpecker lips, but he took at least two closed-fist punches to the face and was having trouble breathing through his nose. He looked wild, and outmatched by his opponent from the Illinois National Guard, who was taller, skinnier, and definitely quicker. When the final buzzer sounded, there was no doubt the SEAL had tasted defeat.

As a disappointed Woody left the mat with Kennedy right behind, a Screaming Eagle took to it. Lehman

Woody the SEAL in the Pankration round.

walked confidently on as Tate took mat one next to him. Both Eagles slapped away at their opponents and earned much-needed victories for the Fort Campbell team. Moments later, Weiner and Josh Landsburg won slobberknockers on the same mats. Just like that, their spirits rose to new heights of anticipation. Maybe they could pull this thing out after all.

Unfortunately, Weiner had to fight almost immediately after winning. He was tired, and it showed when he lost to a soldier named Chino from Hawaii's Tripler Army Medical Center. Moments later, Landsburg also lost to a First Infantry Division soldier from Fort Riley, Kansas.

I couldn't help but wonder how Captain Lauren Shaw would have fared in this round had she advanced. Or how the crowd would have taken a man beating on a woman? Would the crowd have gotten behind her again, or would they ridicule her for getting beaten up in a man's sport? Would they have cringed when she took a shot to the face, or chalked it up as getting what she wanted? And how would her opponent have felt hitting a woman?

I wasn't surprised to hear the disappointment in her voice. "I'm more comfortable striking," she said. "I've boxed a lot and would rather be on my feet trading punches than grappling."

"You wanted to trade strikes with a man?"

"Sure," she said. "I'm here to fight. In the end, I don't want to be looked at differently, you know? We have to get past the stigma that girls are girls and boys are boys. Toughness doesn't have a gender."

Even if she wanted preferential treatment, the Godfather wouldn't have given it to her.

"A soldier is a soldier, man or woman," Larsen said. "If she wants to play, let her play, but we're not going to make any concessions for women."

"Do you think there will be a separate women's division in the future?" I asked.

"No. They're soldiers just like the rest and it took them years to get to that point of equality. If we created a separate women's division, it would negate all of that by saying, 'Look, they're different after all.'"

"What about the stigma of women getting hit by men?" I asked. "Is it appropriate or good for the service?"

"That's not for me to say. That's for some general or public relations expert to decide. I don't have to succumb to fan pressure. We're not under any TV contract and we don't need to bring in fans at the gates to survive like professional MMA promotions. We have to build better fighters, whatever their gender is. In the end, we don't believe in fair fights."

Near the end of the day, just as the brass showed up to see how things were progressing, a soldier took a bad cut over an eye. The gash bled profusely but he insisted on continuing. I wasn't sure if the colonels and sergeants major who were now watching were either upset at the bloody show or admired the kid for marching on.

On mat number 1, the master trainer from Fort Bragg also received a serious injury, but this time to the ribs. The veteran NCO writhed in pain while medics tended to him. I couldn't tell how badly he was hurt, but by his wailing and rolling around, it seemed severe. Seconds later he ran outside and puked.

And then there was controversy. On mat 3, halfway through his match with a cocky kid from Fort Riley, a sergeant first class from Fort Knox had had enough heckling from someone in the crowd and lost his temper. In a display of brute strength combined with a mental lapse in judgment, he picked up his opponent and tossed him into the third row at the heckler. The Godfather and his cadre were on the spot immediately to avoid any further escalation of the conflict and to disqualify the Fort Knox soldier.

"Tempers flare sometimes," Larsen said. "It's like the biggest internal dojo tournament in the world, so guys get emotional. There's a lot riding on it, after all."

On mat 4, Woody was back up. Unfortunately, he was in the consolation bracket, and from the looks of things, that fact damaged his ego. He was flat, showing little of the fire he'd displayed all day. But there were extenuating circumstances, too. Besides the fact that it was his sixth fight of the day, he was facing a teammate from Fort Bragg. For several minutes, the fight, which could only loosely be called that, ebbed back and forth between the two like walruses wrangling over a dead fish. Finally the bell sounded and a decision was reached. Woody raised his hand in unconvincing triumph, earning a shot in the finals for third place. The favorite, normally by his side to support him, was strangely absent for this fight.

"I couldn't watch," Kennedy admitted later. "They're both my teammates, so it was hard. I couldn't take a side." I had thought the inability to take a side was reserved only for Swiss delegates, but apparently even Army Green Berets find an occasion to stay neutral.

The first day of fighting was over. The Screaming Eagles huddled together and took a tally of their position. They had four soldiers still in the competition. Gebhardt was in the 145-pound consolation fight and Lehman made it to the light heavyweight consolation match. Tate, the man who beat Petit, was in the middleweight final, and Specialist Dustin Portillo had advanced to the 145-pound championship.

"We're in third," First Sergeant Lamkins said woefully.

"Hey, that's all right," Coach John Renken replied. "I'm proud of all of you. Here's what we're going to do. We're going to lick our wounds at TGI Friday's. If you're done, you can drink. If not, drink water."

"How do you feel now?" I asked Petit as they headed to their van.

"Fine," he responded in a hollow voice. "I'm okay with it. I didn't think we could catch Bragg. They brought a huge team and have so many good athletes. It would have been nice, but . . ." He shrugged his shoulders as he walked away with his team. Barring an act of God, the glass slipper was broken.

While the Screaming Eagles went to eat, I found a sushi bar called Mikata near the Columbus airport. Being in Georgia, I expected catfish scooped out of the Chattahoochee River served over a bed of peach fuzz and pond scum. Instead, I was pleasantly surprised by the Volcano Roll and Baked Scallop Cali Roll that featured hot scallops served over a cold California Roll. It was creative and tasty and I was amazed to actually hear myself compliment a sushi chef in rural Georgia for his originality and flavorful concoction.

* * * * *

The next day I drove to the Smith Fitness Center through Harmony Church and past the quarters of the Dwight D. Eisenhower family when he was a simple major. Near the gym stood the Infantry's "Follow Me" statue just a stone's throw from the Ranger Memorial. Everywhere I looked was Georgia pine and red clay—and a dead armadillo who thought himself invincible. There were more trucks than cars, which made sense since trucks in these parts were used for everythin', including huntin' and tailgatin'.

The first match was set to start at 1300 hours. By 1230, the stands were nearly full. I walked around the prep area to see how everyone was feeling.

"Everyone has a plan until they get punched in the face," one of Larsen's instructors said as he walked through the warm-up area, which was separated from the main arena by a huge curtain. If he was trying to get under their skin it probably worked. I'd seen professional fighters get worked up over a bout, but this was a new dynamic. These guys wanted to win for more than personal glory. They wanted to represent their units and their installations. They wanted to win it for the Eighty-second Airborne Division and Fort Bragg, not for Joe Schmoe the Paratrooper.

The rules for the day's matches were the unified rules of MMA. There would be two fights in each weight class—a consolation fight for third place and one for the championship.

The Screaming Eagles were confident. They might not be able to catch Fort Bragg, but they could make a statement with the four they had left in the competition. Lieutenant Colonel Petit sat ringside as his first combatant

Matt Larsen referees one of the final bouts.

202

of the day, Private First Class Grover Gebhardt, strode to the ring. He didn't have the dramatic smoke and lights of the IFL or even the red-light walkway of Sportfight, but he had the support of 16,000 soldiers of the 101st Airborne Division behind him, something neither of those venues could provide.

Of course, his opponent had the same, in spades. Private Brandon Sandefur was from Fort Hood, Texas, one of the largest installations in the world. Both men entered the ring bare of sponsors, their shorts having only the word ARMY on the lower left thigh.

Gebhardt came out hard in the first round, but was soon on his back and in trouble. He was able to keep Sandefur in his guard and even attempted an armbar, but it's hard to win a round when you spend the whole time on your back. In the second round Gebhardt's woes went from bad to worse. Sandefur mounted him and bounced his head off the canvas with repeated blows until the fight was stopped. It was a bad start.

With a 5-1 record in the tournament, Woody the SEAL had earned a spot in the 185-pound consolation fight. But he was up against a pit bull in the form of Private First Class Marquez Staton from Fort Riley, Kansas. Staton had brutalized several opponents on his way to this fight and was anything but a pushover. With Kennedy in his corner, Woody looked confident as he removed his shirt and revealed a plethora of tattoos. One was a caduceus with a broadsword running through it that was symbolic of his profession as a combat medic. "If I can fix you, then I can hurt you, and if I can hurt you, then I can fix you," he told me later. "I'm thankful to have the ability to do both or neither."

Staton came out firing bombs as expected, backing Woody into a corner. But the SEAL maintained his cool, and halfway through the first round landed a huge uppercut that rocked his opponent. Staton's knees buckled and his arms dropped, enabling Woody to land more shots that ended the fight. He was disappointed at not taking first place, but at the same time, I suspected that beating the crap out of so many Army soldiers was not without rewards for a Navy SEAL.

Lanky Specialist Derek Lehman was the second of the four Screaming Eagles still in the competition. He'd done well, blowing through most of his fights in the light heavyweight division behind a flexible physique and sizable reach advantage. But there's always a trade-off when everyone is required to weigh the same amount. Lehman was tall and thin, while his opponent was shorter and had considerably more muscle mass. Early in the first round Derek found himself on his back underneath the full mount of Staff Sergeant Benjamin Bradley from Fort Gordon, Georgia.

Lehman did well defending himself against Bradley's peppering punches and even avoided a good omoplata attempt. But Bradley was slick, and when the omoplata didn't work he transitioned quickly into an armbar that Lehman had no way out of. He tapped out, crushing any chances the Screaming Eagles had of moving up in the team standings.

Two Eagles were out. Two to go.

Specialist Dustin Portillo was their next chance to get the honor of waving their unit colors around the ring, but Private First Class Matthew Bray from Fort Riley put an end to their quest almost immediately. He caught Portillo in an Americana (similar to a kimura) and cranked it down.

"Hold on, Dustin!" Renken implored from his corner, but the submission was tight. Portillo had no choice but to tap out or risk breaking his arm.

"I'll get you next year," Portillo said to Bray as he walked away from the ring. Suddenly, not only were their chances of moving up in the standings dashed, but their hold on third place was slipping away, too. Staff Sergeant Marcos Gutierrez took third in the welterweight division and Sergeant Aaron Cooper delivered a ton of punishment to win the middleweight division. Both men were from Fort Benning, which meant their team points were racking up. Out of nowhere, they were on Fort Campbell's heels, with only one hope left for the Screaming Eagles.

Private First Class Gary Tate, the kid who had beat the old man, was all that remained. He was up against Staff Sergeant Jacob South from Fort Knox, Kentucky. Immediately he ran into trouble. Tate took South down and attempted to maneuver for position from his guard, but when he raised up too high, South swung a leg over his head and found a perfectly aligned triangle choke looking at him like a present under his Christmas tree. Tate struggled to get free, but he was a bull being strangled by a giant anaconda. He tapped, and out of disgust, threw his mouthpiece onto the canvas as Renken tried to console him. The last Screaming Eagle was grounded. To add insult to injury, the local Fort Benning team had made enough points in the finals to tie them for third place. They couldn't even enjoy their team trophy to themselves.

Two fights remained, but the crowd knew how uncompetitive they were and almost dismissed them completely. If it weren't for the sheer curiosity of seeing Kennedy work his mojo, they would have left. Kennedy was up against his own teammate from Fort Bragg, First Lieutenant Carpaccio Owens, in the finals. It was a drubbing, but Kennedy seemed to be in practice mode. After getting on top of Owens, instead of raining down massive blows from the dominant position like every fighter is taught to do, he let Owens roll over. Kennedy took Owens's back and choked him out without putting hardly a bruise on his teammate.

"I let him off easy," Kennedy admitted later. "Normally I'd pound someone out when I get the mount, but I didn't want to hurt the guy. I respect him too much."

With that, the tournament was over and along with it everyone's reprieve from the war.

"Is this all about saving lives?" I asked the Godfather of Army combatives as the crowd filtered out. "Is your work all about ensuring soldiers survive?"

"In the end, it's about victory. We have to keep evolving and learning and never let ourselves get to the point where fighting back is not considered an option."

That was another similarity between MMA and the Army. The Army spent an inordinate amount of time studying the enemy and developing ways of defeating him on the battlefield. Say what you want about the war on terrorism, but I can verify that the Army was doing everything possible to get inside the mind of the terrorist and come up with ways to find and kill them. It's a process that consists of three basic tenets: know yourself, know the enemy, know the terrain.

MMA fighters were no different. They spent days and weeks getting to know the strengths and weaknesses of themselves and their opponents and coming up with a game plan to defeat them either in a ring or Octagon under a predetermined set of rules. The goal is no different, though the means may vary.

As the chairs were folded and the floors swept, four skinny privates fresh out of basic training approached Woody like he was Bruce Springsteen.

"Could you sign our shirts, sir?" one asked. He was wearing a plain white T-shirt that was covered in signatures from most of the tournament's winners. I was surprised to see these pimply-faced kids with their heads still shaved asking for an autograph from a Navy petty officer. Here were four kids whose heroes weren't rock stars or cinema legends, but ordinary men who displayed the courage to get into the ring and win. That's why MMA is so big among young soldiers. The generation gap between the older officers and the younger troops was never so wide.

After taking a few pictures with the privates in various submission poses, Woody grabbed his gear and prepared to leave with Kennedy. The favorite had fulfilled his expectation, but the possibility of him defending his title next year was in doubt.

"I'm a staff sergeant with two daughters to support," he said, packing his gym bag. "I love the Army, but if I can make as much in one fight as I can in six months on the job, then why shouldn't I?" Though some might criticize him for being materialistic, it couldn't be said that he didn't do his duty to his country, so I doubt anyone would really fault him for leaving the Army honorably in order to pursue a better life for his family. If anyone was to blame for Tim Kennedy choosing money over duty, it was an overindulged country that would rather pay him more to fight in a ring than fight its adversaries on foreign shores.

"My days of winning this tournament are numbered anyway," he said. "These guys coming up are so talented. They're going to be winning it all soon, and no one will remember me."

I doubted that. So did Matt Larsen.

The Godfather felt for Kennedy, but not just because he knew of the emotional struggle that lay before him. Larsen knew how important it was for the Army to have a combatives champion who was on par with professional MMA fighters. It was the Army, after all. There was a certain amount of pressure to be the best at all forms of warfare, whether it was at maximum weapons range or close quarters.

"Tim's exactly the kind of champion we need," Larsen said as the fitness center quickly emptied. "He's the kind of guy who will get the public to see how hard we're working to make better fighters. But he's going to become a victim of circumstance if he has to choose, and it's all because of the generation gap we have now."

I smirked, knowing what he meant. "Generation gap?" I asked, wanting to hear his take on it.

"The brass don't get MMA. They're not in tune with what the troops are doing these days. You know, we had Matt Hughes out here training troops and when we asked who had heard of him, all the soldiers raised their hands, but not a single officer did. They don't know how important it is to the younger troops. That would certainly change if the Army leadership consisted of officers like Lieutenant Colonel Petit. "Combatives makes everyone feel like killers," he said as his team headed toward the front door. "Support soldiers, like truck drivers and supply clerks, get to get in the ring and tee off on each other. That's what they joined the Army for. Plus it's important that they learn to deal with their fear here instead of after crossing the LD [line of departure]."

"Walk down and fuck them all?" I asked.

"That's right, brother." He smiled and left. In forty-eight hours he'd be on a plane to Iraq—again.

The joke goes like this: A bull and his son are sitting on a hilltop watching a herd of cows.

The son says, "Dad, let's run down there and fuck one of those cows."

The father replies, "No, son. Let's walk down and fuck them all."

VEGAS BABY!

"But the bravest are surely those who have the clearest vision of what is before them, glory and danger alike, and yet notwithstanding go out to meet it."

-Thucydides, *400 B.C.*

It's called Sin City for a reason. The Strip is an American symphony of sensory overload, with all the opulence and narcissism of a Hollywood version of ancient Rome. People from all over the world make pilgrimages here to lose their moral compass in the desert, hoping whatever happens in Vegas stays in Vegas. Usually, it's just their money that stays. In a world of fleeting pleasure, attention deficit disorder, and instant gratification, Vegas is where one comes undone. Its mundane events are on-the-spot weddings, and monumental heat-of-the-moment mistakes, which often are the same thing. It's where naïveté stole the cat's virginity before curiosity killed it. Enough said. You've probably seen it all firsthand, and if not, there's no way I could hope to do it justice without going off on a Hunter Thompson bender that has nothing to do with fighting. Just know that if you never make it here, you will have lived an incomplete life.

When I stepped out of my cab at the front door of the Mandalay Bay Hotel and Casino, the first thing that struck me was Wanderlei Silva—at least his name did. It was at the bottom of a massive red-and-black carpet that stretched across the front of the entryway along with LIDELL, HUGHES, and ST. PIERRE in big, white letters. It was December 26, the day after the Son of God's birthday, but the hype machine was whirring with a different event. Capitalism doesn't take a vacation, especially when the country is in a giving mood.

The Mandalay Bay's size makes it easy to get lost in, which isn't by accident. If poor, hapless souls get turned around on their way to the lobby and drop a wad of cash on a craps table before they get a chance to check in, then the casino deities are appeased. The multitude of restaurants, bars, shops, ATMs, card tables, and slot machines are positioned to suck the money out of your wallet as you transitioned from point A to point B. It isn't as if the Mandalay Bay monstrosity is unique, either. Massive casinos just like it line Las Vegas Boulevard.

The crowds were huge. I wondered where so many people with disposable income came from. It was only one day after Christmas and all across the country, ordinary people were returning ugly socks and oversized sweaters while spending time reminiscing with long-begotten family. Yet Las Vegas was packed. Then again, I had no room to criticize. I was there too.

I'd spent a great amount of time in the valley of the fighter, so it was time to get a view of MMA from the mountaintop. I was here to see the big time, the show, the penultimate moment in MMA, and its wizard behind the curtain. The UFC, the world's largest MMA promotion, has a tradition of showcasing major fights with their marquee names at the end-of-year event in Las Vegas. This year looked to be no different, with the biggest names in the sport on one card.

Here is where the thousands of fighters in rings and cages across the country spend hour after hour sweating and bleeding to get to. All who wish to compete in the Octagon turn toward Las Vegas and pray in the general direction of the Mandalay Bay five times a day. I was lucky. I had gotten an assignment to photograph the event for *Real Fighter* magazine, so I had the luxury of a press credential, which got me into the media room and all media events. I was hoping I could use it to gain decent access to the headliners and get a view of what it's like to be the focus of so much attention. Of course, it wasn't that easy.

I dropped my bags in my room and headed for a prefight press conference and luncheon in the media center underneath the main stands in the Mandalay Bay Events Center, which practically required a GPS to find. It was supposed to start at 2:00, so I was concerned I'd be late when I showed up at 1:55. But we're talking about fighters, so when I found the room nearly empty, I wasn't shocked. Thankfully the lunch buffet was decent and I dug in like a coal miner.

"There was a time when the UFC couldn't drag enough people out here to see this," a scraggly old photographer said as I flopped into a chair next to him with a mountain of food. "Now everybody wants to be here."

"Vemmppfffagaffflddee?" I asked beef-and-rice-fully.

"What?"

I took a moment to swallow. "Then where is everybody?"

"The headliners are back in their own rooms," he said, pointing down a hallway. "They'll come out after everyone eats, and then it'll get started."

I looked down the hallway and spotted Georges St. Pierre disappearing into a room with five guys from his training camp, including Greg Jackson. Georges, or GSP as everyone called him because they were too lazy to pronounce four syllables instead of three, was fighting the most dominating welterweight in MMA history, Matt Hughes, in the main event. The two had fought twice before, with each man winning once. This was the rubber match, the last in the series. The winner would walk away with a title—sort of. The fight was originally supposed to pit Matt Hughes against Matt Serra, the reigning welterweight champion. But Serra got injured during training and was forced to pull out of the fight, leaving the door wide open for GSP to step in. Dana White, the crafty businessman, recognized the significance of it and made it a title fight for the "interim" welterweight title instead of a regular fight. This meant it would last five rounds instead of three, since that's standard for a championship match, and the winner would get an instant title shot at Serra to unify the belts.

But as significant as the Hughes-GSP fight was, it was the other fight everyone was really here to see—a battle of Old Testament proportions that had been in the making for six years. Wanderlei "The Axe Murderer" Silva had been the immovable object in Pride Fighting Championships, where he beat up everyone from Goliath to his own mother in the ring. His aggressive and violent style scared the beejesus out of everyone and earned him a feverish fan base.

While Wanderlei was conquering Asia like Genghis Khan, Chuck Liddell had been building his own kingdom in the Octagon. In early 2007, Liddell had amassed a 20-3 professional record just as Dana White was buying Pride and salivating at the prospect of putting The Iceman up against

The Axe Murderer. For business reasons, the fight didn't happen, and both men lost twice in a row, putting the monumental confrontation on the back burner of White's master plan. But now it was on, and everyone was ready to see it. It was billed as the fight of the year between two extremely adept and exciting strikers, and it posed for the UFC the challenge of living up to its own hype.

Just as the old photog had predicted, the press arrived and, demolished the buffet, and then the fighters emerged to talk. Dana White appeared and introduced them one by one, giving each a chance to say a few words from behind the podium. The headliners were old hands at this and knew how to work the mic. They gave brief, rehearsed lines thanking the UFC for the opportunity and talking about their training, and then they made predictions.

"I will knock out you on Saturday. You're going to see," Silva said to Liddell.

"I promise you, like I said before, I'm gonna knock you out," Chuck returned to Wanderlei. I couldn't resist the opportunity to be a smart ass. "That's what LL Cool J's momma said, too," I told the old guy.

To which the look on his face replied, "El who?"

"I'm not the guy out there chasing paychecks. I'm the guy out there wanting to scrap," Matt Hughes said.

"I hope it's going to be a great show and I'm ready for a war," GSP said.

It was all very civilized. The conference broke down into questions about the headliners' conditioning and mental state, but only one comment really caught my ear. GSP, who classed the place up by being the only guy to wear a collared shirt, was asked why he wasn't smiling.

"I'll be nervous Saturday," he said. "Right now I just chill. I just came off the best training camp of my life. I was training for the Olympics. I took this fight because I'm a MMA fighter. It's more important to be the UFC champion than being in the Olympics."

My head reeled backward like he'd just punched me. Really? I thought. You would rather fight for the UFC than represent your country in the pinnacle of sports competition?

I was in shock. I had read that GSP was a talented wrestler and

Greg Jackson gives an interview before UFC 79.

was considered a shoo-in for the Canadian Olympic team, which was a remarkable achievement for a guy who hadn't wrestled growing up. I had a hard time believing that a UFC belt was more important than an Olympic gold medal; maybe because I'm a military man who places duty to his country above all other priorities. I had thought I was on the verge of understanding the fighter's mind, but GSP blew my perceptions out of the water. Either he was making a lot of money from this fight or he had no patriotism at all, but either way I thought his priorities were all wrong.

In the corners of the media room were life-sized cardboard cutouts of each man in menacing poses. As the conference broke up and the buffet ran dry, I noticed a scruffy half-bearded man being interviewed in front of GSP's poster. It was Greg Jackson.

Since I'd left Albuquerque, Jackson's fighters had been tearing through MMA. Duane Ludwig, Julie Kedzie, Rashad Evans, and Joey Villasenor had all posted victories, and Keith Jardine had defeated Chuck Liddell in an upset victory just a few months prior. With GSP joining Greg's gym, he was getting a major league dose of the hype machine's love in the media room, not his first, by any means. When his interview was done, I chatted with him for a few minutes, but it cost me. While I wasn't looking, GSP snuck out.

"Dammit," I said as I caught a glimpse of his back disappearing out the door.

"What?" Greg said.

"I wanted to ask Georges a few questions. Can you get me some time with him?"

His face contorted and I knew the answer before he said it. "I don't know. He's very private right before a fight, but I'll see," Greg said. "You can hang out with me all you like, though." Flattering, but I didn't want to get in the way, especially on the eve of such a massive event. The last thing I wanted was for GSP to lose because his trainer was spending too much time with a nosy Army guy.

"I'll catch up with you later," I said.

Outside the media center, I ran into Dean Lister. His nickname was the Boogeyman because once when his opponent got hurt the day of a fight, the promoter went through a Rolodex of alternate fighters, and none of them stepped up to the plate. His trainer commented that he must have scared them all away like the Boogeyman and the nickname stuck. His weight cutting wasn't going as well as he wanted, so the Boogeyman wasn't in the best mood.

"How far do you have to go?" I asked.

"Sixteen pounds," he responded.

"Sixteen pounds? Are you going to make it?"

"Oh, yeah," he said. "I'll get there."

The constant ups and down of weight gain and loss must have a long-term effect on the body that hasn't yet been discovered. I'm sure researchers will link it to cancer, diabetes, or persistent hemorrhoids one day. He was going to lose sixteen pounds in twenty-four hours. I needed comfort food just thinking about it.

In the middle of the casino was J-Pop sushi, an expensive sushi bar equitably crowded with slot-machine losers and well-to-do high rollers (also losers). The Mandalay Bay roll was decent, but not worth the $18 price. There was a pattern here—don't eat sushi named after the place where you are. The South Beach roll in Miami and now the Mandalay Bay roll in the Mandalay Bay Hotel sucked. By that logic, a California roll anywhere but California was okay, and since I was in Vegas I got one and chased it with a Sapporo beer. The tab was fifty bucks and I left unsatisfied.

Typical Vegas.

*   *   *   *   *

It was the day before the fight and nothing was happening until the weigh-ins at 3:00. I had heard most fighters go to the arena to step on the scale early to gauge where their weight is, so I headed downstairs to check it out. On one end of the arena was a massive black curtain that hid three-quarters of the venue behind it. In front of it was a small stage occupied only by a lone scale. No fighters were in the arena, and the media center was likewise deserted. But I spotted a room marked with an interesting sign, "THQ Filming." I poked my head inside.

"How are you?" a tall, thin guy in a black shirt said.

"Uh, fine. And you?"

"Good. I'm William. I'm the project manager." William was in charge of the coolest project in the entire world! THQ was developing a video game based on the UFC and were in the media center to film fighters with those high-tech ping pong balls on them in front of a green screen. William showed me a minute-long sample of the game that pitted Chuck Liddell against Quinton "Rampage" Jackson that was, in video gamer speak, sick! It was uncanny how real the action was.

"How many people does it take to make this?" I asked.

"We have seventy just writing the software itself," William answered. "There was a UFC game a few years ago, but it didn't do well because the market just wasn't ready for it. Now the UFC is huge, and the market is ready."

THQ, like the comic books of the twentieth century, was making ordinary men into superheroes, giving them extraordinary talents and knockout artwork. William said Rampage was scheduled to come in for filming, so I decided the THQ room was the place to hang out for the day. Unfortunately, Rampage's manager had other ideas, and his filming didn't happen. Boredom set in and I wandered back out toward the arena, but before I got there an entourage, moving together like a school of fish, blocked the way.

It was Wanderlei Silva and his camp. He was going to step on the scale.

Suddenly, GSP and his own entourage (minus Greg Jackson) emerged from the arena, and the two camps met. GSP and Wanderlei shook hands and nodded politely as they passed. Then GSP and two of his guys walked straight toward me. As they approached, I made sure my press credential badge was clear so he didn't think I was a hack or a stalker.

"Georges, you got a minute?"

"No. I am going to cut weight," he said, not even slowing his stride.

"Uh, okay," I stammered. "Good luck with that," I said, like a complete idiot. Good luck with that? I thought. What are you, a teenage girl waiting to get a glimpse of Leif Garrett? I wandered back into the media center, reassembling my dignity, when I ran into ANDERSON SILVA!!

I stopped in my tracks as the UFC middleweight champion passed in front of me in a velvet beige sweat suit. He was there to give THQ his time and graciously did so for almost thirty minutes. I watched from a corner as they took hundreds of photos from every angle possible while his interpreter translated requests: "show me happy," "angry," "sad," "excited," "throw a punch at the camera," "what do you want for lunch?" Silva shook hands, thanked everybody, and left. I wandered back out to the scales to see if I could catch another fighter. Instead I found a lawyer.

"Let me see your shorts sometime today," a guy in a suit told Bulgarian fighter Jordan Radev.

"What for?" I asked as I walked up reflecting the stadium lighting into his face with my oversized press badge. He gave me the once over before deciding I was okay.

"Sponsorship rules. Their shorts have to be in accordance with our guidelines." His name was Mike Mersh, the UFC's lawyer.

"What guidelines are those?" I asked.

"Well, they can't have certain things on their shorts, like alcohol, pornography, tobacco, the names of nightclubs, that kind of thing."

"What else is there?" I asked. "You've taken all the fun stuff away."

He laughed. "They can have their own sponsors as long as it isn't one of those or a competing sponsor."

"A competing sponsor?"

"Yeah. We have official sponsors, like Toyo Tires, Mickey's, Xyience—they can't be competitors of those companies or another casino, because the owners of the UFC also own Station Casinos."

"Do they get reported to Homeland Security?"

He smiled the way a lawyer does before he whips out some big words and starts speaking Latin.

I thanked Mersh and ran down Dean Lister, the Boogeyman, whom I spotted leaving the arena.

"How many pounds now?" I asked.

"Seven."

"In three hours? You gonna make it?" I asked.

"Yeah. Shouldn't be a problem. It's all water," he said.

I wandered around a little more, all the while expecting security to hustle me out by the elbows before I could flash my badge. The massive black curtain that hid the rest of the arena from the stands also drew the curiosity of the nosy. Feeling like Dorothy in The Wizard of Oz, I walked over to peek behind it.

On the other side lay the symbol, the very figure of big time MMA— the Octagon. It was the ultimate shark tank in all its glory. I can't say a beam of light shone down on it from the heavens or a chorus of angels sang in my head, but it was a beautiful sight. I hesitated, then stepped past

Chuck Liddell cuts weight.

the curtain. I would have run around the cage with my arms held high, pretending the crowd roared as Bruce Buffer called out my name through thundering megawatt speakers, except for two problems—a hundred arena workers and Chuck Liddell.

At first I didn't notice him. He ran around the empty floor of the arena in sweats that covered his face. The workers still hadn't put the floor seats out, so all around the Octagon was open space—perfect for breaking a sweat. His training partner, Antonio Banuelos, ran sprints nearby.

Now this is real backstage access, I thought as I watched the pair get their heart rates up. A thin wire ran from underneath his hoodie to his ears and he sang what I think was something by Rage Against the Machine, oblivious to anyone around him. I watched for a while then returned to the other side of the curtain to wait for the official weigh-ins, satisfied that I got to see something few others did.

The crowd came early, the most ardent of supporters getting the first few rows where they could reach out and touch their favorite fighters. To keep the crowd entertained, Anderson Silva, along with a translator, answered questions from fans for about an hour. The youthful crowd made me glad I wore a baseball cap to cover my balding head. I didn't see a single fan over forty. Only time would tell if this meant MMA would have a lifelong fan base and eventually become the sport parents told their kids about.

The fighters filed in, and all disappeared behind the giant curtain of doom with their trainers. The first man was supposed to be on the scales by 3:00, so at 3:30, the dalliance was bringing the crowd close to prison-riot mode. On several giant TV screens, a "Countdown to UFC 79" video rolled to keep them pacified. Suddenly someone threw open the curtain and I could see Greg Jackson sitting in the stands with Julie Kedzie.

I remembered how he'd said I could hang out with him all I wanted to. My badge got me through and I quickly headed over to sit with them.

"What's the hold-up?" I asked.

"Medical checks, paperwork, you know," he responded.

I didn't, but nodded anyway. About a hundred feet away, I picked out GSP getting poked and prodded by medical personnel—definitely not a good time for an interview. I had Greg though.

"Is all this attention a distraction?" I asked. "I mean, does it make it hard to concentrate on the fight itself when so many people want to talk to you and take pictures and such?"

"It is, but it's necessary, too. I mean, we wouldn't be here if it weren't for the fans. They're the ones paying their money to see more of us, you know? Would I rather just concentrate on fighting, yeah, but I like hanging out with people, too."

We sat there for another ten minutes, during which I asked Julie Kedzie what she thought about women fighting against men in the Army tournament. "It sounds like it's good for them," she said. "But I don't think it would be good for professional MMA."

Finally the first fighters made their way to the scales and I left to take some pictures. One by one, the athletes came out and got on the scale while Joe Rogan introduced them and called off their official weights. Dean Lister, who was seven pounds heavy just a few hours before, had to endure the Bartimus torture of getting naked behind a skimpy towel. Only this time there weren't two hundred people watching—there were two thousand!

"One hundred eighty-five pounds!" Joe Rogan announced as Dean tried to find his underwear. After each pair of fighters weighed in, it was time for one of the most entertaining features of MMA—the stare-down.

The stare-downs are actually a critical element of the fight. It's an opportunity for a fighter to get into his opponent's head. Sometimes it works; sometimes it doesn't. For the most part, the undercard fighters just posed, smiled, shook hands, and exited the stage. But James Irvin had a message to send to his opponent, Luis Cane. Irvin made it clear he meant business and got in Cane's face for a few seconds.

But the true bad blood of the evening was between Melvin Guillard and Rich Clementi. They'd been in a street fight, and the animosity between them was palpable, with Guillard being the clear instigator. He weighed in and approached Clementi with a few choice words at close range before the two had to be separated. The crowd loved it. I suspect that 95 percent of the time MMA fans appreciate a gentlemanly handshake, but the other 5 percent of the time they want to see a good old-fashioned grudge match. As much as I prefer the gentlemanly approach of a Randy Couture, I have to admit that I was suddenly more interested in the bad-blood matchup.

Chuck Liddell and Wanderlei Silva had mastered the stare-down. They had truly fearsome looks, and their stare-down that had been anticipated for the past six years. The uproarious reaction of the crowd for Wanderlei was surprising. I had thought Chuck would enjoy a home-field advantage over the Brazilian, but the fans clamored for Silva almost as much as they did for Liddell. Only inches from each other's face, they played a game of intimidation chicken. Chuck stood perfectly still while Wanderlei shuffled back and forth on his feet like a psychotic gorilla staring at a female in heat. After ten seconds, Wanderlei head-faked at Chuck, who didn't flinch. I guess no one told him Chuck doesn't take kindly to taunting. Liddell backed away to give Wanderlei a full view of his middle finger. The two almost erupted into a brawl on the stage.

Matt Hughes and GSP then got on the scale to finish the event with no incidents.

Afterward, most of the fighters made themselves available in the media room, but GSP bolted quickly, frustrating me yet again. Getting close to the marquee fighters was damn near impossible, even with a press credential. They moved quickly from place to place. I really wanted to get into GSP's head and find out if he was nervous, calm, irritated, hungry, homesick, whatever. I wanted to know how the headliner was treated compared to all the guys who were struggling for a three-and-three.

In addition to the constant moving I discovered another reason the headliners are so hard to get to when, moments later, the crowd broke through the doors, having caught a glimpse of Chuck Liddell leaving the media center. Suddenly he was gone, as his crew and the Mandalay Bay security team escorted him through a black door that seemed to lead into another dimension.

Rock stars, I thought. *That's what they are here.*

Upstairs hundreds of fans waited for Chuck to emerge, not knowing that he was currently being ushered through secret corridors beneath them. I wondered if maybe I was wrong to assume I could get to see MMA from the top of the food chain. Maybe this sport, like other mainstream sports, had already made elitists of its athletes.

With the weigh-ins complete, there was nothing left to do but wait for the fights. All the training, studying, training, cutting weight, training, mental preparation, and more training was done. Most of the fighters were now sitting in their rooms waiting, thinking, and trying to rest. For me it was like sitting on an airfield waiting for a plane to take you to Afghanistan. If you hadn't learned something by now, it was too late.

* * * * *

Fight day at Starbucks, my coffee cup ran dry just as Greg Jackson and Julie Kedzie walked past heading toward the events center.

"No underground tunnels?" I joked.

"It sucks, but we wouldn't get anywhere without them. You should have seen the crowd that assaulted Diego Sanchez during the finale of The Ultimate Fighter," Greg said. "It was crazy! It might not be the right thing to do, but the timeline they have us on makes it tough to get anywhere without them."

A crowd was already gathering outside the events center and several recognized Greg and Julie. If I was going to beg for a favor, I only had a few seconds left before they swarmed him.

"Can I get some time with GSP before the fight?" I asked.

"Dude…," he said, the answer already obvious. "It isn't me, okay? He's a few hours away from his title shot and his crew…"

I cut him off. "I got it. How's he looking?"

"Great. He's focused."

"He's definitely ready," Kedzie added.

Then the fans descended like sailors on shore leave. Greg took a few photos and headed into the events center to pick up credentials, read tarot cards, roll chicken bones—the normal things trainers do before a fight.

Later near the elevators I ran into former UFC heavyweight champion Tim Sylvia. "Why don't you take the tunnels to get around?" I asked.

"I probably would if I was fighting," he responded. "Sometimes you need to get yourself focused and that means alone time. But I got nowhere to be, so I'll stroll through here and talk with people."

No sooner had he answered me than a small crowd of people assaulted him for pictures and autographs. I was beginning to think the sport was growing too big for its britches, especially since I couldn't seem to nail down GSP, but Greg Jackson and Tim Sylvia put things into perspective.

When they weren't fighting, the athletes were out there, gripping and grinning with fans and helping keep the sport moving forward at the grassroots level. Watching Liddell and the others take the tunnels to avoid the fans may have been distasteful to me, but I had to admit there was a practical reason to do so. In fact, it could even be viewed as irresponsible to the fans if Liddell had spent all of his time with them instead of preparing for the fight. They wouldn't have gotten their money's worth if he entered the Octagon at anything less than peak performance.

But what about me and my press badge? What about the view from the mountaintop I had come for? Actually it suddenly looked like I would get my chance. After months of requests, the director of public relations at the UFC, Jennifer Wenk, granted me time with Dana White. From everything I'd heard about him, I felt like I'd scored a home run and been sent to death row at the same time. His business model was simple: sign all the best fighters in the world, reinvest in the company, and crush the opposition. The press portrayed him as a Doctor Evil, wildly obsessed with taking over the world, but armed with F-bombs instead of witty banter.

"You get to shadow him while he goes through the prefight preparations," she said as we entered the empty arena. "Then you get one-on-one time."

"No blindfold and cigarette?" I joked.

He sat next to the Octagon, an Orwellian presence in a long-sleeved

The most powerful man in the sport. UFC President Dana White.

black T-shirt, overhead lights gleaming off his bald head. His bodyguard, Tom, an earpiece with a pigtail cord draped over his shoulder, gave me the once-over without a smile. I looked around for a bald Mini-Me, but didn't see one.

"Add the overhead shot of Chuck knocking Randy out," White told the production crew. He went through each of the headliners' highlight reels as staffers and cameramen rehearsed the walk-ins from the dressing rooms. He had detailed instructions about every piece of video footage that was going to be seen that night, both in the arena and on pay-per-view. Nothing went out unless he approved it first. It was extreme image control.

"Did you see that?" he said to no one in particular when watching the weigh-ins for the third time. No one answered. He turned to me. "Did you see that?" he asked again. I shook my head. "Chuck didn't even fucking flinch." Someone rewound the tape to when Wanderlei did his head fake at Chuck's face. Sure enough, Liddell didn't flinch.

"Fucking stone nuts, man," White said.

"Wanderlei's isn't ready," a guy with headphones reported. "They need twenty minutes still." I took a step back, not wanting to get bits of soundman on me when White launched a Hellfire missile into his chest.

"Okay. Get it when you can," White said nodding.

"Shannon Lee is out front," someone told him.

"Shannon Lee? Let her in," White responded. Moments later, the only surviving child of the legendary Bruce Lee gave White a hug, and the two chatted like old friends. He showed her more respect than the President, which I couldn't blame him for. I felt like standing at attention myself and snapped two photos, though the lighting sucked. White turned to me.

"You want a picture?" he asked.

"What?"

"You want a picture with Shannon?"

"Uh, sure," I said. He took my camera and popped two photos of Shannon Lee and me.

Someone pull me out of the twilight zone, I thought. *This guy's not supposed to be this nice.*

After Lee left, he gave an interview to a pair of Japanese journalists that garnered some funny quotes.

"Don't ask me why I'm not in Japan," he said laughing. "I know that's what you want to know, but you know why I'm not there. This was a big year for us. Our growth is evident in the growth of the smaller businesses like TapouT and all the other clothing companies. Fighter of the year? Probably Anderson Silva. Most disappointing? Tito was the most disappointing fighter of the year. He's the big pussy of MMA. He pulled out of a fight because he said he was hurt when he wasn't. Fedor is the joke of the year. He's fighting Hong Duk Dong tonight. Whooppee do. I feel sorry for him because he has bad management. Rookie of the year has to be Roger Huerta."

Twenty minutes later, I was in a locker room below the arena. If what follows is long, I apologize, but I waited a long time to get an interview with the most powerful man in MMA. Squandering the opportunity to ask questions that he'd already answered many times would have been irresponsible.

"I have nothing to do with the death of boxing," White said about killing his former love. "Boxing has been doing this to itself. It's the corruption, man. It's the fucking promoters who only give a shit about, 'How much money can I put in my pocket right here, right now.' Nobody is taking money out of their pocket to secure the future of the sport. We take money out of our own pocket. We spend money to make this sport grow. You know how much fucking money we lost going into the UK in 2007?"

I didn't.

"We got beheaded!" he continued. "We lost so much money it's crazy. Now I could have been a boxing promoter and I could have just kept doing fights here in the U.S. and stuffing money in my pockets, but we want to grow the sport."

It was true. The boxing promoters let networks like HBO or Showtime pay for everything, so there is no risk and they rake in more profits. Boxing promoters by and large don't reinvest money back into the sport because they don't have to. Boxing has been around for over a hundred years and enjoys a robust and loyal following. But White pursued several networks throughout 2007 for a broadcast deal, and he couldn't make one happen, which is one of the reasons for the disparity in fighters' pay. The UFC has a lot more bills to pay than boxing promoters do.

There was a lingering anger in White against boxing. Maybe a promoter screwed him out of a paycheck. Maybe his dreams were crushed by an unscrupulous manager. Whatever the reason, he had no desire to hide his disdain.

"We're not sitting around like fucking greedy fat pigs like these boxing promoters have for years," he said. "These bloated, fucking corrupt dirtbags. And it's not just the promoters; it's the sanctioning organizations, some of the networks. A lot of fucking greed and corruption going on there. So boxing has a lot of problems, more than just the fights aren't exciting."

Speaking of exciting . . . "There are thousands of fighters out there struggling to make it into the UFC," I said. "Is it better for them to have an exciting loss or a boring win?"

He didn't even hesitate.

"Boxing became the sport where you had to build this guy up to 42 and 0 with 39 knockouts. There had to be this invincible aura about guys. Nobody's invincible. It got to the point where you buy these boxing matches and you get all pumped up for the fight and get all excited and you buy the fight for fifty dollars and the fuckers didn't fight. Tonight, tickets are a thousand bucks for ringside. The pay-per-view is forty-four dollars. So when you put down your forty-four dollars or your thousand dollars for the ticket, I fucking guarantee you, you're going to see guys come in and fight, you know? And that's why I give these guys incentives. Each guy involved in fight of the night tonight gets fifty thousand dollars. Knockout of the night, fifty thousand. Submission of the night, fifty thousand."

He didn't answer the question, but he hit on something else I wanted to know. In early 2007 while I was commiserating with Ivan Salaverry, the standard entry pay was three and three. But over the course of the year, salaries had steadily increased, and just a month earlier at the finale for *The Ultimate Fighter* season six, it had gone up to eight and eight, and bonus money had risen from $15,000 to $50,000.

"You hear a lot of shit about us," he said, mocking a critic. 'These poor guys that fight on the card only make three and three, and four and four . . .' Guess what? That's more money than most boxers make when they're on their way up. Those guys get a hundred bucks a round and they fight four-rounders. That's four hundred dollars. You're gonna train your ass off and get paid four hundred fucking dollars a fight? How does that even make sense? You know? Winning four thousand after training for months isn't a lot of money either, but . . . it's the way you pay your dues."

By that logic, though, MMA headliners should have been getting more than boxing headliners, which wasn't happening. Floyd Mayweather reportedly made $11 million for his fight against De La Hoya, and no MMA fighter had ever made anything close to that. But there was no denying the salaries were steadily increasing, and for a young sport that was growing quickly, that meant 2008 should be a banner year for the pocketbooks of UFC fighters.

The most important lesson I'd learned about MMA was that fighters weren't the stereotypical thugs that many perceived them to be. Most at least.

"I don't want any guys out there getting arrested, getting into street fights, things like that," White said. "Ninety-five percent of the guys aren't like that. But there's always gonna be the five percent that are. Most of these guys are good guys. Tito's the biggest fucking scumbag on planet earth, okay? This guy is a fucking scumbag. Hold on one second, I gotta . . . ," He took a text message and responded quickly, moving his thumbs faster than a junior high kid.

"My point is," he continued, "there's good guys, there's bad guys, there's guys who like to hurt people, there's guys who just like to compete and look at this thing differently. You have to let every guy be who he is, you know?"

The revelation I had while training with Kenny Florian was that right before a fight, the athletes aren't in their normal frame of mind and tend to say things they regret. Was it okay to stick a camera in someone's face at this critical time before a fight?

"When it comes to how you think and what your mind frame is when going into a fight . . . I want to hear it," White said. "I want to hear that shit. This is how he feels before he goes out. People will hate him for that and people will love him for that. But you gotta let the guy be who he is."

That was understandable, but White was controlling when it came to the UFC's image, as I'd seen with his insistence to review and approve all videos before the public did. A bad blood fight could get fans more interested in watching and pull in huge crowds, but what if the rivalry came at the expense of the sport's reputation?

"Every fight can't be, 'I hate this guy and I fucking wanna kill him,' and every fight can't be, 'Hey, man, I love this guy, he's great.' What makes it great is that you have both. Melvin Guillard and Clementi. They hate each other. They actually got into a street fight outside, which isn't good for the sport, either. That's bad shit. That's like a couple of thugs that met each other in the street, but . . . it's the fight game."

The conversation turned to the UFC's competition.

"Now the new guy is Mark Cuban," White said, leaning forward like his fellow Bostonian Mark DellaGrotte did when he got excited about a topic. "Mark Cuban's got some money, smart guy, done some good things. But Mark Cuban is dancing with the stars, he's sitting at the Mavericks game, he's all about the Mavericks. I heard he's trying to buy the Chicago Cubs. He owns HD Net television network, and now he's involved in MMA. Do you know what I do? I do MMA twenty-four-fucking-seven. It's all I care about. It's all I think about. I have an infrastructure. I have a hundred and ten fucking employees and that's all we do. As hard as I work, they all work that hard too. He ain't gonna fuck with us. He ain't gonna come close."

He smiled like Jack Nicholson in *The Shining*.

"He thinks MMA is the right content to help pull HDNet out of the shitter. MMA will help him spend a lot more of his money. So I love it. I welcome it. I want Cuban to come in and drop, twenty, thirty million in MMA. It's good, you know? And Floyd Mayweather is running around with seventy million in his pocket right now too, looking to get into something. I love it. I get out there and I'll talk a bunch of shit, and piss them all off. Floyd loves to spend money. I mean how many more fucking cars and rope chains can he buy? Let him start investing some money in MMA. It's good for all of us. All these younger kids get experience, get paid, build their records up, and they're all gonna end up with me at the end of the day anyway. I'll end up with all of them."

That last sentence made me think White knew how much he actually benefited from the smaller MMA promotions that fed the UFC with new talent. The smaller promotions offered fighters a venue to sharpen their skills so they could come to the UFC ready for prime time. They also solidified the UFC's position as the big dog in the yard.

"Do you feel that you actually need those smaller promotions out there?" I asked. "If you're going to be head and shoulders above the rest, doesn't there have to be a 'rest'?"

"People talk about negative things . . . bad things that we've done, okay? We've never lost a court battle, ever. Never in seven years. The reason is because everything we do is on the up and up. Not only are we good people, but we do everything by the book."

I thought it odd to equate moral integrity with legal victories, but everyone has a different measure of success. White had always found a way to defeat his competition. It was his calling card. He was savvy with killer instincts and a scorched-earth, leave-them-nothing-but-their-eyes-to-cry-with business model. Fans of Pride Fighting Championships had a bad taste in their mouths, and with good reason, after he bought the mighty Japanese promotion. Despite his pledge to leave Pride the way it was, he let it wither and die on the vine, erasing his last major competition and bringing all of its best fighters to the UFC. There were plenty of people who didn't like his tactics, but in the end it was business, which made it necessary to find ways to survive.

"I can either be your best fucking friend and your greatest ally or I can be your worst fucking enemy," he said. "You pick which one you want me to be. I'm cool with everybody. We do a lot of good things with a lot of people and people get dumb, people get greedy, and people just plain do stupid stuff. And if that's where you want to go with me, then I'll go to the fucking death."

General George S. Patton, Jr. was the same way. The standard operating procedure of Patton's command was, "In the absence of orders, attack, attack, attack." He rose through the ranks riding a bold, audacious ego and an affinity for violence of action. Without a doubt, the brash, cursing, in-your-face General Patton of MMA is Dana White. White is one of the few generals of the MMA world; there are only three in my opinion: White, Kurt Otto at the IFL, and Terry Trebilcock who runs King of the Cage. Otto has a revolutionary vision for MMA, the balls to follow his dream, and the business acumen to be successful, even if the IFL is perennially one step behind the UFC. Trebilcock and King of the Cage has proven staying power and boasts a roster of the world's best MMA fighters.

These heavyweights of the sport define and shape MMA through crafty business decisions, powerful lawyers, and high-profile events. They cultivate fans, establish policies, and put on big-time fights. But Dana White is clearly the five-star of the generals. He is the man who had the vision to take the sport to new heights and the courage to use whatever means necessary to get it there. Love him or hate him, White got results.

After World War II, Patton envisioned invading the Soviet Union immediately after Germany surrendered. He was called crazy for it, but history eventually recognized the genius of his plan. White also has a vision that seems overly ambitious…today.

"We think that this is probably the only sport that can actually be a global sport," he said. "I'll give you an example. There's nothing bigger in this country than the NFL. I don't give a shit if you didn't watch one football game all season, everybody watches the Super Bowl. It's huge. It spent millions of dollars to try to break into Europe, and it can't. You know why? Because kids don't grow up playing it. They don't know a fucking fourth down, punt, kick, pass. They don't know what any of that means. They don't get it. It's like saying cricket's gonna go wild over here in the United States. It's never gonna happen.

"Now I take two guys, put them in the Octagon, and they can use any martial art they want . . . people get it. It's like if you're flipping around on the Mexican channel and there's two Mexican guys in there banging it out, right? You don't give a shit what [the commentator's] saying. I know what's going on. There's a fight and it's a good one!"

I ended my time with Dana White unhating him, if that's a word. On a personal level, he was accommodating and sincere. He wasn't as belligerent as I'd imagined, and if anyone loved the sport of fighting, it was him.

My seat for UFC 79 was in the section no one should ever have to pay for. I was there to photograph the event for the magazine and got banished to the nosebleed section with about ten other paparazzi.

The undercard fights were underwhelming and proved how unpredictable the sport of MMA can be. The matchups looked good on paper, but none delivered much excitement. Still, Nate Mohr did scream loud enough to be heard all the way up in our section when Manny Gamburyan secured a tight leglock and dislocated his knee. The slow motion replay on the six Jumbotrons made the moment all the more cringe-worthy.

James Irvin's injury was different. The biggest difference between the rules of the now-defunct Pride Fighting Championships and the UFC was the "no knees or kicks to a downed opponent" clause. It had been criticized by websites, bloggers, and fans alike. But when Luis Cane connected with a knee to Irvin's forehead while Irvin was on his knees, and he slumped to the mat for several minutes, not a critic of the rule was to be found. Irvin lay motionless while Cane was sent to a neutral side of the cage.

Striking your opponent hard enough to make him lose consciousness is the goal, but even in the darkest days of MMA, it wasn't as dangerous as boxing, a socially accepted sport. Boxing's goal is to pummel a man in the head and torso until he can no longer carry on. In mixed martial arts, there is at least a choice to take the fight to the ground and submit an opponent without resorting to striking. The brutal image of MMA really is undeserved, especially compared to boxing.

Finally Irvin got to his feet. Cane was disqualified for an illegal strike and went home disgraced. For all the hype, the Super Bowl of MMA wasn't really providing the crowd with edge-of-your-seat excitement.

After the intermission, the lights dimmed again and Bruce Buffer yelled into the microphone. "Ladies and gentlemen…we are live!"

The first fight of the main card was the bad blood that had been building between Rich Clementi and Melvin Guillard. Their hatred for each other got the crowd amped. I had to admit, I was jacked to see these two go at it. But I expected it to be more of a no-technique slugfest than an MMA match. Early in the first round, Clementi slammed Guillard to the mat but couldn't capitalize on it. Near the end of the round, though, he got Guillard down, gained a dominant position and secured a rear-naked choke. Guillard had no choice but to tap out. But it didn't end there because some people are just plain old sore losers.

The moment the bout ended, Guillard got up and went after Clementi, forcing the referee to step in and restrain him. Clementi coolly waved goodbye to his foe, who was accosted with boos. Once again, the MMA crowd upheld its standards and showed disaffection with Guillard's poor attitude. I wondered if I should have spent time in Guillard's gym to find a guy who was in MMA for the wrong reasons.

The African Assassin was expected to put on a good show for the crowd. Rameau Thierry Sokoudjou, a native of Cameroon, was another Pride standout. He was an accomplished judokan who could dazzle a crowd with his striking ability as well as his perfect smile, ripped abs, and fancy dreadlocks. A soft-spoken hype machine dream, he even showed a hint of character when he entered the arena wearing a Predator mask—very cool.

Lyoto Machida was the opposite. He was as plain as a K-Car, a clean cut Brazilian with formidable ground skills, and a perfect record, including a win over BJ Penn. Yet he was the underdog because Sokoudjou's stand-up striking was so feared. It was a contrast of styles and another microcosm of the question the UFC was built to answer—which style was better.

The first round was predictable. Sokoudjou threw punches and kicks, but Machida was smart. He backed away from the imposing African's powerful hands and waited for his moment to go for a takedown. Once he did, it was just a matter of time. Ironically, it was a punch that got Sokoudjou off of his feet. Machida was known for having great counter-punching ability, and he connected with a big right on Sokoudjou's chin, got on top of him, and worked step by step until an opportunity presented itself.

"Here it comes," I said, seeing Machida pounce on Sokoudjou's exposed arm, a mortal mistake when fighting a BJJ expert. With his right arm in the air, Machida put his head into Sokoudjou's armpit, wrapped his own arms around Sokoudjou's neck, and squeezed like an anaconda. The African Assassin feebly tapped his arm twice, an indicator that he was on the brink of unconsciousness.

The crowd was impressed; Machida was good. But after seeing what Sokoudjou was capable of on TV, they had wanted to see the same knockout power live. It's bloodlust. It's also the risk of hyping a fight. They don't always go the way they're expected to. The next fight was rather boring. Eddie Sanchez beat up Australian rookie Soa Palelei. Though the fans' bloodlust was appeased when Palelei's nose broke, its appetite for close fights wasn't. Palelei could barely muster a decent defense against Sanchez's constant punching. He bled everywhere and mercifully the referee stopped the fight.

It had to be disheartening to train for months and get booed. I wondered if Americans were arrogant or the Japanese were tolerant because they never booed. Did we have short attention spans, or did the hype machine build our expectations too high? So far we'd seen two boring decisions, a boring TKO, a win that would be remembered more for its sore loser, and a disqualification. If the UFC was going to make new fans, the headliners would have to get the job done.

When the lights dropped, the crowd roared for The Axe Murderer, who entered the arena to techno pop.

Then the hero was called out. The lights dropped and Chuck entered, more magnificent than Elvis. The fervor was at its highest point, like the bottom of the ninth, fourth and goal, three-point shot at the buzzer, all in one. And the fight hadn't even started.

Like Las Vegas, if you haven't seen this fight, I won't be able do it justice here. It was an epic confrontation worthy of the Roman coliseum.

Chuck Liddell (right) connects on Wanderlei Silva.

It was a brutal melee of fists and feet and a rare takedown that stunned the crowd. Almost the entire fight was a striking exchange, with neither man wanting to go to ground until, inexplicably, Liddell took Silva down in the third round. I couldn't remember a time when he'd done that to anyone, yet suddenly he did it to a man with a BJJ black belt on the biggest stage in the sport. The crowd was a living entity, seething back and forth between CHUCK! CHUCK! CHUCK! and SIL-VA! SIL-VA! SIL-VA! They chanted like Gregorians and waved like a wheat field with the ebb and flow of the fight.

It was a defining moment in the UFC. It had achieved the impossible. It lived up to the hype of an all-out war. I had scorned fighters for using the term "war' to describe a match, but after that fight, I gladly ate my words like crow with ketchup. Silva and Liddell appeased most everyone's desire for entertainment that night, whether it was a bloodlust, a striking clinic, or a close fight—everyone got to see what they wanted. Except, of course, a knockout. The fight went to the judges, all of whom decided victory belonged to Liddell. Thousands of fists were thrust into the air. He was their hero—Hercules, Achilles, and Odysseus rolled into one. Dana White's night was salvaged and all his sins were suddenly forgiven.

"He's a tough guy," a swollen and dazed Silva told the crowd. "He win. I do my best." I don't think the term tough applies to human beings. Seriously. It's a term that should be used to refer to cattle products, such as beef jerky and leather. Men who ignore pain and continue to fight are enduring. They have a threshold that's very difficult to reach. Tough is a measure of thickness. Endurance is a measure of human ability. Someone once called me tough for graduating U.S. Army Ranger School, when in fact I just had a high threshold for bullshit.

It would be almost physically impossible for the GSP-Hughes fight to deliver such extraordinary emotion as Liddell and Silva had conjured up. But they were both champions, and the potential was there. I was more nervous than excited. I had gotten to know Greg Jackson, and my heart was in my stomach, hoping he wouldn't fail.

Hughes came out southpaw, his right leg forward instead of the normal left. GSP seemed confused at first and stayed cautiously away from Hughes's fists until he decided to take the former welterweight champion down. On the ground, GSP imposed his will on Hughes until the horn ended the first round. Since this was a five-round fight and both men wanted to have enough energy to go the distance, the first round was more of a feeling-out process. Neither man had taken much damage.

As GSP sat on a stool being attended to by Jackson, someone spilled water over him that cascaded onto the mat. The water added to a large puddle that had grown from fight to fight. But it wasn't just water. There was blood, too, and a lot of it after the Liddell-Silva throw down and the Sanchez-Palelei fight. I found it ironic that the headliners had to fight in this ever-growing coating of fluids and shoe dirt.

In the second round, it was more domination by the French Canadian. He peppered Hughes with shots and returned the fight to the ground with a perfectly executed hip toss that brought Hughes's legs high into the air and earned a sympathetic groan from the crowd. Once GSP got on top, the end felt near. With only a few seconds left in the round, GSP attempted a kimura. Hughes rolled smartly to get out of it, but as I learned at Jackson's MMA, every good move has a backup, and GSP easily transitioned to the

GSP moments after winning the title. Matt Hughes in the background.

dreaded armbar. Matt Hughes's right arm was trapped, and his left looked caught on GSP's leg.

"Tap! tap! tap!" he said to the referee.

It was over. Moments later, Bruce Buffer informed the crowd of what they already knew.

"Ladies and Gentlemen, referee Steve Mazagatti calls a stop to this contest at 4:54 of the second round for your winner by verbal tapout due to an armbar. Interim UFC welterweight champion of the world . . . Georges 'Rush' St. Pierre!

Dana White strode forward and strapped the belt around GSP's waist, but it didn't stay there long.

"I am going to take off this belt," GSP said suddenly. "It's an honor, but it does not mean nothing. The real champ is Matt Serra. Until I beat him I do not consider myself the champion."

Big brownie points! The crowd cheered his deep desire to defeat Serra. But after hearing his comments at the prefight press conference, I was thoroughly confused. The title means nothing? If this meant nothing then why did he ignore the Olympics to be here?

I chalked GSP's comments up to postfight nonsensical dimwittedness and cruised downstairs to the media center, which was only half full but held one of the most impressive sights I'd ever seen. Mandy Moore, singer and MMA fan, stood in the middle of the room sipping water while soda bottles spontaneously popped their tops around her. Some people look completely different in person.

The athletes entered the room, beaten and bruised. Chuck sported a black eye, and Matt Hughes only had the use of one since the other was quickly swelling shut. They mounted the stage and began talking, but I wasn't listening. Greg Jackson entered the room, flanked by GSP's manager carrying his interim title belt, so I ambled over to hang with him.

"How are you?" I asked.

"Better than I was three hours ago," Greg responded with a smile. "Did you see he came out southpaw?"

"Yep. What did you guys do to adjust?"

"I didn't have to tell him much. He was on his game so well."

"You happy to have that belt?" I asked, pointing to the welterweight title that GSP's manager was toting around.

"Hell, yeah."

GSP's manager had trouble holding it while she answered her cell phone.

"Let me hold that," I said, grabbing the heavy belt. It was solid leather and brass. I wanted to put it around my waist to see what it felt like, but decided not to disrespect the man who'd just earned it.

The belt was merely a symbol, but one that held true meaning for a small group of people. They're the ones who ignore the basic human instinct of self-preservation, the ones who throw themselves into harm's way and disregard their own personal safety to achieve a goal that others find...crazy.

* * * * *

"How are you feeling, Soa?" I asked the next morning as I got in the elevator and spotted Soa Palelei. Wearing a hoodie and sunglasses, he looked like the Unabomber with an MP3 player.

"I'm all right," he said. "I think I let the crowd get to me, you know?"

The only other person in the elevator, a woman of about fifty, flinched. With her back to us, she started to look over her shoulder, but stopped.

"I'll be back," Soa said. "I'll be better next time. My pride's hurt worse than my body."

That seemed to be the way of it. Losing a fight, whether it was in a parking lot or in front of thousands of people, hurt our souls more than our bones. In a way that was why so many people associated fighting with negative emotions. It wasn't the physical pain that stuck with us, but the emotional trauma of having to face our peers after being on the wrong end of a beatdown that really hurt.

"Good luck," I said to Soa as we exited the elevator and went separate ways.

When he was out of earshot, the woman on the elevator made a snide remark. "Another fighter," she said as she shook her head in disgust at Soa and turned toward the convenience store across from the elevators. She went to the magazine rack while I grabbed a cold coffee, her discriminating comment boiling my blood. She looked like the nicest grandmotherly figure, but her crack at my new favorite sport was insulting. She knew nothing of MMA except that she hated it and everyone in it. Prejudice based on one's occupation isn't a new concept, but it was the last thing I expected to experience in the heart of Sin City.

At the register, the woman paid for a Good Housekeeping magazine and a candy bar while another man, straight from the casino, drank a Bloody Mary. Next to him, a twenty-something who had clearly been out all night bought two beers. It was eight o'clock in the morning and the only person purchasing a healthy beverage was fighter Jeremy Horn, who placed a bottle of water on the counter.

I walked out of the Mandalay Bay Hotel and Casino for the first time in three days and stopped on the oversized UFC carpet in the entranceway. My journey through MMA was complete. I waited for an epiphany to happen; a summation of all the places I'd been and people I'd met. Maybe the world would spin like it does in movies when the camera goes around and around the main character while he has a blinding moment of clarity.

Didn't happen.

But I did know that thousands of men and women were waking to a new day, sore from their last workout, eagerly awaiting their next training session. Years ago a friend of mine had a poster in his office at Fort Stewart, Georgia. It was a picture of him standing in a field, dressed like a ninja, holding a katana blade in menacing fashion. Underneath the picture it read, "Somewhere, someone is training harder than you . . . and he will beat you." It was corny, and I always gave him shit about it, but it was also completely true. The man who is destined to shock the world and defy all expectations is out there training his ass off somewhere. It doesn't matter if he's using duct tape to hold together a worn-out pair of gloves or is hooked to multitudes of physiological monitors in a cyborg production facility; he's out there and his training and endurance will someday carry him to his own title shot.

Kelly A. Crigger is a Lieutenant Colonel in the U.S. Army with Bachelors degrees in Political Science and History from Kansas University and a Masters degree in International Relations from Troy State University. He has served in a variety of assignments worldwide, including the 1st Special Forces Group and the 3rd Infantry Division, and has completed the Army's grueling Ranger school. A longtime fan of MMA, he began writing on the sport in 2006.